Answers to ANOREXIA

A Breakthrough Nutritional Treatment That Is Saving Lives

D1231386

(handwritten notes)
111 — Zn
128 — 2
107 — Link to Zinc
135 — 30 mg day Zinc

James M. Greenblatt, MD

SUNRISE
River Press

Sunrise River Press
39966 Grand Avenue
North Branch, MN 55056
Phone: 651-277-1400 or 800-895-4585
Fax: 651-277-1203
www.sunriseriverpress.com

Edit by Karin Craig
Layout by Monica Seiberlich

ISBN 978-1-934716-07-6
Item No. SRP607

Library of Congress Cataloging-in-Publication Data

Greenblatt, James.
  Answers to anorexia : a breakthrough nutritional treatment that is saving lives / by James Greenblatt.
     p. cm.
  Includes index.
  ISBN 978-1-934716-07-6
  1. Anorexia nervosa--Diet therapy--Popular works. 2. Anorexia nervosa--Treatment--Popular works. I. Title.
  RC552.A5G72 2010
  616.85'2620654--dc22
                                2010021106

Printed in USA
10 9 8 7 6 5 4 3 2 1

Contents

Dedication

To the patients and families who have suffered the tragic consequences of anorexia nervosa.

To the staff of Walden Behavioral Care and clinicians around the world who have dedicated their careers to supporting and treating patients with anorexia nervosa and related eating disorders.

To the individuals who will continue to look for answers to anorexia.

Acknowledgments

I would like to thank Sunrise River Press for their support in publishing this manuscript. Thank you to my wife and children for their patience and understanding during my many morning and weekend disappearances to work on this project. I also want to thank my parents, who have provided a lifetime of unwavering support, encouragement, and the "It's ok to think outside of the box after you graduate medical school" messages. Finally, this book could never have been written without the research, writing, and editing help of Lee Yuan, Virginia Taylor, Deborah Elbaum, Nancy Monson, and Suzanne Stoterau, MD.

Foreword

"The greatest obstacle to discovering the shape of the earth, the continents and the ocean was not ignorance but the illusion of knowledge."
— *Daniel J. Boorstin, The Discoverers*

It is estimated that up to 24 million people in the United States experience an eating disorder, with nearly 50 percent of Americans familiar with someone who is suffering from this problem. Yet only 10 percent of men and women with eating disorders obtain treatment. Even so, roughly 80 percent of females who receive treatment for their eating disorder do not get the intensity of treatment needed in order to stay in recovery. In many cases patients are released from treatment while their weight is still below 85 percent of what is considered normal. Furthermore, the relapse rate is a staggering 50 percent. Treatment usually involves a combination of poly pharmacy and counseling with nutritional goals focused on increasing calories as the mainstay. Virtually everyone involved, family and professionals alike, knows how difficult, significant, and widespread the emotional toll of this disease can be.

Currently, the nutritional aspects of an eating disorder treatment will address obvious deficiencies and correct them—a great beginning. But increasingly, research is pointing toward a much more sophisticated relationship between food, mental states, and genetic expression. With such a high relapse rate, any lifestyle intervention (which includes nutritional information) that poses far less risk of adverse effects, as compared to medications, begs exploration to improve outcomes.

This book represents an approach that aptly addresses this complex medical, social, and psychiatric problem in a whole-person approach. It represents an evidence-based perspective on how alternative and complementary medicine can be implemented in the treatment of eating disorders without sacrificing the best of conventional treatments. This integrative approach, now recognized as integrative psychiatry, adds more dimensions to improving and personalizing medical treatment. Furthermore, clinical studies are beginning to demonstrate that this approach heightens patient empowerment—a key vulnerability in many with an eating disorder.

In psychiatry it is becoming evident that environmental, nutritional, and genetic influences have much more interplay than we suspected in affecting mood states. Understanding this fact helps to shed light on why some individuals experience continued symptoms despite optimizing therapy and psychotropic medications. Having this information, spelled out as it is in the book, will potentially further raise awareness of the heightened importance of diet as a therapeutic intervention.

In sum, this book introduces a new paradigm for approaching a difficult and increasingly more common psychiatric disorder. The information helps broaden the therapeutic focus away from poly pharmacy and diagnosis, without sacrificing care, to including useful lifestyle interventions that can create a lasting transition into mental, physical, and emotional wellbeing.

Roberta Lee, MD
October 2010

Roberta Lee, MD, is Vice Chair of the Department of Integrative Medicine at Beth Israel Medical Center. Dr. Lee is a recognized expert on the use of alternative, integrative therapies and botanical supplements in optimizing wellness and managing chronic disease. She is currently developing new strategies for stress management that incorporate a unique blend of mind/body exercises, lifestyle changes, and botanical supplements. She is the author of The SuperStress Solution.

Preface

In this book I propose a new way of treating anorexia nervosa. Fundamental to this treatment is the acknowledgment that anorexia is a genetically based illness with a complicated biology that results from self-starvation. The treatment protocol described in this book has worked for many patients. I am not offering a quick fix, rather, a foundation from which to treat this disorder of self-starvation. From this foundation, patients and their families can draw suggestions, and physicians can establish guidelines for their medical practices. This approach clearly has relevance to all eating disorders, including bulimia nervosa, binge eating disorder, and obesity.

Over the years as a specialist in the treatment of eating disorders, I have witnessed the tragic loss of life and irreversible medical and psychological scars in innocent, young adolescents and adults. What I have watched has heightened the urgency for the need for scientific research and insights from other fields that would help illuminate the mechanisms of this deadly disease.

My daughter is particularly adept at putting together complicated 1,000-piece jigsaw puzzles. My skills have always been limited in this area. I've worked hard enough at them to break into a sweat, but I still can't put a puzzle together, let alone a few pieces. Through the years I've learned to contribute by offering support rather than trying to manage on my own. When my daughter begins a new puzzle, I help by separating the colors and the edge pieces. This very basic start helps her move on to put the entire puzzle together with amazing speed.

In presenting my thoughts about anorexia, I hope to provide the edges and separate some of the colors of the puzzle. With deep respect for patients, their families, and professionals, I hope that we will work together to solve this complicated puzzle in its entirety and to eliminate the most lethal psychiatric illness.

Our current treatment model for anorexia nervosa is inefficient, costly, and—tragically—woefully unsuccessful. Anorexia is a debilitating psycho-biological illness that affects body, mind, and spirit. It robs patients of emotional and physical freedom to make decisions about what to do and what to eat, and it tortures them with obsessive ruminations.

This book aims to help you understand how nutritional deficiencies affect brain function and the expression of genes, and their relationship with anorexia nervosa.

"Nutritional deficiencies with anorexia nervosa?" Is this a ridiculous question? Perhaps, but nutritional deficiencies are still an obvious and neglected component of our current treatment model!

During the more than 20 years I have practiced psychiatry, I have been on a professional journey to find and integrate valuable insights from different fields as they relate to eating disorders. I hope you'll join me on the journey to explore the complex terrain of this disorder and the tools we now have to treat and even to prevent it. The stakes are high. Anorexia nervosa threatens lives. It exacts the highest level of stress on caregivers and carries the highest suicide risk of any mental health disorder. The longer people struggle with anorexia, the less likely they are to recover. Our patients can't wait.

A majority of young women diet, but only a small fraction develops an eating disorder. Why? What triggers anorexia?

Genetics appear to be behind more than half of the risk, but our genetic makeup is not our destiny. Our genes are more accurately described as our biological liability. Scientists are discovering numerous influences on our genetics. These include emotions, stress, environmental toxins, and nutrients we eat or don't eat.

We are all unique, not only in the way we look and in our past experiences, but also in our metabolism and biochemistry. No two individuals have exactly the same thumbprint, not even identical twins. Rather than being random, these differences are often the result of predictable differences in genetics and an interaction between our genes and the environment. In fact, one-third of genetic variations are associated with the body's ability to utilize and absorb nutrients. These variations mean that every individual has unique metabolic needs and that the metabolism of essential nutrients varies across individuals.

I speak with patients every day whose powerful stories make clear to me that every patient suffering from anorexia is unique. However, it is not their uniqueness alone that captures my attention. It is the disturbing "sameness" of their treatment. Over and over, my patients relate to me the endless list of medications they have been prescribed, medications that have been useless in combating their debilitating disease. They relate to me the endless treatment programs they have tried and the contradictory and conflicting information they and their families have received from their teams.

Is it any wonder that patients and families are disheartened, confused, frustrated, and scared?

As a physician, I have been trained to use the medical model as the lens through which I view disease and health. But the medical profession has observed restrictive eating patterns for hundreds of years without truly understanding them. The medical community has based its treatment model for anorexia nervosa on the belief that it is a psychological disorder triggered by the idealization of a cultural icon of beauty; a disorder that is precipitated by high stress, high family conflict, and a focus on issues of separation and sexuality.

So, why does the professional community for eating disorders continue to treat anorexia as primarily a psychological disorder? This stubbornness recalls the long and tortured history of other psychiatric disorders that we now understand to be biologically based. Depression. Schizophrenia. Obsessive Compulsive Disorder. For years, psychiatry viewed these as disorders of psychological conflict, repressed memories, or aberrant sexual thoughts.

Now we know more. Now we know better.

It is time for change.

The treatment of anorexia nervosa has not benefited from our heightened scientific enlightenment. It is as if the medical community is blind to what is directly in front of them. We observe our patients in a state of malnutrition after extensive starvation of all major food classes, yet anorexia is rarely treated as a nutritional deficiency disorder. Instead, it is treated as a psychologically based disorder, and patients are asked to understand their feelings around not eating, often to tragic results. Of all the major psychiatric disorders, anorexia has the highest mortality rate.

Psychiatry has made tremendous strides in treating many psychiatric illnesses with medications, yet there is not one drug approved for the treatment of anorexia! Antidepressants such as Prozac, Paxil, and Zoloft are commonly prescribed, but research has demonstrated that these medications are not effective for anorexia nervosa.

Despite the fact that these medications have consistently been shown to be ineffective in treating anorexia nervosa, the majority of patients with anorexia continue to be placed on many different medications. Polypharmacy is the rule, not the exception.

In this book you will learn about Referenced-EEG. Referenced-EEG is a new, exciting tool for the treatment of eating disorders. It is emerging from a growing body of research and clinical practice as an effective tool for psychiatrists who are considering medications for patients with eating disorders. Referenced-EEG (rEEG) provides a neurophysiologically based treatment for predicting medications for eating disorder patients—medications that can effectively relieve the depression and obsessive ruminations.

Recently, academic research has begun to demonstrate a genetic, biologically based contribution to anorexia. In the *American Journal of Psychiatry*, one of the most well-respected physicians in the field of eating disorders, Dr. Walter Kaye, described the struggle of anorexia and its impact on families:

"Many families get burned out during the seemingly endless struggles during the ill state. To prevent families from giving up, it is important to explain to them that many individuals with eating disorder do get better, but only after many years. Unfortunately, a subgroup of patients with eating disorders have a persistent chronic course and high mortality. Such findings raise the question of whether physiological factors contribute to outcome."

My goal in writing this book is to help individuals with eating disorders, their families, and mental health professionals understand that anorexia nervosa is a brain-based disorder of profound malnutrition. The physiological factors are related to malnutrition.

I have treated more than a thousand patients with anorexia nervosa over many years. They are without exception profoundly malnourished. Yet, their most vividly articulated distress continues to be how fat they are and how they need to lose weight.

No issue of sexuality, parental conflict, or separation can cause such a distortion of perception and priority. What is going on in the anorexic is a physiological dynamic. The patient is literally starving herself to death. The pieces of the puzzle are diverse. Yes, there is a powerful psychological component to anorexia. But there is also a profound physiological one.

The factors that may contribute to the onset of anorexia nervosa may be unrelated to the physiological dynamics that sustain the illness and cause such emotional turmoil for patients and their families. Anorexia is a nutritional disease. Understanding this points us in a therapeutic direction—anorexia has nutritional solutions.

A family with a loved one diagnosed with cancer is often provided with a well-organized system of care, including adequate health insurance coverage. A family who is trying to find help for their child's eating disorder often has a treacherous journey without professional consensus or even a clear understanding of what direction to take. Last year as I was driving through New Hampshire, I heard my daughter yell from the backseat, "We are off the map!" As we had turned onto a small mountain road, the GPS system went blank. There were no street lines, parks, or water to be seen. The screen was empty.

Many of my patients' families have shared similar feelings while struggling to find their way in recovery from anorexia nervosa. No GPS, no navigation, unclear where the next turn will be, lost on a frightening road—the behavioral, biochemical crossroads of anorexia nervosa and medical treatment.

Optimal nutritional support and correcting nutritional deficiencies are the first steps in recovery. What follows is a clearer path to health and recovery. Patients with nutritional support experience improved mood, better sleep, greater focus on school or work, and fewer obsessions around food. They become more resilient to stress and more responsible for lifestyle choices.

Most of the patients I meet with understand the lifestyle and dietary changes they *should* make to regain health. It is easy to know what to do, but it's a very different concept to have the capacity to make the behavioral changes that are necessary.

Correcting nutritional deficiencies will help optimize brain function. Correcting nutritional deficiencies will help patients recover.

Nutritional medicine is no longer considered to be "alternative medicine." Rather, what we eat is acknowledged to be the foundation of optimal health care and a healthy brain.

A healthy brain creates a mind that defines our uniqueness, and our uniqueness creates our psychological freedom.

This book is about hope.

The pieces of the puzzle are there. It is time to put them together in a clearer picture.

Chapter One

A New Approach

Flanked by her weary parents, 25-year-old Monica sat before me looking careworn and impoverished. Her eyes were sunken in deep hollows, and baggy clothes draped over her skeletal frame. For 12 years—almost half of her young life—Monica had struggled with issues related to eating.

I heard despair, frustration, and hopelessness in the voices of Monica and her parents as they described her problems. Monica's entire life was organized around the restriction of food. Elaborate, compulsive rituals accompanied every bite. Monica was haunted by negative, obsessive thoughts about her body and her size and suffered from chronic anxiety that sometimes escalated to extreme panic.

Through the years, Monica had been given several diagnoses from various health professionals, including depression, anxiety, obsessive-compulsive disorder, attention-deficit hyperactivity disorder, and anorexia nervosa. A total of 14 medications had been prescribed to treat her symptoms, but the only apparent effect was to make Monica feel "drugged." She had participated in individual psychotherapy, dialectical behavioral therapy, cognitive behavioral therapy, group sessions, and family therapy. In addition, she had spent months in residential programs and had been hospitalized many times. In fact, the hospital door had become a revolving door. During the two years prior to my first meeting with Monica, she had been hospitalized four times, sometimes for as long as four weeks.

Monica's family could afford the best treatment programs and took her to the most experienced professionals in the eating disorders field. And, unlike some patients with eating disorders, Monica was compliant. She committed herself wholeheartedly to each course of therapy, cooperating with everything that was asked of her. Yet inexorably, over a decade, her condition had worsened.

When Monica's family brought her to my office, I was the latest in a long parade of medical professionals. And Monica was one of the countless patients I had seen who had been let down by conventional eating disorder treatment. Clearly, a new, more effective approach was needed.

The Current State of Anorexia Nervosa Treatment

The medical profession has failed Monica and thousands of other patients with anorexia nervosa, a life-threatening illness of self-imposed starvation.

Our approach has long been to throw everything but the proverbial kitchen sink at our patients in order to get them to eat. We measure and weigh them to a fraction of an ounce. We overwhelm them with therapy, hoping against hope that they will eventually want to eat and gain weight. We prescribe a variety of medications, including antidepressants such as Prozac and Zoloft, stimulants like Adderall and Ritalin, and antipsychotics such as Haldol, Zyprexa, and Seroquel. We try medications with mood-stabilizing effects, such as Lithium and Lamictal, and anti-anxiety medication like Ativan and Klonopin. Yet many still succumb to the disease. Our failure is not a failure to act. It is a failure of imagination—a failure to acknowledge that our treatments have not been effective and that we need to find a new approach.

Our understanding of anorexia nervosa has remained nearly static since the disorder was first diagnosed in the late nineteenth century, and this limited vision has had devastating consequences. Anorexia nervosa has the highest death rate of any disorder treated by psychiatrists: one out of every five patients dies within 20 years of being diagnosed. Most of these deaths are due to suicide. A higher percentage of patients with anorexia nervosa take their lives than those suffering from severe depression or schizophrenia, a fact that surprises even medical professionals. Although there have been significant advances in treating other psychiatric disorders, the alarming death rate seen in anorexia nervosa persists. As Swedish researcher Fotios C. Papadopolous and colleagues noted in a recent study of anorexic patients published in the *British Journal of Psychiatry* (2009), "The increased mortality from both natural and unnatural causes that persists through their lifetime is astonishing."

A New Understanding

My own journey as a psychiatrist has led me to take a different approach to treating anorexia nervosa. When I entered medical school, I was fascinated by nutrition and the possibility that nutritional interventions could prevent and treat disease. But I was obligated to follow the existing curriculum, which did not emphasize nutrition. I finished my medical training at Johns Hopkins University as a "psychopharmacologist," meaning I was trained to treat psychiatric problems by prescribing medications.

But eventually I realized that anorexia is not primarily a psychiatric disorder, but rather a biological illness of starvation. The starvation leads to malnutrition, and it is malnutrition that produces the psychological symptoms we associate with anorexia nervosa. Correcting this malnutrition is the key to successfully treating anorexia.

One of the major obstacles to recovery is the pervasive focus on weight gain that is characteristic of most eating disorder treatment programs. Weight gain has become the sole significant and objective measure of progress for patients with anorexia nervosa. It is the primary goal of treatment and the primary measure of success.

The majority of professionals treat anorexia by cajoling patients to eat and then hoping for the best. Yet, as many as 50 percent of anorexic patients who gain weight while hospitalized relapse within one year.

Nobody with anorexia nervosa wants to gain weight. Patients want to stop the obsessive thoughts in their heads and decrease their anxiety. Many patients find brief solace in exercise, art, hobbies, or work. Some find it in sex, drugs, and alcohol. But the simplest way of calming the anorexic brain is to restrict food, and this becomes the default for almost all patients. "The thoughts bother me less when I don't eat," they'll say. Or, "My brain is calmer when I restrict." Most patients are eventually treated with psychiatric medications, including the ever-popular selective serotonin reuptake inhibitors or SSRIs (e.g., Celexa, Paxil, Prozac, and Zoloft). But recent studies provide little evidence that these drugs are effective in anorexia nervosa. In fact, no drug has ever been approved by the FDA for the treatment of anorexia nervosa.

Zeroing In On a New Treatment Concept

Of the smorgasbord of anorexia nervosa treatments now available, none can be considered the standard of care. Even individual psychotherapy and family therapy have been found to be effective in less than half of the patients we treat. But what about nutritional approaches?

As I began to explore nutritional approaches to the treatment of anorexia, I discovered that studies show striking evidence that a deficiency in the essential mineral zinc may play a key role in the development of anorexia. Symptoms of zinc deficiency include decreased appetite, weight loss, altered taste perception, depression, and missed menstrual periods—all symptoms associated with anorexia! Research also suggests that celiac disease, a genetic intolerance to the protein gluten, may lead to a predisposition to anorexia due to subsequent nutritional deficiencies like zinc, folic acid, B12, and essential amino acids. Correcting these, determining the underlying causes of nutritional deficiencies in an individual, and restoring a person's nutrient balance are necessary for effective treatment.

Probiotics ("friendly" bacteria) can also be crucial to the refeeding process. Patients frequently complain about bloating, stomach cramps, gas, and extreme discomfort with eating. My professional colleagues attribute these complaints to the eating disorder. But patients with anorexia truly feel pain and discomfort, and the abdominal distention is real! Prolonged periods of malnutrition make it physiologically difficult for the body to digest food and utilize nutrients. With starvation, the body makes fewer of the enzymes required to break down food. There is also a complete change in the bacteria that inhabit the gastrointestinal (GI) tract. There are far fewer friendly bacteria, the kind that enhance digestion. When I prescribe digestive enzymes and probiotics to patients, their physical discomfort and bloating dramatically decrease. More comfortable, patients then have an easier time resuming regular eating schedules.

The longer I work with eating-disorder patients, the more I realize that recovery is not just about food and weight gain. Correcting nutritional imbalances and consuming adequate amounts of vitamins, minerals, amino acids, and fatty acids are absolutely crucial factors in restoring brain health and laying the foundation for a long-lasting recovery. These strategies also help psychotherapy and medication work more effectively.

The Plan: A New Approach to Anorexia

The plan for treating anorexia described in this book evolved from the field of Integrative Medicine. My comprehensive approach integrates nutritional therapies and a new, highly effective approach to selecting the right medication along with psychotherapy. It can pave the way for true sustained recovery from anorexia and create a state of mental wellness. In addition, this book offers safe and natural ways to reduce and reverse the medical complications of anorexia nervosa, restoring both the brain and body to vibrant good health.

First, an accurate understanding of the problem is critical. Anorexia has long been seen as a psychiatric illness brought on by skewed cultural values that prize thinness over happiness. To this day, some psychiatrists *still* view it as a schoolgirl fad! But what we today call anorexia has been around for much longer than the values of our diet-obsessed culture. Further, although a majority of young women diet, only a small fraction will develop an eating disorder.

Anorexia is a major, life-threatening, very complex illness. Many factors—genetic, biological, psychological, and sociocultural—contribute to an individual's susceptibility to developing the disease. Genetics appears to be responsible for more than half of an individual's risk for developing the disease, but genes are not destiny! They are simply a biological liability that can be countered by eating the right nutrients, which, in turn, affect the way genes are expressed.

New information from the fields of genetics, neurobiology, and neuroimaging support the realization that anorexia nervosa is based in biology. We can no longer view eating disorders as a lifestyle choice, and we need to stop blaming magazines, rail-thin models, or overly controlling parents. The truth is that anorexia is a medical disorder caused by starvation, and it must be treated first and foremost by feeding the malnourished brain with nutrient-dense foods and nutritional supplements.

My approach has evolved over years of seeing many hundreds of patients. With every new patient I am reminded that not all individuals with anorexia are the same. Although a treatment plan needs to be specific for every individual, each plan starts with a comprehensive nutritional evaluation. Then, the nutrition-based treatment is implemented in conjunction with individualized medications. This approach transforms the treatment of anorexia from conventional hit-or-miss medication trials to focused interventions. Following my recommendations, testing for underlying conditions and implementing necessary treatments can and will result in clinical improvement in your child or loved one.

The five major aspects of this new approach to anorexia include:

- Optimizing zinc levels
- Evaluating deficiencies in digestive enzymes
- Correcting any underlying nutritional deficiencies
- Evaluating for celiac disease
- Choosing medications based on Referenced-EEG testing

Optimizing Zinc Levels

Over the past decades, research has shown more and more that a deficiency in the mineral zinc plays a critical role in the development of anorexia. When people have low levels of zinc, they often demonstrate decreased appetite, weight loss, altered taste perception, depression, and amenorrhea (missed menstrual periods). Do these symptoms sound familiar?

Adolescents typically do not eat foods that are high in zinc, such as meat and fish, and consume foods high in substances that inhibit zinc absorption from the GI tract, such as pasta. Having a zinc deficiency can be disastrous. Not only are appetite regulation and brain function impaired, but zinc is needed for every living cell in the body! Fortunately, testing for zinc deficiency involves a simple taste test. If needed, zinc supplementation is easy and can greatly enhance recovery.

Evaluating Deficiencies in Digestive Enzymes

Specific digestive enzyme problems can contribute to some symptoms of anorexia. Enzymes are substances in our digestive tract that break down the food we eat into smaller pieces. If a particular enzyme called dipeptidyl peptidase IV is inactive or deficient, then foods containing dairy and/or wheat ingredients cannot be fully digested. These undigested dairy and/or wheat proteins can still be absorbed into the bloodstream and travel to the brain. There they can cause psychiatric symptoms such as increased anxiety and intrusive, obsessive thoughts that can hinder effective treatment.

Determining whether a person has a deficiency and/or inactivity of this specific enzyme requires a simple urine test. This condition is treated by taking a digestive enzyme supplement as well as limiting dairy and/or wheat in the diet. When underlying digestive enzyme deficiencies are treated, the resulting changes in individuals with anorexia can be dramatic!

Correcting any Underlying Nutritional Deficiencies

"You are what you eat." It sounds simple, yet in the case of anorexia, this principle is particularly relevant. Underlying nutritional deficiencies affect the body; without essential nutrients, the body cannot build cells, grow normally, or heal properly. Chapters in this book will discuss the importance and necessity of minerals, vitamins, amino acids, fatty acids, and antioxidants.

Individuals with anorexia suffer from nutritional deficiencies as a result of starving themselves. Simple blood and urine tests can reveal a person's specific nutritional needs, and supplements can then be prescribed to optimize health. Fortunately, most patients with anorexia are comfortable taking nutritional supplements because they contain few calories. Once patients begin taking supplements necessary for their bodies, they often start to feel less anxious, more focused, and better able to participate in therapy.

Evaluating for Celiac Disease

When a patient presents with anorexia, a medical workup should be done to make certain that no treatable medical conditions are contributing to the clinical illness. Celiac disease, an autoimmune disorder in which the body is so sensitive to a certain food protein that it actually attacks and damages itself, can cause severe malnutrition and digestive discomfort. It often occurs in people with anorexia.

A blood test and, occasionally, a biopsy of the small intestine are used to test for the disease. Celiac disease is managed by eliminating a food protein called gluten—found in wheat and other grains—from the diet. Treating celiac disease can contribute immeasurably to the treatment of anorexia.

Choosing Medications Based on Referenced-EEG Testing

Researchers have yet to identify any psychiatric medications that can successfully and consistently treat patients who are suffering with anorexia. Instead, most psychiatrists continue to use a trial-and-error approach when prescribing medications for individuals.

Now an innovative and exciting technology called Referenced-EEG (rEEG) can identify which specific psychiatric medication(s) have the best chance of helping a particular individual with anorexia. A patient's brain-wave patterns are examined in a non-invasive manner, and the information is compared against a database. This database allows us to see which medications have previously been successful in other patients with similar EEG brainwave results. In this way, medication choices can be determined by the physiology of each individual's brain. With this guided medication selection, patients no longer have to be subjected to costly, unnecessary, and time-wasting trials of medications.

Brain Health is the Goal

Health should not be defined solely by the weight a person registers on a scale, or by the amount of food contained in a meal plan. Health has to be understood as a state of psychological freedom and physiological homeostasis.

In this book, you will learn safe and natural methods you can use with your child or loved one to restore health and arrest the downward spiral of the medical complications of anorexia nervosa. The foundation of my program is brain health; by ingesting essential nutrients, vitamins, and minerals, the brain will work in harmony with the mind. Obsessive thoughts about food and body image are a biological phenomenon and can be most quickly overcome with proper nutritional support and medications.

My treatment of eating disorders integrates nutritional supplements with psychiatric medicines. Many of my colleagues believe they have to be entrenched in one camp or the other; they either recommend nutritional support or prescribe medications. Why does it have to be one or the other? Prescribing multiple drugs based on symptoms without supporting scientific literature is as ridiculous as taking bottles of vitamins because you watched an infomercial on TV.

The treatment model for anorexia nervosa in contemporary medical practice is not grounded in any scientific reality. There is a huge disconnect between the scientific literature on eating disorders, anorexia nervosa in particular, and the treatment models we are asking patients and families to embrace. The professional leaders in the eating-disorders community insist that genetics, biology, and physiology need to be considered in treatment. Is anyone listening?

I cannot overstate the importance of a sound nutritional program in the treatment of eating disorders, particularly anorexia nervosa. With optimal physical health, patients will find the strength, confidence, and emotional energy to engage in treatment that will help them deal with the critical emotional, relational, developmental, and spiritual issues of long-term recovery.

I am *not* suggesting that a vitamin pill can erase psychological stresses or negative emotions, nor that nutritional supplementation alone will cure the disease. I am well aware that long-standing relationship struggles and dysfunctional family dynamics need to be addressed for successful recovery. What I *am* suggesting is that with a proper biological foundation and a nutritionally optimal environment, a complete recovery is possible. The healthiest brains have the greatest advantage when engaging in psychotherapy to work toward recovery.

Monica's Story Revisited

To undo the effects of a decade of malnutrition, I designed a treatment program for Monica that incorporated essential fatty acids, zinc, and vitamin B12 supplements; two psychiatric medications determined by rEEG testing; and outpatient psychotherapy. Since following my plan, she has not returned to the inpatient hospital unit. Best of all, Monica has begun to live a life that is no longer defined by her eating disorder. With a new job, friends, and a social life, she has fully integrated into the outside world. The fact that Monica could recover after 12 years of struggling with anorexia should signal hope to patients everywhere! With targeted nutritional therapy and a personalized medication plan, those who suffer from anorexia nervosa can get well.

Chapter Two

Anorexia 101

Anorexia nervosa is a life-threatening disorder that is poorly understood and often ignored by medical researchers. Anorexia is a complex, pernicious, and difficult-to-treat disorder. Those who have the disorder are masters at hiding it. Only when there are dramatic, outward manifestations do others become aware of the problem. Because our culture values thinness so highly, the anorexic generally receives praise in the earliest stages of the disorder. She is complimented for being thin and healthy, for eating properly and exercising. It's not until she grows sickly thin that people begin to whisper that maybe this is no "ordinary" diet.

To most people, deadly illnesses are conditions like cancer, AIDS, and heart disease. But self-starvation? The thought might never cross your mind. Yet the death rate from anorexia nervosa is more than 12 times higher than the annual death rate from all other causes combined for young women ages 15 to 24. According to the National Association of Anorexia Nervosa and Associated Disorders, 5 to 10 percent of those with anorexia die within 10 years of diagnosis, a figure that increases to 18 to 20 percent by the 20-year mark. Suicide accounts for approximately 20 to 30 percent of these deaths—a painfully frightening statistic that is often ignored by professionals, families, and patients themselves.

Anorexia nervosa is a serious disease in which a person has an extremely low body weight, sharply restricts her intake of food out of fear of gaining weight, and suffers from a distorted body image. Ninety percent of those with anorexia nervosa are women, most of them adolescents or young women, with onset most commonly occurring between the ages of 15 and 19. However, the disease is appearing increasingly in women older than 25, and it is seen in men.

In the United States, about 1 in 100 girls and women, and 0.3 to 1.20 percent of the overall population, suffers from anorexia. Although this may seem like a small number, this deadly disease actually affects millions, with estimates ranging from 8 to 11 million people struggling with eating disorders in the United States. Conservative estimates suggest that more than 25 percent of high school girls are affected by dietary practices of disordered eating. And the sad fact is that only 30 to 40 percent of those with anorexia will successfully recover.

Symptoms of Anorexia

There are several physical and psychological symptoms of anorexia, and, as we will see, almost every one of them is a direct result of starvation. They include the following:

Physical Symptoms
- A very low, unhealthy body weight (less than 85 percent of optimal weight for height, or a lack of increase in weight with age)
- Anemia (low iron level in the blood)
- Swelling of the feet and hands
- Bone loss
- Brittle, dry nails and hair
- Difficulty concentrating
- Fatigue, weakness
- Feeling cold all the time
- Growth of baby-fine hair all over the body
- Heart disease
- Irregular heart rate
- Liver abnormalities
- Low blood pressure
- Missed menstrual periods
- Nerve damage
- Sleep difficulties

Psychological Symptoms
- Fear of eating and refusal to eat, even when hungry or craving food
- Intense fear of weight gain
- Altered body image (believing she is "fat" when she is in fact emaciated)
- Obsessive thoughts regarding body image and appearance, food, calories, meals, or weight
- Secretive behavior (such as refusing to eat in front of other people)
- Anxiety
- Depression, withdrawal
- Irritability
- Psychological symptoms that become more apparent as more weight is lost, such as attention difficulties, memory problems, anxiety, and depression

Anorexia's Effects on the Body

Anorexia is much more than just being "too skinny," as it affects literally every major body system.

Cardiovascular system: The heart rate slows, blood pressure decreases, and the heartbeat can become irregular.

Digestive system: The speed at which food is digested and eliminated decreases, resulting in constipation and stomach pain.

Endocrine system: The complex and subtle balance of chemicals and hormones in the body is thrown off balance. For girls and women who have begun to menstruate, this can cause cessation of the menstrual cycle, which affects both fertility and bone density.

Immune system: Low white blood cell counts can occur, leading to a compromised immune system that increases vulnerability to infection.

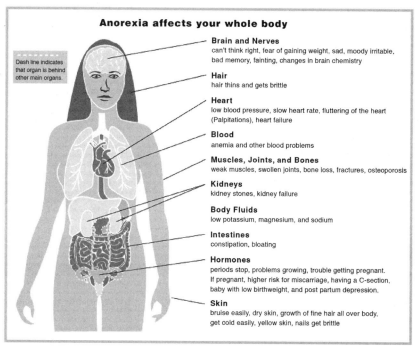

Illustration used with permission of the U.S. Department of Health and Human Services, Office on Women's Health. www.womanshealth.gov/faq/anorexia-nervosa.cfm#e.

Skin, hair, and nails: Due to a lack of protein and essential fatty acids, the skin becomes dry and flaky, the hair dry and fragile (in some cases, it falls out), and the nails brittle.

Nervous system: The space around the brain that holds the cerebrospinal fluid is enlarged, while the gray and white matter of the brain appears to be reduced.

Cognitive problems relating to attention, concentration, memory, and visuospatial ability can result. In addition, a research team in London found a reduction of blood flow to a region of the brain associated with emotion, appetite regulation, memory, motivation, and perception in 75 percent of adolescent anorexic patients. Unfortunately, even after a healthy weight is restored, brain abnormalities can persist in varying degrees.

Diagnostic Criteria for Anorexia Nervosa

According to the Diagnostic and Statistical Manual of Mental Disorders IV (DSM-IV), there are only four criteria for the diagnosis of anorexia nervosa:

1. The refusal to maintain body weight at or above a minimally normal weight (85 percent of ideal body weight) for age and height.
2. An intense fear of gaining weight or becoming fat, even when underweight.
3. Self-perception that is grossly distorted and weight loss that is not acknowledged.
4. In women who have already begun their menstrual cycle, at least three consecutive missed periods (amenorrhea), or menstrual periods that occur only after a hormone is administered.

There are also two sub-groups in the criteria for anorexia nervosa:

The restricting type. The restricter maintains a low body weight solely by severely restricting her food intake.

The binge-eating/purging type. The binge eater/purger eats large amounts of food, but maintains a low body weight by inducing vomiting, or abusing laxatives, diuretics, or enemas.

Midlife Women Are Not Immune to Anorexia

Age, too, is not a clear-cut criterion of anorexia. Typically, it's been assumed that as women age, eating disorder problems become less common—but it appears that the pressure to be thin never fades. Today the new standards of beauty for aging women are celebrities who flaunt their bodies onstage and in magazines and TV stars who maintain rail-thin bodies for the express purpose of pursuing younger men. Aging women are now expected not only to fight the inevitable expansion of their waistlines, but to compete with younger women in terms of looks.

The sad fact is, no matter what their age, most women struggle with body image. Faced with the super-slim ideal promoted by the media and celebrities—images that have been enhanced by photo manipulation, good lighting, and Spanx—most women have no hope of living up to this ideal. In fact, the average American woman is 5 feet 4 inches and 140 pounds, compared to the 5 feet 10 inches tall and 120-pound models they see in magazines and on television. Not surprisingly, many women in their 40s, 50s, and 60s suffer from poor body image and are unhappy with their weight. Some even suffer from eating disorders. A recent report from Austria found that among a random sample of 475 normal-weight women ages 60 to 70, most said they felt very or moderately fat and made efforts to manage their weight. Over half said they were dissatisfied with their bodies, and 4 percent (18 women) met the diagnostic criteria for an eating disorder.

Some midlife women with eating disorders may have had these problems continually since their youth, while others experience recurrences of eating disorders suffered in their teens, 20s, or 30s. Others may develop problems for the first time as they age in response to aging itself or to a traumatic life event (menopause, children going off to college, or the death of a spouse). Because these events can make a woman feel that she has little control over her life, she may focus intensely on her eating and exercise habits, which are things she can control. Many older women also use bingeing, purging, and restricting food as ways to cope with anxiety, anger, or depression.

Men and Anorexia

Although eating disorders are generally considered "female" diseases, men are not immune. Of the 8 million Americans with eating disorders, it's estimated that about 1 million are male. However, many clinicians believe this figure is low. The results of a survey of nearly 10,000 people conducted by researchers at the University of Toronto showed that males accounted for

1 of every 6 people who qualified for a full or partial diagnosis of anorexia.

Although men with eating disorders may share the same desire to be thin as women, the driving forces behind eating disorders in men can differ from those in women. While women simply desire to be thin, men seek well-defined muscles and an overall sculpted physique, and they will overexercise and restrict their food intake to build toned muscles and eliminate unwanted body fat. This can make it difficult to recognize the symptoms of an eating disorder. Most people wouldn't register concern about a man working out relentlessly, thinking "he's just trying to get fit." If he also restricts his diet, he's just "being healthy." And, since eating disorders are considered a "woman's disease," many men fail to realize or don't want to admit they may have this devastating disorder.

But the consequences of eating disorders in men are very real. Like women, men with anorexia suffer from low self-esteem and distorted body image. They struggle with issues of perfectionism and control. Physically, anorexic men suffer from dehydration, cardiac irregularities, thinning hair, and osteoporosis like their female counterparts. And ignoring the eating disorder can lead to death.

Other Eating Disorders

Anorexia nervosa is one of several categories of eating disorders. Each of these disorders leads to physical and emotional damage and can even lead to death. The other major disorders in addition to anorexia are bulimia nervosa, binge eating, and eating disorder not otherwise specified.

Bulimia nervosa. This is an eating disorder that involves eating unusually large amounts of food, then purging (ridding the body of that food) through self-induced vomiting, taking laxatives, or excessive exercising. The goal of bulimia, like anorexia, is to lose weight or, at least, prevent weight gain. Unlike people with anorexia, those with bulimia are typically of a normal weight for their height. Still, it can be a devastating disease. Bulimia can lead to fatigue, depression, dehydration, constipation, irregular heartbeat, electrolyte imbalance, and damage to teeth, gums, and cheeks due to repeated exposure to gastric acid during vomiting. (Some patients with anorexia nervosa may also indulge in bingeing/purging.)

Binge eating. This is commonly seen in eating-disordered patients, although it is not recognized as an eating disorder by the American Psychiatric Association's Diagnostic and Statistical Manual 4th Edition (DSM-IV), the diagnostic guide of the psychiatric and psychological professions. Binge eaters, who are typically overweight or even obese, repeatedly gorge themselves with food. They generally can't stop eating until they are overly full. Then, once they're done eating, they struggle with feelings of shame and guilt. They may suffer from fatigue, joint pain, high blood pressure, high cholesterol levels, heart disease, type 2 diabetes, and/or gallbladder disease.

Eating disorder not otherwise specified (*EDNOS*). Because most patients treated for anorexia nervosa don't exhibit all of the criteria for the disease listed in the DSM-IV (see below), 60 percent of all cases fall into the "non-diagnosis" category of "Eating Disorder Not Otherwise Specified" (EDNOS). Eating disorder not otherwise specified includes disorders of eating that do not meet the criteria for any specific eating disorder; the following are examples:

- For female patients, all of the criteria for anorexia nervosa are met except that the patient has regular menses.
- All of the criteria for anorexia nervosa are met except that, despite significant weight loss, the patient's current weight is in the normal range.
- All of the criteria for bulimia nervosa are met except that the binge eating and inappropriate compensatory mechanisms occur less than twice a week or for less than three months.
- The patient has normal body weight and regularly uses inappropriate compensatory behavior after eating small amounts of food (e.g., self-induced vomiting after consuming two cookies).
- Repeatedly chewing and spitting out, but not swallowing, large amounts of food.

The majority of patients with eating disorders are given the vague and unhelpful diagnosis of EDNOS. This diagnosis tells a clinician little about the patient except that she failed to meet the strict criteria of either anorexia nervosa or bulimia nervosa. An adolescent who meets all other criteria for anorexia nervosa with the exception that she continues to menstruate, would be given a diagnosis of EDNOS. This would put her in the same category as a woman who binged daily and suffered from obesity.

Despite the vast disparity among patients who have EDNOS, the fact remains that most eating-disorder cases are diagnosed as EDNOS. A study published in the journal *Behaviour Research and Therapy* estimated that 60 percent of eating disorder cases are diagnosed as EDNOS.

Many clinicians complain that the imprecise diagnostic criteria in the Diagnostic and Statistical Manual of Mental Disorders (DSM) is to blame for so many unhelpful diagnoses of EDNOS. The definition of each eating disorder has changed with each new edition of the DSM. In the DSM-III, an underweight individual who binged would have been given a diagnosis of both anorexia nervosa and bulimia nervosa. In the current DSM, DSM-IV, these same individuals would be classified as anorexia nervosa binge-purge subtype. These changes might seem small, but they have a significant impact on a patient's diagnosis and treatment. Without an accurate way of communicating among the medical community, how can we even begin to develop comprehensive, consistent treatment plans for patients? All medication and treatment trials rely on accurate diagnoses. If we cannot consistently categorize a disorder, then any research findings become nebulous and difficult to interpret.

Debate over the diagnostic categories has increased as a new version of the DSM is being prepared for release in May 2013. With this new version, major changes are being proposed for each of the eating disorders. Many clinicians suggest changing the criteria for anorexia nervosa, in particular, by eliminating the requirement for missed menstrual periods (amenorrhea). To clarify eating-disorder diagnoses, some clinicians suggest removing the subtypes for anorexia nervosa and creating new diagnostic categories, such as purging disorder and binge eating disorder. By changing the criteria, some of the current cases of EDNOS could be reclassified as either anorexia nervosa or bulimia nervosa.

The confusion evident among the professional community is magnified in the countless roadblocks patients and their families encounter in seeking help. How can we prescribe a treatment, offer informed care, or instill hope? The sad reality is that the professional community has been treading water with little progress for many, many years.

Co-Existing Illnesses Hinder Treatment

Effective treatment of anorexia nervosa is complicated by the presence of other psychiatric disorders in patients with anorexia. Adults and adolescents with anorexia and other eating disorders share similar rates of co-existing psychiatric illnesses. Many anorexics suffer from depression and anxiety disorders, including generalized anxiety disorder, obsessive-compulsive disorder, social phobia, panic disorder, agoraphobia, or post-traumatic stress disorder. Depression is typically seen in those with anorexia, with estimates ranging as high as 88 percent. Anxiety disorders are also prevalent in individuals suffering from eating disorders. In the largest study conducted to date, involving 672 patients with eating disorders, close to two-thirds (64 percent) were found to have a lifetime history of one or more anxiety disorders. In comparison, people without eating disorders had rates up to 31 percent.

Substance abuse is also common in patients with anorexia nervosa. The National Center on Addiction and Substance Abuse at Columbia University found that approximately 50 percent of individuals with eating disorders abuse drugs or alcohol, compared to 9 percent of the general population. Individuals with anorexia, particularly those who binge and purge, are far more likely to use drugs or alcohol than the general population. The reverse is also true. Nearly 35 percent of individuals with a substance use disorder have an eating disorder, compared to 3 percent of the general population in the United States.

Substance use disorders tend to develop after an eating disorder has been established. Anxiety disorders and depression, on the other hand, often begin in childhood before the onset of anorexia, suggesting that these mental illnesses make people more vulnerable to an eating disorder, again acting as a kind of gateway for the expression of anorexia. Furthermore, when one or more of these illnesses occur together, they tend to exacerbate the severity of all of these problems.

The Danger of Eating Disorders

What has become very clear recently is that all of the eating disorders are serious psychiatric illnesses with high mortality rates. In a recent study published in 2009 in the *American Journal of Psychiatry*, Dr. Scott Crow and colleagues reported that mortality rates for bulimia and EDNOS were as frighteningly elevated as those reported in anorexia nervosa.

Anorexia, bulimia, and EDNOS are arbitrary names for pathological eating patterns. These eating behaviors have several disturbing features in common: they cause tremendous suffering, prolonged treatment attempts are ineffective and costly, they are chronic conditions that tend to recur, and they have higher mortality rates than other psychiatric illnesses.

These features underscore the importance of changing our fundamental approach to treatment.

Another important fact is that frequently many patients' diagnoses do not remain static. Over the course of their illness, some patients initially diagnosed with one eating disorder will later meet criteria for another disorder. The two recognized eating disorders, anorexia nervosa and bulimia nervosa, share several clinical features and characteristics. Most patients with anorexia nervosa will later meet criteria for bulimia nervosa. This shifting of diagnoses is referred to as "diagnostic cross-over."

Although all eating disorders demand urgent attention, anorexia nervosa is the primary focus of this book. Anorexia nervosa is the most lethal of all disorders treated by psychiatrists. Once you witness the tragic effects this disorder has on its emaciated victims and their families, you can never forget. I can't.

Before I discuss alternative solutions, I'd like to explore a more comprehensive, yet often ignored, discussion on the science of anorexia nervosa.

The Emerging Science of Anorexia Nervosa

Anorexia nervosa affects every organ system in the body, including profound changes in the nervous system and the brain. Structural abnormalities in the brain are one of the earliest physical consequences of anorexia in adolescents. Studies using computerized tomography (CT) and magnetic resonance imaging (MRI) to view the brain have found that young women with anorexia have reduced brain mass. Long-term weight recovery may reverse some of these abnormalities, although persistent brain abnormalities to varying degrees can still exist. In other words, these changes in brain structure are not always fully reversible, even after an adolescent with anorexia makes a full recovery.

These physical brain abnormalities have consequences. Those with anorexia often have cognitive problems relating to attention, concentration, memory, and visuospatial ability. As with the structural brain changes, some—but not all—of the cognitive problems disappear once these young women regain weight.

It's not known, however, exactly how these structural brain changes are related to cognition. A study published in the *International Journal of Eating Disorders* found a 75 percent reduction in blood flow to key areas of the brain in patients with anorexia. The London-based research team found reduced blood flow to the temporal lobe and nearby areas that are associated with emotion, appetite regulation, memory, motivation, and perception.

Rather than solely examining the physical changes in the brain, researchers are now interested in the various proteins and receptors in the brain. One of these proteins is brain-derived neurotrophic factor (BDNF), which plays a critical role in the development and function of nerve cells in the brain. Recent research using laboratory animals has revealed that BDNF also plays a role in regulating eating behaviors. Several recent studies published in the *European Journal of Human Genetics* and the journal *Psychological Medicine* have found significantly decreased BDNF levels in the blood of patients with eating disorders, specifically patients with anorexia nervosa. Although decreased levels of BDNF have also been implicated in depression and anxiety (common co-existing conditions in anorexia), BDNF levels may provide new insight into detecting and treating anorexia as well as other eating disorders. The function of BDNF is highly dependent on the mineral zinc, which you will learn more about in the next section.

There is evidence to suggest that altered brain serotonin function may be contributing to traits seen in anorexia. Altered serotonin function has been documented in patients with anorexia during the height of their illness. Patients suffering with anorexia have reduced amounts of serotonin metabolites (the byproducts that remain after serotonin is used) in their cerebrospinal fluid, indicating that they have overall decreased amounts of serotonin in the brain. Brain-imaging studies also show that individuals with anorexia have altered amounts of receptors for serotonin. Serotonin receptor abnormalities can also be reproduced in animals by feeding them diets deficient in omega-3 fatty acids. Disturbances in serotonin can contribute to the dysregulation of appetite, mood, and impulse control in anorexia.

There are also some scientists who believe anorexia nervosa is an autoimmune disorder. There is growing research showing that those with anorexia possess antibodies against the proteins that control appetite and stress responses. A study published in the journal *Proceedings of the National Academy of the Sciences* found that three-quarters of patients with eating disorders, in particular anorexia, have antibodies against peptides in the brain that regulate emotion and appetite. There appears to be a correlation between the level of these antibodies and the severity of the disease; higher concentrations coincide with more severe forms of anorexia nervosa.

Although the details are beyond the scope of this book, there is a growing interest in looking at the biochemical and genetic abnormalities seen in anorexia nervosa. As you will learn, however, many of these abnormalities can be traced to the underlying nutritional deficiencies addressed in the coming chapters, specifically the essential fatty acids and zinc. These core nutrients regulate critical aspects of our genes and the cellular functions that occur in the brain.

Chapter Three

Misplaced Blame

You may be reading this book because your teenager's eyes, once bright, now look hollow and frightened. Or maybe you're close to someone who is an emaciated skeleton under baggy clothes, a parody of the slender frame our culture idealizes. Seeing her this way breaks your heart; trying to reason with her perplexes and frustrates you. You ask her to eat, and she looks at you as if you have asked her to do something more terrifying than die.

Anorexics have the longest hospital stays, highest suicide risks, and highest mortality rates of any psychiatric patients—10 percent die from the disease within a decade. The disease transforms carefree little girls into young women who are disgusted by their bodies and morbidly afraid of gaining weight. The disease also affects men, as well as midlife women, most of whom suffered from eating disorders as young girls. But whether young or old, male or female, the results are the same. These individuals waste away, refusing food while insisting they are fat, even as jutting bones and emaciated bodies testify otherwise. It's a sad fact that although this disease has been documented for nearly 700 years, the medical profession has not provided adequate treatments.

Possible Causes of Anorexia

Health professionals will tell you that anorexia nervosa results from a combination of social, genetic, psychological, and family traits that combine to produce a disease that can be treated with psychotherapy. While social, genetic, and psychological factors are relevant, they are most certainly not the sole, or even primary, causes of the disease. Let's take a look at each of these to understand why.

Societal Pressure to be Thin

Traditionally, anorexia nervosa has been seen as a psychiatric illness triggered by our culture of thinness. People in our society often measure a woman's personal worth by her weight and body shape. Glossy magazine covers glorify super-skinny models and celebrities, and thanks to airbrushing, Photoshopping, and other tricks, they appear perfect. Yet these "perfect" models and celebrities can easily fall into the anorexia pit as they struggle to live up to impossible ideals. In 2004, Ana Reston, a 5-foot 8-inch, 112-pound Brazilian model, was told she was too fat. Two years later, she died of anorexia nervosa. Similarly, Luisel Ramos, a prominent model in Uruguay, collapsed and died of self-imposed starvation immediately following her runway walk during Uruguay's Fashion Week. Her sister, also a model, died of anorexia the following year.

The cultural pressure to be thin not only permeates the world of international modeling but affects many other arenas: If a girl wants to be a gymnast, dancer, model, actress, or athlete, she must attain and maintain a lean body. And it trickles down to virtually all socioeconomic and age groups, including the very young. Surveys of schoolchildren have shown that:

- 45 percent of those in grades 3 through 6 say they want to be thinner, and 37 percent have already dieted.
- More than three-quarters of 10-year-olds are afraid of being fat.
- 53 percent of 13-year-olds report that they are unhappy with the way they look.
- 78 percent of 18-year-old girls are unhappy with their bodies.
- The most frequently expressed wish of American girls between the ages of 11 and 17 is not to have a pony or an elaborate party, but to lose weight.

Many girls and young women feel an inordinate amount of pressure to conform to the ideal of a thin body as the ultimate in feminine beauty. They may believe that they aren't worthy unless they are as thin and gorgeous as the women in the magazines. And if that means they have to diet, they will diet. Dieting is something of a ritual among women in America, and although most lose small amounts of weight on diets, they eventually gain back more than they lost in the first place. Thus dieting just increases body dissatisfaction.

Young people bombarded with the media glorification of thinness can develop what is called normative discontent. This means that their dissatisfaction with their bodies is typical; it's the norm. We might conclude that normative discontent causes anorexia nervosa. A brief history, however, shows that what we now call anorexia nervosa has been around much longer than the values of our diet-obsessed culture. This history supports our increasingly clear awareness that although body dissatisfaction may be a factor in anorexia, it is not the fundamental cause of the disorder.

Genetic Influences

Eating disorders, like red hair or flat feet, run in certain families. Many family studies have confirmed that those with a family member who has anorexia have 10 times the risk of developing anorexia themselves, compared to those from families with normal eating behaviors. Moreover, there is an increased risk of developing anorexia when a family member has other kinds of eating disorders; those with a family member who has bulimia are at 12 times the normal risk of developing anorexia.

The heritability of eating disorders is most apparent in studies of twins as they share the same set of genes. A study in the *Archives of General Psychiatry* of 31,206 Swedish twins born between 1935 and 1958 found that more than half (56 percent) of the risk for anorexia can be attributed to genetic make-up. Similar studies have shown that the risk can range from 48 to 88 percent.

What are those suffering from eating disorders inheriting that could possibly lead to anorexia, bulimia, or other eating disorder behaviors? Many personality traits, such as shyness and—in the case of anorexia—a drive for thinness, obsessionality, and dietary restraint, have been shown to be heritable.

It is not just the genes that are related to personality traits that researchers believe are responsible for anorexia. Potential alterations in genes associated with mood and behavior (such as neurotransmitter genes) and appetite and hunger (such as leptin and ghrelin genes), may also be inherited. Many studies are exploring whether changes in the function of these genes are found in those with eating disorders. The genetic links are so profound that most of today's researchers focus on inherited causes of the disease.

However, despite a wealth of genetic findings, it is very clear that genes are merely a biological liability: They do not predetermine that an individual will become anorexic. A host of other factors, including hormonal changes, nutrition patterns, and stress can trigger the expression or, more likely, the "misexpression" of these genes.

Personality Traits

Temperament, otherwise known as our innate personality traits, remains relatively stable over the course of a lifetime and greatly influences how the brain interprets external events. For instance, temperament may determine whether a child is open to new experiences or fearful of them, or whether she is able to "think outside of the box" and problem-solve rather than follow the rules all of the time. Research shows that the "anorexia temperament" can be found across different cultures, races, and ethnicities and is often observed when the individual is as young as two or three years old.

The most common traits linked to anorexia nervosa include:

- Perfectionism
- Neuroticism (emotional instability)
- Harm avoidance (a passive, careful approach to life)
- Anxiety
- Insecurity
- Non-novelty seeking (desire to avoid new situations)
- Rigidity
- Need to control
- Chronically low self-esteem
- Lack of self-direction

Patients with eating disorders have long been described as having personalities characterized by perfectionism, anxiety, and low self-esteem. Evaluations of women with anorexia nervosa have shown that they have increased traits related to harm avoidance and decreased traits related to cooperativeness and self-directedness. Individuals with high harm-avoidance traits are extremely careful, passive, and insecure and are also prone to react to stressful events with a high rate of anxiety and depression. Low self-directedness is related to chronically low self-esteem and a struggle with identity. It's believed that these personality traits may make an individual vulnerable to an eating disorder.

The medical and therapeutic professions, as well as the lay public, remain convinced that anorexia and other eating disorders are psychological diseases. They claim that the personality traits listed above combine with our culture's extreme emphasis on thinness and physical attractiveness to create a destructive cycle that spirals out of control. The result is a distorted body image and a morbid fear of weight gain.

Family Dynamics

Another popular theory holds that family dysfunction lies at the core of anorexia, in particular the "enmeshed" family style, in which members become so interdependent that they identify more as members of the family than as individuals. One particularly destructive manifestation is an almost morbid fear of growing up.

In families described as enmeshed, members tend to become over-involved in each other's lives, and boundaries between individuals are not

---

clear. They tend to speak for each other and intrude into each other's feelings. Family therapists have hypothesized that adolescents in enmeshed families may become anorexic in a desperate attempt to control the small domain left to them: their bodies and their diets.

Dieting

We all live in a society that puts a high premium on thinness, and many of us come from troubled families or wrestle with anxiety, depression, or low self-esteem, but only a few of us develop anorexia. This is true even when all of these factors are present and the individual has a genetic predisposition toward eating disorders. So why does one person at high risk of anorexia develop the disease while another with a similar set-up doesn't?

Often the deciding factor is dieting. The intentional attempts to restrict food intake are detrimental to both mind and body and can promote anorexia by:

- Encouraging obsessive thoughts and behaviors about eating.
- Fostering an "all-or-nothing" attitude.
- Promoting hyper-controlled, rigid behavior.
- Contributing to depression, anxiety, and poor self-esteem.
- Promoting isolation.
- Increasing the likelihood of nutritional deficiencies that contribute to anorexia.
- Interfering with the body's signals of hunger and satiety (fullness).

The inextricable link between mind and body is clearly evident in the dieting process. When the food supply dwindles, both mind and body go into survival mode. The body lowers the metabolism and burns energy more frugally, trying to hang on to each calorie as long as possible. The mind focuses solely on one purpose: getting food. Suddenly, the dieter can think of nothing but food, diets, and eating. She may plan menus, clip recipes, cook elaborate meals or dishes for others (while declining to eat them), and dream about food at night. The body wants food, and so does the mind.

Depression and anxiety set in after just a few days of extreme restriction of the food supply. This is partially due to changes in neurotransmitters like serotonin, but it may also be a pleasure void—something that was very pleasurable (eating) has not been replaced by anything else. There is an increased desire to spend time alone, as it's just too energy-draining to interact with others, and the isolation just increases the depression. Self-esteem begins to plummet, thinking becomes distorted, and anxiety rises, leading to even more obsessive thinking about food. Stress levels rise dramatically; she feels out of control and responds by restricting her food intake even further. On the physical side, existing in a state of semi-starvation drastically reduces the rate at which the stomach empties, so just one piece of bread, for example, can cause an uncomfortable feeling of fullness and take a long time to digest.

In short, dieting leads to food obsessions, depression, anxiety, and isolation, which contribute to increased stress, negative thinking, poor self-esteem, more food obsessions, and problems with digestion, all of which can lead to further restriction of food. It's a vicious circle.

The True Cause of Anorexia Nervosa

While societal pressure to be thin, genetic makeup, certain personality traits, family dynamics, and dieting are all important factors in the development of anorexia, the true cause of the disease is the malnourishment of the brain. The process of self-starvation brought on by systematic food restriction is the root cause of anorexia nervosa. Unfortunately, the psychological effects have received more attention than the starvation process, although not for lack of evidence.

The Minnesota Starvation Experiment

More than 60 years ago Ancel Keys, a physiology professor at the University of Minnesota, launched a landmark study of the effects of starvation on the body. Thirty-six men, all conscientious objectors to World War II, participated in what became known as the Minnesota Starvation Experiment. For 24 weeks, their caloric intake was severely restricted, and they were forced to walk 22 miles a week. The result was extreme weight loss, of course, but more interesting were the psychological effects of starvation. Like those with anorexia, the men became obsessed with food and eating; they constantly thought about food and even dreamed about it. They even took pleasure in watching others eat and continually chewed gum—sometimes as many as 40 packs a day.

As the starvation phase continued, the men displayed even more of the typical psychological characteristics of anorexia nervosa: depression, obsessive-compulsive behavior (in this case, rituals involving food), anxiety, irritability, and delusional thinking. Like anorexics, they lost interest in sex, their family and social connections began to fray, their ability to concentrate was diminished, and their comprehension and judgment faltered.

Thirty-two of the men made it through the starvation stage to the recovery stage, at which time their caloric intake was slowly increased. However, they continued to suffer psychological effects, with many experiencing severe emotional distress and depression. Three weeks into recovery, one individual suffered a horrendous reaction—chopping off three of his fingers with an ax. Although 50 years later he was unsure whether or not the action was intentional, he did vividly recall that he was not psychologically stable at the time. The researchers attributed his actions to a severe degree of "semi-starvation neurosis."

The Minnesota Starvation Experiment clearly showed that eating too little food for a prolonged period of time causes psychological symptoms, and many of these symptoms are similar to those described by patients with anorexia nervosa. The psychological symptoms didn't cause anorexia; they emerged as a consequence of starvation. The men who participated in Keys' experiment were determined to be psychologically healthy at the beginning of the study. This, of course, does not mean that all individuals whose restricted eating spirals downward to anorexia were psychologically healthy to begin with. But Key's results clearly showed that whatever psychopathology was present to begin with, the malnutrition that comes from self-starvation is sure to exacerbate it.

Toward a New Understanding of Anorexia Nervosa

The treatment of anorexia nervosa has remained essentially static for more than five decades. After years of treating patients with eating disorders, it's become painfully apparent to me that psychiatry misunderstands anorexia. Psychiatrists have confused the obvious effects of anorexia nervosa (depression, anxiety, obsessive-compulsive behavior) with its causes. Thus, they're treating depression, panic attacks, compulsions, obsessive behavior, and other psychological conditions in an effort to quell anorexia, when it's actually the starvation that is causing these conditions in the first place.

This new understanding of anorexia is beginning to draw support among researchers around the world. Cecilia Bergh, PhD, and Per Sodersten, PhD, at the Karolinska Institute in Stockholm have written about this and direct a treatment program founded on the hypothesis that the symptoms of anorexia are a consequence of starvation rather than a mental disorder. A 2003 article by Shan Guisinger, PhD, in *Psychological Review* concludes that psychological treatment for anorexia "has had too little to offer" and concurs that the symptoms of anorexia are biological responses to low body weight.

Guisinger proposes that anorexia actually reflects an ancestral adaptation to times of starvation. As our ancestors were most likely foragers, humans were at one time exposed to periods of starvation and famine. In response to these adverse situations, our bodies respond by declining our metabolic rate by as much as 40 percent and developing behavioral and neuroendocrine mechanisms that increase our desire for food. For short periods of time these are advantageous to survival, because they make individuals more efficient at conserving energy and seeking food. Prolonged periods, however, are detrimental, as individuals become lethargic and obsessed with eating. This scenario mirrors anorexia. Guisinger argues that part of the failed treatment of anorexia stems from professionals who fail to take into account the evolutionary roots of anorexia. Understanding anorexia requires more than just looking at its symptoms.

Approaching anorexia nervosa as a psychological disorder does not take into account the brain's physiological response to a shortage of essential nutrients. Regardless of culture, psychological traits, or family pressures, the results of starving remain the same: a malnourished mind. This is where so many experts and researchers go wrong. Incorrectly assessing the root cause makes it impossible to find an effective treatment. It's like smacking your head on an open cabinet and taking lots of aspirin to relieve the pain. When a CT scan reveals that you actually have a small brain bleed, you realize that you've not only treated the wrong root cause, but you've actually made things worse because aspirin can cause further bleeding.

The medical field has pursued treatment after treatment for anorexia nervosa while misunderstanding the cause of the disorder, which is a nutritional deficiency syndrome. If professionals were less focused on blaming the culture, the patients' psychological problems or the functioning of their families, perhaps we could have recognized 50 years ago that a malnourished brain is a critical and, I believe, the primary cause of anorexia nervosa.

Conquering anorexia nervosa can be achieved by restoring the malnourished brain with nutritional supplements during the course of therapy and psychological treatment.

Chapter Four

Confusing Cause and Effect

It is important to understand that anorexia is not an illness that people choose. We may choose to diet and lose weight, but we don't choose to become delusional about our health and weight. We don't choose to incessantly obsess about food and how and what we eat. After eating patterns are altered, brains are changed. This spurs on further weight loss and pathological eating behaviors. Anorexia nervosa is complex, puzzling, and biologically and emotionally malignant.

Harriet Brown, a parent writing in *The New York Times* about her family's ordeal with anorexia, described the disease as "a vicious demon." It was as if her daughter was possessed by an evil spirit, and they were engaged in a battle of wills for her body. The daughter, Kitty, was not strong enough to fight back against the voice in her head that told her she was disgusting and fat, making her choke on every bite and clutch her stomach in pain. "Her anxiety was so great that there was no reward that could motivate her to eat," Brown wrote. Only the threat of being put into the hospital and fed with a tube would make Kitty eat.

Having treated hundreds of patients with anorexia nervosa, I find it difficult to imagine that attitudes about sexuality, parental conflict, or separation could explain the devastating consequences I witness firsthand.

It is time for change.

Is it such a huge leap of logic to surmise that patients with a disorder of self-starvation require additional nutritional support?

The case for the nutritional perspective I am promoting is well documented, but it has been overwhelmed by a treatment culture that has deep historical roots. A brief review of the history of anorexia nervosa is both fascinating and helpful in trying to unravel many misperceptions about the underlying cause and treatment for anorexia.

A Brief History of Anorexia Nervosa

Cases of anorexia nervosa have been chronicled through the centuries, well before strikingly thin models became the ideal of female beauty. The earliest documented case of self-starvation comes from the Middle Ages. In the fourteenth century, a female saint, Catherine of

Siena, became emaciated from an extreme form of fasting and eventually starved herself to death. Other Italian female saints of the same century followed a similar path. They seem to have been motivated not by an intense fear of being fat, but by a desire to deny the claims of the flesh in order to perfect their spirit. Whatever their professed motivation, and despite the intervening centuries, we can recognize from the lives of these female saints familiar symptoms: depression, anxiety, obsessive thoughts, and compulsive behaviors. These saints are sometimes called "holy anorexics" because they believed their starvation was infused with religious meaning.

While there is disagreement about whether or not the holy anorexics of the Middle Ages really suffered from what we now call anorexia, there is common agreement that by the end of the seventeenth century there existed eating disorders that very closely mirror modern sufferers of anorexia.

In 1689, Richard Morton, MD, described an illness marked by its relentless pursuit of thinness; a pursuit for which he could not determine any medical cause. He concluded that the illness was the result of "violent passions of the mind."

Morton assigned some nuance to the disease, understanding that there was a seductiveness to the illness, that it "flatters and deceives the patient" in its early stages. Certainly, modern therapists hear echoes of their own understandings in his words!

Writing nearly two centuries later, in 1868, the English physician Sir William W. Gull found himself confronted by:

"A peculiar form of disease occurring mostly in young women, and characterized by extreme emaciation... At present our diagnosis of this affliction is negative, so far as determining any positive cause from which it springs... The subjects [are]...chiefly between the ages of 16 and 23... My experience supplies at least one instance of fatal termination... Death apparently followed from the starvation alone... The want of appetite is, I believe, due to a morbid mental state... We might call the state hysterical."

Convinced that this strange and disturbing disease was the result of a mental "hysteria," Gull named it anorexia nervosa—nervous loss of appetite. He was certain, with all the certainty a physician of the Great Empire could possess in the late nineteenth century, that anorexia nervosa was the result of a psychological dysfunction. So certain, in fact, that he embedded the cause for the disease firmly in the name he gave it.

And he was wrong.

As a psychiatrist, I can understand Gull's perspective—and I even have a great deal of sympathy for it. It must have been disturbingly frustrating to see an otherwise healthy patient essentially starve herself to death. I sympathize because it is the same feeling many therapists feel even today. What I have more difficulty understanding is how, in the ensuing 140 years, so little has changed in our treatment and our understanding. Our frustration has not changed. Through the Industrial Revolution, Darwin's publication of *The Origin of Species*, the advent of motorized travel, airplanes, the Roaring Twenties, the Great Depression, two world wars, nuclear weapons, walking on the moon, the growth of psychopharmacology, and on and on, we still cling firmly to Gull's fundamental premise even though it fails to adequately encompass anorexia nervosa or point to effective treatments.

Another prominent physician, Charles Lasègue, writing in the 1860s around the same time as Gull, confirmed the perception of anorexia nervosa as "hysteria linked to hypochondriasis." Lasègue described anorexia as "…that mental perversion, which by itself is almost characteristic, and which justifies the name which I have proposed for want of a better—hysterical anorexia."

So, by the 1870s, Gull and Lasègue had established the pillars of our understanding of anorexia, the pillars that have informed our theoretical and therapeutic understanding of anorexia up until today.

Curiously, the demands of the culture seem to have played much less of a factor in the diagnosis of anorexia in the nineteenth century. That time period certainly did not hold thinness as the ideal of beauty. Quite the opposite. Even a cursory look at the art of the time shows voluptuous women as the image of feminine beauty.

Anorexics of the nineteenth century were not responding to a cultural image of thinness. They were opposing a cultural image of beauty. Lasègue's patients seemed to share more with Catherine of Siena and other religious ascetics than might have appeared at first glance. They did not try to lose weight due to a morbid fear of being fat, as modern anorexics do, but instead placed moral value on their weight loss. They engaged in starvation behavior for "positive" reasons to elevate themselves.

For the next century, eating disorders seemed to exist just below the radar of most psychiatrists and psychologists. In 1947, John M. Berkman at the Mayo Clinic in Rochester, Minnesota, called attention to anorexia nervosa in girls or young women between ages 16 and 30. He attributed the condition to starvation that results from psychic disturbance brought on by relationships with parents or other disappointments in life. According to Berkman, "Among adolescents the cause for the psychic upset can often be traced to a parent. However, the disturbing factor may originate in school, with a teacher, or in disappointments far removed from the parent and home life."

But it wasn't until 1973, when Hilde Bruch published *Eating Disorders: Obesity, Anorexia and the Person Within,* that the pursuit of thinness, already a strong, cultural dynamic, was raised in the common consciousness. Although Bruch's understanding of the disease had nothing to do with the religious motivations of earlier times, it was more nuanced than simply, "the pursuit of thinness." She understood the centrality of the drive for thinness in modern society, but she also placed that drive within a larger psycho-cultural context and the rapidly evolving role, status and image of women.

In Bruch's world view, the drive for thinness is a concrete manifestation of the anorexic's "failed quest for autonomy." Without diminishing the challenges women face in defining themselves in and against a difficult culture, this understanding continues to place the drive for thinness in the psychological or the cultural realm.

The medical and psychological communities have long blamed anorexia on our culture's emphasis on slimness and the exaggerated response this emphasis elicits from certain vulnerable women. Thus, anorexia has traditionally been viewed and treated as a psychological disease.

What we now know about malnutrition and starvation, however, makes it clear that our culture's unhealthy preoccupation with slimness—while it is a factor in body dissatisfaction and dieting—is not the root cause of anorexia nervosa.

The medical profession has been observing restrictive eating patterns for hundreds of years, yet we still do not have a basic answer as to why it starts and how to treat it. The death rate of anorexia nervosa is staggering. The irreversible medical and psychological complications are tragic.

Medical Professionals and Nutrition

Why are medical professionals slow to recognize the nutritional contribution to disease and health? Why have medical professionals been slow to acknowledge evidence that anorexia nervosa is fundamentally a disorder of starvation and malnutrition? I believe there are at least five reasons:

1. Physicians are not taught or trained to think about nutrition.
2. Severe nutritional deficiency was thought to have disappeared in the 1940s with the advent of food enrichment.
3. There is a lack of funding or financial incentive to research non-patentable, non-profit-generating nutritional products.
4. Physicians who focus on nutrition are segregated from the rest of medicine as "Complementary and Alternative" practitioners.
5. The "Tomato Effect" exists in medicine.

Physicians Are Not Trained in Nutrition

A study conducted by the National Academy of Sciences in 1985 determined that physicians in U.S. medical schools received inadequate nutritional education. A broad survey in 2006 reached the same conclusion: American medical students do not receive the training they need either to understand the importance of nutrition or to counsel their patients. In fact, researchers report a substantial decline in the perceived relevance of nutritional counseling the longer students are in medical school. Graduating seniors consider nutrition less relevant than do entering freshmen! Other studies have found that far too many physicians in current practice—even cardiologists whose primary focus is the human heart—lack basic knowledge about the influence of diet on cardiovascular health.

Severe Nutritional Deficiency Is Thought to Have Disappeared

In the early part of the 1900s, nutritional intervention played a significant role in medicine. As Casimir Funk coined the term *vitamine* in 1912, there was growing interest in the medical community in using these vitamins for the treatment of many diseases. Vitamins were important aspects of medical practice after the discovery and treatment of vitamin deficiency disorders in the early 1900s. However, with the fortification of food starting in the 1940s, the use of vitamins in the field of medicine was slowly phased out. It was believed, and still is, that enrichment of food with vitamins and minerals is enough to overcome any deficiency.

The Vast Majority of Psychiatric Research Today Is Funded by Pharmaceutical Companies

Pharmaceutical companies invest millions—if not billions—in research, hoping to generate substantial profits. Nutritional substances like zinc, however, are inexpensive and non-patentable. In other words, nutritional substances aren't profitable, and investing in nutritional research will not lead to the big payoffs that pharmaceutical companies seek. This is a likely reason why research on zinc for the treatment of anorexia was never explored further after the initial studies in the 1980s.

Physicians Who Incorporate Nutrition Into Medical Treatment Are Considered Outside The Mainstream

Nutritional medicine has always been considered "alternative medicine," and for most physicians it isn't part of their practice. Psychiatry and mental health treatment has continued to lag behind the rest of medicine in incorporating nutritional therapies into treatment. Physicians often face colleagues who question nutritional interventions, and it usually is easier to maintain "conventional wisdom."

The Tomato Effect

A phenomenon labeled "the tomato effect" helps explain the reluctance of the medical community to embrace nutritional therapies for anorexia nervosa.

The tomato effect was first identified by Dr. James Goodwin in the *Journal of the American Medical Association* in 1984. He wrote, "The tomato effect in medicine occurs when an efficacious treatment for a certain disease is ignored or rejected because it does not 'make sense' in light of accepted theories of disease mechanism and drug action."

The rejection of a potentially effective treatment because "everyone knows it won't work" is named for Americans' persistent belief—from the sixteenth to the nineteenth centuries—that tomatoes were poisonous.

Although tomatoes were first eaten in the Americas, throughout the 1600s and 1700s they were considered inedible decorative plants. It was believed that they were poisonous because they belonged to the nightshade family of plants, among which belladonna and mandrake are, indeed, toxic. But Americans also knew that Europeans were serving and eating tomatoes at the dinner table.

The fate of the tomato in America changed in 1820, when a man named Robert Johnson of Salem, New Jersey, consumed a basketful of tomatoes in public to prove they were safe to eat. When he neither dropped dead nor even suffered any apparent ill effects, the witnesses to his experiment slowly began to open their minds. By the end of the decade, American gardeners in the Northeast were growing tomatoes for food.

Considering the omnipresence of the tomato in the American diet today—in salads, sandwiches, ketchup, pasta sauce and salsa—it is hard to believe that the tomato was once shunned as inedible!

The Tomato Effect and Medical Treatments

Dr. Goodwin coined the term the tomato effect to explain the rejection by American medicine of therapies that do not fit with currently accepted theories of disease and treatment. He believed that the tomato effect had delayed the acceptance of vitamin and mineral supplementation. This type of intervention is outside the familiar medical paradigm, which has no place for a disease or disorder caused by a deficiency, a negative cause. In fact, Goodwin believed that the particular resistance to micronutrient treatment went beyond skepticism. After studying prominent medical texts written between 1948 and 1995, he identified an angry tone in descriptions of nutritional supplementation, a departure from the unemotional language that is typical in these texts. For instance, R. J. Harrison, writing in 1970 in *Textbook of Medicine*, cites the physician's temptation to prescribe vitamins and minerals as "a simple way to protect patients from the small chance that they may develop deficiency states." He concludes that this practice is "wasteful... to be deplored" and is often based on "an insidious marketing device that cannot be justified."

Understanding the human tendency to reject a treatment outside one's frame of reference—even in the presence of contradictory evidence—should help us identify the medical profession's persistent resistance to recognizing the importance of nutritional deficiencies in anorexia nervosa. Still, we cannot afford to remain under the spell of the tomato effect. Patients and their families are waiting for physicians to break free from our long-held, but mistaken, assumptions.

From the Past to the Present

Astonishingly, the only thing that seems to have changed from Lasègue to Bruch is the cultural definition of the ideal female body. Still, that single variable fits in perfectly with our current, common narrative that anorexia is an extreme desire to meet a cultural ideal and serves to fuel an understanding that the surge in cases of sufferers of eating disorders is the result of young women and men with body image issues, a dysfunctional family, anxiety, and low self-esteem becoming victimized by societal pressures.

This understanding is a disservice to the people who struggle with anorexia and a barrier to those who struggle to truly understand and treat the disorder. Anorexia is not simply a desire to be thin taken to an extreme—whatever the motivation for that desire. Certainly, the fact that anorexic behavior has existed over the centuries should serve as a caution to such deceptively easy understandings.

A good scholar, Bruch tried to find a commonality between sufferers of anorexia through the ages. Unfortunately, the commonality she sought remained founded—and continues to founder—on Gulls' nervosa, on the psychological.

It would have been more insightful and of greater benefit to have examined more closely those religious ascetics of the Middle Ages and how their determined and faith-based fasting spiraled into an emaciation that we would recognize immediately as being anorexia nervosa—the demon that has controlled too many of our loved ones.

In other words, we should recognize that the psychological and cultural motivations are changeable but that the physiological dynamic remains the same.

The anorexic patients we see today are separated by years, cultures, and religious sensibilities from Catherine of Siena and the other Italian women saints and from the men of the Minnesota Starvation Experiment. Yet they have something very essential in common: They all restrict their eating, often in conjunction with exercising vigorously. And when they do this, they eat less, not more, until they became malnourished. Dwelling on the reason that a person stops eating is beside the point. It's far more important to understand the effects of starvation on the brain and the resultant biochemical changes that affect behavior.

Confusing cause and effect is dangerous; it's like looking through the wrong end of a telescope. Rather than bringing distant objects closer, nearby objects appear to be far, far away. It is time to turn the telescope around and bring the problem into focus.

Chapter Five

Therapy Is *Not* the Answer

Elise is a 25-year-old woman with a 13-year history of restrictive eating behaviors. She reports that she was first put on a "diet" by a family pediatrician at age 11 because she was "10 pounds overweight." Both her parents and her doctor commented on her weight and said she was "fat." By age 12, Elise was chewing and then spitting out her food in an attempt to restrict her caloric intake. Elise remembers being "forced to be on a diet" until she was 18 years old. She recalls her food intake consisting of fruits, vegetables, and ice cream during these adolescent years. She lost 20 pounds in her eighteenthth year.

Elise currently restricts her calories to no more than 600 to 800 per day. She has no self-initiated ability to monitor and manage her own eating behaviors and patterns. She automatically spits out whatever she has chewed and finds it hard to swallow at times. She is terrified of someone else telling her she is fat. Elise weighed 92 pounds when we first met and was at 80 percent of her ideal body weight of 115. Her hair was thinning, and her face was wrinkled and sunken. Elise appeared much older than 25.

Elise wishes "all of this had never happened. All I do is think about how to eat less. I hate my parents and wish I had just been born a skinny person." Elise works part-time and has been unable to maintain full-time employment due to her illness.

Elise reports a long history with therapy and "shrinks," including individual and family therapy for years. "We just talked," explained Elise of the multiple treatment attempts in residential and outpatient eating disorder programs. She now sees a psychotherapist, internist, nutritionist, and DBT (dialectical behavioral therapy) coach. Yet Elise and her family don't participate in family therapy. Elise explains, "I have given up on family therapy; they just don't get it."

Elise is trying to be compliant with recommendations for treatment, yet when I saw her, her hopelessness and despair were evident. After 13 years of treatment, very little has changed for Elise.

For more than 200 years, anorexia nervosa has been considered a psychological illness. It seems logical, then, that psychotherapy would be a good way to treat it. Yet most kinds—whether traditional "talk" psychotherapy or behavioral therapy—have proven inadequate in treating and relieving anorexia and its accompanying depression, obsessive-compulsive behaviors, and other problems. That's not surprising, considering there is relatively little information from randomized clinical trials to guide psychological treatment for anorexia and prevent the relapse that currently occurs in up to 35 percent of those who reach near-normal weight.

To be blunt, the current forms of psychological therapy—which form the basis of standard treatment for anorexia—are not nearly as effective as they should be, or as they could be. The sad truth is that well over half of all people with anorexia are at serious risk of relapsing, spiraling downward, and even dying because of over reliance on psychological therapies which, by their very nature, cannot help the anorexic until her brain is "ready to listen."

Underlying Problems with Psychotherapy for Anorexia

Doctors and therapists are supposed to offer their patients the therapies that are most effective and appropriate for them. For example, when combating a bacterial infection, the doctor uses lab tests to identify the type of bacteria causing the infection, and this knowledge will help to determine the kind of antibiotic that will work best. Similar approaches are used for many other diseases, and the results of scientific research can reveal which treatment is most likely to be effective. But when it comes to treating anorexia with psychotherapy, whether individual, group, family, cognitive behavioral therapy (CBT), dialectical behavioral therapy (DBT), or other approaches, we're really operating in the dark. The truth is that there is no body of scientific research demonstrating that one therapy is superior to another, or that one type of therapy is best for one type of patient while another form of therapy is best for another. We really don't know which therapy is best for which patient.

Not only are doctors and therapists unsure which form of psychological therapy is most effective for a given type of patient, but they tend to offer their patients and clients the kinds they are most familiar with.

Why continue to insist on using what so often fails? It's often because the choice of psychological treatment depends on the provider's preconceived notions of what works, no matter how many times that built-in prejudice is proved wrong.

That's not to say that many of the standard forms of psychological therapy cannot be useful. They can, in fact, be very helpful.

Let's take a quick look at three of the major forms of therapy used for anorexia, their approaches, and weakness. Then I'll explain how they can be made much more effective than they currently are.

Cognitive Behavioral Therapy (CBT)

Cognitive behavioral therapy (CBT) centers around identifying distorted thinking patterns and behaviors, challenging them, and replacing them with more rational thoughts and beliefs. In individuals with eating disorders, the distorted thinking mostly concerns eating, body size, and the self.

Distorted Thought Patterns

Distorted thought patterns are ways of thinking that guide behavior, even though they are incorrect, out of proportion to the situation, or otherwise erroneous and potentially harmful. Some examples of the distorted thought patterns and erroneous beliefs that CBT addresses in anorexic patients include:

- All-or-nothing thinking ("If I'm not thin, I won't ever have any friends or a boyfriend.")
- Nonsensical thinking ("If I eat chocolate, my thighs will instantly get bigger.")
- Overgeneralizing ("I used to eat carbohydrates and I was fat, so I can't eat carbohydrates at all.")
- Catastrophizing ("If I gain two pounds, none of my clothing will fit me.")
- Overpersonalizing ("I heard two people laughing as I walked by, and I knew they were calling me a fat cow.")

CBT, which developed as a combination of cognitive therapy and behavioral therapy, is built on the premise that behavior follows thoughts. If you have "normal" thoughts, your behavior will be normal, while if your thinking is "distorted," your behavior will be abnormal.

CBT does not rely on a single model or approach. Instead, it incorporates several approaches, including a gradual increase in exposure to a feared activity or object (such as flying or spiders), keeping a diary of events, feelings, thoughts and behaviors to increase understanding of the relationship between thoughts and behaviors, and techniques for distracting and relaxing the patient.

How Effective is CBT?

CBT has shown great success in treating depression, anxiety, and insomnia, but it has had decidedly mixed results in patients with eating disorders. Although there are very few studies, and even fewer involving large populations, CBT appears to be more helpful in patients with bulimia than anorexia, and more successful in adults than teens.

One problem with CBT is that irrational feelings often persist even after a patient reaches a normal weight. These feelings can resurface at a particularly stressful point in life—a romantic break-up, college graduation, the death of a loved one, moving to a new home—which can precipitate a relapse of anorexia. In spite of receiving months or even years of CBT, many patients never relinquish the irrational ideas that they should be thinner than they are or that being fat is something to be feared. They can also continue to harbor bad feelings about themselves long after treatment ends.

Dialectical Behavior Therapy (DBT)

Dialectical behavior therapy (DBT) is similar to CBT and based on the same principles. However, instead of emphasizing changes in thought and behavior, DBT emphasizes acceptance and validation of the patient as a means of helping her to change. It includes several different types of interventions: individual psychotherapy, group skills training, and telephone coaching.

DBT was first developed in the early 1990s by Dr. Marsha Linehan, a psychologist who worked with borderline personality disorder patients, "cutters," and patients with suicidal ideation. While treating her patients, Dr. Linehan encountered significant resistance to the incessant emphasis on change inherent in the CBT process. She discovered that many patients dropped out of CBT-based treatment because they felt their therapists didn't understand how difficult it was for them to change their behavior or how much they were suffering.

In response to these complaints and concerns, Dr. Linehan added acceptance strategies to her CBT therapy, some of which she'd learned from the practice of Zen Buddhism. It must be emphasized, however, that in no way does DBT suggest that the patient's behavior is acceptable. It simply allows the therapist to validate the patient's thinking, acknowledging that it makes sense in the context of the way the patient perceives her world and her place in it. The therapist, however, does not agree that this is the best way to handle the situation.

DBT seeks to help the anorexic patient develop greater emotional and behavioral control. The patient is taught to "be" with painful thoughts and distressing situations rather than numbing herself by refraining from eating or exercising excessively. By listening to her feelings instead of running from them, she learns that she can become more adept at dealing with life circumstances. Along the way, she learns new skills and behaviors for healthy eating and how to apply them to everyday situations. DBT also aims to help the patient and family overcome relationship problems that have arisen in response to the disease.

How Effective is DBT?

To date, no controlled studies of DBT's effectiveness in treating anorexia nervosa have been performed, although anecdotal studies have found it effective in managing both bulimia and binge eating disorder.

In my clinical experience, many anorexic patients enjoy DBT and other forms of psychotherapy, and they participate cooperatively in the process. But even when they seem to show improvement, they inevitably end up struggling with the anxiety and obsessive thinking about food, weight, and distorted body image.

Family Therapy

While CBT and DBT focus on the individual, family therapy works primarily with the patient and her family in order to correct the interactions between family members that may have contributed to the development of anorexia and its associated ailments.

As with other types of therapy, there are different models of family therapy. One type of family therapy that has had some success is the Maudsley model. Named for the London hospital where it was developed more than 20 years ago, the Maudsley model involves the entire family—patient, parent(s), and siblings—all of whom meet with a therapist for twenty 50-minute sessions over the course of a year. During these sessions, the family is asked to band together to confront and ultimately solve the problem of anorexia nervosa, which affects all of them.

The Maudsley model consists of three phases: refeeding, returning control of eating to the patient, and encouraging a healthy relationship between patient and parents.

- *Refeeding:* In this phase, parents are taught to present a united front and to compel their child to eat. They must prepare meals for the child containing adequate calories for weight restoration and be willing to sit with her until she finishes. Initially, it can take hours for an anorexic to finish a meal, and parents must not only sit through it, but withstand bouts of intense emotion and recrimination from the child. Still, there can be no negotiation. The refeeding phase is so intensive and time-consuming that one or both parents may need to reorganize their work schedules or even take a leave of absence to spend the necessary time with their child.

- *Returning control of eating to the patient:* Approximately ten sessions into the treatment, when the patient is at 90 to 95 percent of her ideal body weight and no longer needs to be compelled to eat, she is gradually allowed to regain control of her eating habits and return to "normal" teen activities. This phase usually lasts from two to three months.
- *Encouraging a healthy relationship between the patient and the parents:* The final therapy sessions focus on establishing autonomy and family relationships with normal boundaries and dealing with typical age-related issues (e.g., going away to college and dating).

How Effective is the Maudsley Model of Family Therapy?

The Maudsley model has shown some success with patients who are younger than 19 and have had anorexia for less than three years. One British study published in the *Archives of General Psychiatry* compared the Maudsley method to individual supportive therapy in 57 patients with anorexia nervosa and 23 with bulimia nervosa who had received treatment, gained weight, and been released from the hospital. After a year, the Maudsley family therapy model proved more effective than individual therapy. A higher percentage of the adolescents who underwent the Maudsley model of family therapy maintained their weight and were free of eating-disorder symptoms for five years after treatment, as compared to those who participated in supportive therapy.

The success of the Maudsley model is significantly less clear for adult women. Current studies suggest that other therapies tend to produce better—though far from acceptable—results for this group. We still do not know which patients will benefit most from which types of therapy.

Kate, diagnosed with anorexia at age 12, is a 15-year-old I recently saw for a medication consultation. She has been hospitalized three times and has spent 60 days in a residential treatment center for eating disorders. For the past three years, Kate and her family had been battling about food.

When I asked Kate why she thought she was doing better and what kept her from returning to the hospital, she responded quickly, "They make me eat. I have no choice."

Kate and her family had participated in Maudsley therapy for only six weeks when we first met. It was clear that the hierarchy in the family system had shifted and concern about basic health and nutrition was controlled by her parents, the beginning step in the treatment of anorexia and restoring health.

Psychotherapy Is Only Part of the Answer

Psychotherapy can be valuable, especially in addressing the depression, low self-esteem, and self-destructive behaviors that arise in tandem with anorexia. It can also help repair family relationships and help the recovering anorexic face life without the crutch of restricting her food.

Although many different forms of therapy are available to those with eating disorders, there are few randomized, controlled trials examining the effectiveness of each therapy for anorexia nervosa. There are no clear studies suggesting that any one form of psychotherapy is superior to another.

To study the effectiveness of two common psychotherapies for anorexia, CBT and interpersonal psychotherapy, Virginia McIntosh, PhD, and colleagues enrolled 56 women with anorexia nervosa in their study published in the *American Journal of Psychiatry*. The women were randomly assigned to one of three treatment groups: CBT, interpersonal psychotherapy, or a control treatment. The control treatment consisted of a combination of clinical management (encompassing education, care, and support in fostering adherence to medical treatment) and non-specific supportive psychotherapy (consisting of praise, assurance, and advice).

Over the course of 20 weeks, the women completed 20 hours of therapy sessions. For the 35 women who completed therapy, nonspecific supportive clinical management was more effective in minimizing eating disorder symptoms than the two specialized therapies, CBT and interpersonal psychotherapy. Of those who participated in non-specific supportive psychotherapy, 56 percent reported improvement in eating-disorder behaviors such as drive for thinness, weight concerns, and eating concerns as compared to 32 percent and 10 percent of those who participated in CBT and interpersonal psychotherapy, respectively. Patients who only received support fared much better than those who participated in specialized therapy programs!

Scientific studies and decades of frustrating experience have made it clear that psychotherapy is not the solution to anorexia. Indeed, psychotherapy cannot be the solution because the brains and bodies of nutrient-deficient patients with anorexia simply cannot respond to the message offered by their therapists, fully embrace the therapies, or make the needed changes. Until zinc levels have been restored to normal, until essential fatty acids and other nutritional imbalances have been corrected, until taste and desire for food have been restored, and until the gut can digest and process food without physical distress, anorexic patients cannot fully benefit from psychological treatment.

However, restoring zinc and the other nutrients to the proper levels can "unclog the ears" of anorexics and let the message get through. When that happens, psychotherapy can be effective. But insisting on using psychotherapy on patients whose nutrient levels are low can be futile—which is why so many millions of anorexic patients have not been cured by psychotherapy, despite our best efforts.

Chapter Six

Trial-And-Error Polypharmacy

Not one medication has been approved by the FDA for the treatment of anorexia nervosa. Years of research and clinical experience underscore that point: There is no convincing evidence that any medication effectively treats the illness. So why then are medications so commonly prescribed?

Psychotropic medications are drugs designed to act on the central nervous system to alter brain function. These drugs can affect perception, mood, and behavior, and over the past decades they have greatly benefited individuals suffering from a wide range of psychiatric disorders. These medications have helped many, many people live happier, less anxious, and more productive lives. Having seen these medications help so many other patients, psychiatrists tend to believe they will work in every situation. And even though anorexia has proven to be resistant to all forms of medication, psychiatrists continue to prescribe medications to try to diminish symptoms such as anxiety and depression that may be contributing to the illness and prolonging recovery.

Relying as much on hope as on medical evidence, psychiatrists strive to find the right medications, prescribing one after another to their anorexic patients. Of the more than 30 different psychiatric medications currently available, I have seen each and every one prescribed for anorexia nervosa at one time or another. So many medications are prescribed that many of my patients are as well-versed in psychopharmacology as my colleagues.

A perfect example is Kristen, a 22-year-old woman who has been struggling with anorexia since the age of 14. With remarkable nonchalance, she is able to rattle off the names of a dozen drugs—both brand and generic names—prescribed to her during her years of treatment. In fact, she and the other patients like to refer to their psychiatrists by their preferred medications (i.e., "Dr. Cymbalta" and "Dr. Prozac"). Kristen can immediately tell you from experience what was "okay" about each drug and what wasn't. And in every case the result was the same: it didn't work.

Speaking with my colleagues around the country has reinforced the notion of this haphazard pattern of prescribing medications for anorexia. One eating-disorder program may favor antidepressants as a first-line medication; another hospital five miles away may first prescribe anitpsychotics; and a third may hold off on all medications, claiming instead that "food is medicine."

This wide variability leads to the crux of the problem. Without clear-cut scientific evidence, a psychiatrist has to make his or her best educated guess based on clinical experience and the patient's symptoms when treating a patient with anorexia. The patient might be started on one medication, but when she soon fails to improve or relapses—as will often happen—new medications are added, or dosages of existing medications are increased. All the while, the original medications are continued. Soon, a patient can be on three, four, or five psychiatric medications, all with significant side effects. Still, the patient may struggle and require hospital-level care!

Yet sometimes the psychiatrist is not fully to blame for a patient being on multiple medications. Patients become attached to certain medications, believing they will suppress their appetite and contribute to weight loss. For example, believing it will help them stay thin, patients with anorexia frequently ask for the medication Topamax, which has been associated with mild weight loss in some studies. Although Topamax probably contributes very little to a patient's weight loss, patients will "doctor shop" until they find someone to prescribe it for them.

Similarly, patients may complain about attention and concentration problems with a goal of getting a physician to prescribe an amphetamine like Ritalin, used to treat ADHD. These stimulant medications are appetite suppressants, and, frankly, have no business being prescribed for a 16-year-old, straight-A student who had no attention issues before starving herself. But once a patient has found a doctor to prescribe a stimulant, she will often ask the physician to increase the dosage until she has no desire to eat so that she can restrict food without difficulty.

This chapter will discuss not only the types of medications commonly prescribed to patients with anorexia, but also relevant research demonstrating which medications may be beneficial in certain circumstances, and which ones are not.

Medications Used to Treat Anorexia

There are four categories of medications that are often prescribed for patients with anorexia:

- Antidepressants
- Anti-anxiety medications
- Antihistamines
- Antipsychotics

Antidepressants

Because nearly 90 percent of patients with anorexia suffer from depression, it is no surprise that antidepressants are the most frequently prescribed psychotropic medication. Psychiatrists prescribe them for patients with anorexia, hoping that alleviating a patient's depression will also relieve the anorexia.

Antidepressants work by acting on neurotransmitters, or chemicals in the brain, that carry signals from one nerve cell to another. These chemicals, called serotonin, norepinephrine, and dopamine, are constantly being released into the space between nerve cells and then reabsorbed back into the nerve cells. Higher levels of neurotransmitters are associated with an improvement of mood. Different categories of antidepressant drugs affect different neurotransmitters, slowing their reuptake, which allows their levels to build up in the brain and have a mood-elevating effect.

Currently, there are three major classes of antidepressants.

Tricyclics. The tricyclic antidepressants, or TCAs, were discovered by chance in the 1960s by researchers who were searching for a more effective medication for schizophrenia. TCAs treat depression by prolonging the mood-enhancing effects of norepinephrine and serotonin in the brain. Unfortunately, their action also negatively impacts other chemicals, causing a high incidence of side effects.

TCAs have been associated with a heightened risk of arrhythmias, or irregular heartbeats. The poor nutrition that is part of severe anorexia can also often lead to compromised heart function. One always needs to consider the possibility of a drug overdose in depressed patients. The cardiac side effects of TCAs combined with cardiac arrhythmias in anorexic patients due to low potassium levels could lead to a dangerous situation.

TCAs are also associated with weight gain, a side effect that frequently deters patients from agreeing to take this type of medication.

TCAs can be effective in treating depression. In addition, as one side effect of TCAs is weight gain, they are sometimes prescribed to both ease depression and facilitate weight restoration. But do they cure anorexia? Elavil (amitriptyline) was evaluated in a double-blind clinical study published in the *Journal of Clinical Psychopharmacology*. In this study, no significant differences or overall improvement was seen when patients with anorexia were treated with Elavil.

Selective serotonin reuptake inhibitors (SSRIs). The SSRIs, which were developed in the 1990s, slow the reabsorption of serotonin into the nerve cells of the brain, allowing this neurotransmitter to build up and exert its antidepressant effects for a longer period of time. The SSRIs act primarily on serotonin and not on other neurotransmitters. They are currently the most frequently prescribed psychotropic drugs in the United States.

Because they do not influence other brain chemicals, SSRIs usually produce fewer side effects. However, they have been linked to an increased risk of suicide in young patients. This has prompted the FDA to order all SSRIs—for example, Celexa, Prozac, Luvox, Paxil, and Zoloft—to be labeled with a "black box" warning to physicians, patients, and parents, stating that some children and adolescents who have taken SSRIs experience an increase in suicidal thoughts and may be at risk for suicide. The black box warning does not, however, explicitly advise against the use of SSRIs in adolescents; instead, it suggests that young patients on SSRIs receive more frequent follow-up and monitoring.

Early studies examined the potential effectiveness of SSRIs as a medication that could prevent relapse in anorexia. Patients who had successfully regained weight were treated with SSRIs and followed. The encouraging results from early case reports, however, were not substantiated by later and larger clinical trials. However, despite the fact that these early results were not corroborated, many psychiatrists continue to prescribe SSRIs for patients with anorexia. Based on what I have seen clinically, I estimate that about 80 to 90 percent of patients with anorexia are being improperly treated with SSRIs!

Let's examine the scientific evidence against a role for SSRIs in anorexia.

Cecilia Bergh, PhD, and colleagues wrote in 2003 in the journal *Current Opinion in Pediatrics*, "SSRI[s] have no effect on the psychopathology of [anorexia nervosa] and can reduce body weight."

In 2005, Kristian Holtkamp, MD, and colleagues found that treating anorexic patients with SSRIs was ineffective, even in those patients who had already gained weight. They commented in the *Journal of Psychiatric Research*, "We could not find any differences in the rates of readmissions to inpatient treatment within six months after discharge between patients who received SSRIs and those who did not."

A third study, led by researcher Scott Crow, MD, concurred that Prozac had proved to be disappointing for treating anorexia, and warned physicians to be wary of prescribing SSRIs for their anorexic patients.

The largest medication trial of SSRIs in patients with anorexia to date was reported in the *Journal of the American Medical Association* in 2006. The goal of the study was to determine whether fluoxetine (Prozac) could promote recovery by prolonging the time-to-relapse among patients. The participants were outpatients who had regained weight after treatment in an inpatient or day program. Forty-nine patients were randomly chosen to receive fluoxetine for one year, and 44 patients were treated with a placebo for one year. All patients also received individual cognitive behavioral therapy. To follow progress, the patients were weighed weekly, and questionnaires and assessments measuring disturbed eating behaviors, disordered thoughts, depression, anxiety, and self-esteem were obtained monthly. On nearly all of the measures, including time-to-relapse, body-mass index, and clinical measures of depression, the two groups were not significantly different. The researchers concluded, "This study failed to demonstrate any benefit from fluoxetine in the treatment of patients with anorexia nervosa following weight restoration."

Accordingly, after reviewing the results of this and other studies, the American Psychiatric Association recommended against the use of SSRIs in treating underweight patients with anorexia.

There are many possible reasons why the SSRIs have not proved effective for anorexia. One may be that malnutrition and decreased protein intake results in the brain not having enough of the essential amino acid tryptophan that is required to make serotonin. This will be discussed in more detail in Chapter Twenty. Several researchers have also pointed to too much serotonin activity as a potential cause of certain personality traits in anorexia, including extreme harm avoidance and an obsessive temperament. If this is correct, then a medication such as an SSRI that increases serotonin could actually worsen a patient's illness. Although there is no scientific research to support this hypothesis, this is what I commonly see, and it's why I believe SSRIs hinder progress in patients with anorexia.

Atypical antidepressants. Atypical antidepressants act on different neurotransmitters (dopamine, serotonin, or norepinephrine, or a combination of two of them) and have varying mechanisms of action. For instance, the medication Wellbutrin affects dopamine by blocking its reuptake, and the medications Effexor and Cymbalta affect both serotonin and norepinephrine by blocking the reabsorption of both neurotransmitters.

Similar to the SSRIs, some of the atypical antidepressants, such as Wellbutrin, Remeron, Serzone, and Effexor, have a "black box" warning to physicians, patients, and parents. Children and adolescents who take these medications may experience an increase in suicidal thoughts, placing them at a higher risk for suicide.

Some atypical antidepressants are not recommended for patients with eating disorders, particularly those with bulimia. A well-cited study reported on the dangers of treating bulimic patients with Wellbutrin. Sixty-nine nondepressed patients with bulimia were treated with Wellbutrin, and four of them—who did not have any prior history of seizures or predisposing medical conditions—experienced grand mal seizures. This rate of seizures (5.8 percent) was 14.5 times higher than the rate seen in other groups of patients taking Wellbutrin (0.4 percent). Although it seemed as though Wellbutrin could be effective for treating bulimia before the study was terminated due to the patients' seizures, the risk of this side effect is usually considered to outweigh the benefits. Currently, Wellbutrin is not typically recommended for patients with eating disorders.

Anti-Anxiety Medications

Some physicians treat the anxiety and panic associated with mealtime, eating, and weight gain with a class of medications called benzodiazepines. These include Ativan, Klonopin, Xanax, and Valium. Although extremely effective for non-eating disordered patients with anxiety and panic disorders, these medications should not routinely be used to help patients with eating disorders.

Although benzodiazepines can be calming for brief periods of severe anxiety and panic, I have not found them to be significantly helpful. In fact, I have seen many patients on extremely high doses of benzodiazepines who continue to experience chronic anxiety around eating and food. Also, these medications are potentially addictive. People can develop a tolerance to them, requiring increased amounts to achieve the same benefit.

Antihistamines

Antihistamines have been studied for use in patients with anorexia nervosa with surprisingly promising results. Initially, their appetite-stimulating effects were discovered in patients with asthma, who had significant weight gains and height increases after being treated with these medications. Antihistamines oppose the actions of histamine, a chemical substance that has effects throughout the body. Some antihistamines also block the action of serotonin. Most of the time, antihistamines are used as allergy medications to counteract symptoms that are caused by increased histamine activity, including itchy rashes, runny nose, and watery eyes. Only minor side effects such as dizziness and transient drowsiness have been reported.

Several studies conducted in the 1970s and 1980s showed the anti-histamine cyproheptadine to be a safe and effective medication in patients with anorexia. Cyproheptadine was found to stimulate the appetite as well as to quickly facilitate weight gain, especially in those with severe anorexia. One study found cyproheptadine to also have an antidepressant effect. Even at low doses, the medication was beneficial.

When I feel that an antihistamine could benefit a patient with anorexia, I most often recommend Vistaril, 25 to 75 milligrams (mg), 1 to 3 times per day. Although Vistaril is commonly used for allergies, it can be helpful to patients with anorexia by causing mild sedation that decreases anxiety and facilitates eating.

Antipsychotics

In contrast to depression and anxiety, psychotic disorders such as schizophrenia and bipolar disorder are often characterized by delusions, which are fixed, false beliefs. Although they appear absurd to a rationally thinking person, delusional beliefs preoccupy a patient's thinking. Those suffering from anorexia can similarly have a delusional thought processes. Anorexics may harbor striking misperceptions about their own size and shape, insisting that they are fat when in reality they are dramatically underweight. Many anorexics also describe an "inner voice" ordering them to refrain from eating.

Addressing these psychotic-like symptoms with medications can provide another way to potentially reach a severely ill anorexic patient. By loosening the strangling hold of irrational beliefs, a patient can slip out from the grips of delusional thinking. Less anxious, less depressed, and less agitated, she may be more open to treatment. Another reason antipsychotic medications may be helpful to anorexics is that these medicines are commonly associated with weight gain. While this side effect may not be desirable in patients with schizophrenia, it may benefit patients with anorexia.

Commonly prescribed antipsychotic medications include Haldol (haloperidol), Zyprexa (olanzapine), Risperal (risperidone), Abilify (aripiprazole), and Seroquel (quetiapine).

Some researchers have expressed concern that antipsychotic medications may be associated with diabetes. One study, published in the *Journal of the American Medical Association*, looked at antipsychotic medications in 272 children with schizophrenia, mood disorders, or disruptive or aggressive behavior disorders. The results showed that more than one-third of the children gained enough weight to be classified as overweight or obese within 11 weeks. On follow-up laboratory testing, many of the children had significant lipid profile abnormalities, which can be associated with potential hypertension, diabetes, or cardiovascular diseases. Based on this and other similar studies, the FDA recently released an advisory, cautioning the use of olanzapine (Zyprexa) for the treatment of bipolar disorder and schizophrenia in teenagers.

In the psychiatric community, there is currently a mixed opinion about using antipsychotics to treat anorexia nervosa. Psychiatrists and families alike may shy away from antipsychotic use, believing anorexia to be dissimilar to an illness like schizophrenia.

I have found antipsychotics to be helpful in severely ill anorexic patients who have been chronically resistant to treatment. I have had success with small doses of these medications, even in children. When a child is so sick that she may die without treatment, using an antipsychotic in the short term can mean the difference between life and death. Here is a brief example: A 12-year-old girl was admitted to a local hospital for failing to eat, resulting in a low heart rate and electrolyte abnormalities. Her elaborate food rituals and her weight loss continued in the hospital, much to everyone's dismay. After many months of continued weight loss and inability to engage in individual and family therapy, I prescribed a very low dose of Zyprexa—only 1 mg per day—and within a week she was eating, and after three months her weight had returned to normal.

Although a small number of studies have shown that antipsychotics may benefit patients with anorexia, Zyprexa and Seroquel have been most studied. They have been found to decrease depression, reduce anxiety, and decrease distorted body perceptions. Taking them, patients also often gained weight, were less agitated, slept better, and were more compliant with treatment. These medications appeared to be well tolerated without reported side effects.

The largest and most well-conducted trial of Zyprexa was undertaken by Hany Bissada, MD, and colleagues in Canada and involved 34 patients with anorexia. Sixteen patients received Zyprexa, and 18 patients received a placebo. After 10 weeks, those receiving Zyprexa had a greater increase in body-mass index (a measure of weight gain) than those who had received the placebo. Both groups of patients became less depressed, less anxious, and had fewer obsessive thoughts. Other studies and case reports have corroborated these findings; not only is Zyprexa associated with weight gain and a decrease of depression and anxiety, but it can also improve a patient's overall functioning so that she can better comply with treatment.

Another antipsychotic medication I may prescribe when treating severely ill patients with anorexia is Seroquel. While this medication has not been approved for the treatment of eating disorders, it has been given to patients with anorexia with promising results. Open-label trials of Seroquel, in which patients knew they were receiving the medication, showed that it helped patients with anorexia by reducing depression and anxiety, and facilitated weight gain. One study found that after taking Seroquel for eight weeks, severely ill patients with anorexia had fewer restrictive eating behaviors as well as fewer disordered thoughts.

For treatment refractory patients, I may use very low dosages of Seroquel, such as 10 mg before each meal. As it is less than the amount in the lowest-strength pills available by the manufacturer, this dose needs to be made by a special compounding pharmacy.

Antipsychotic medications are rarely prescribed for patients suffering with anorexia nervosa. As you will learn, the majority of the patients I see benefit from nutritional therapy. However, antipsychotic medications should not be dismissed in patients requiring extensive hospitalization for a disorder that has consumed all rational thought processes regarding health leading to life-threatening decisions.

You Can't Beat Anorexia with Medication

Leslie is a 28-year-old nurse who suffered from depression and restrictive eating behaviors for more than 10 years. She recalls her first bout of depression, which happened just after she turned 18. She had just broken up with her boyfriend when she learned that she was not admitted to her first-choice university. Thrown by the combination of events, Leslie found that she had no appetite. By the second week of eating very little, Leslie had lost weight and found she enjoyed the compliments from her friends about how she looked. Having lost five or six pounds, Leslie felt so good about herself that she kept restricting her food intake. But her good feelings eventually gave way to dark and obsessive thoughts.

Before taking her to college, Leslie's parents insisted she see the family physician for her weight loss and mood changes. The doctor prescribed Prozac and encouraged Leslie to follow up at the school's health clinic. Not feeling better, Leslie discontinued her Prozac after a few months. Later, when she became ill with the flu and went to the health clinic, a nurse prescribed Celexa for Leslie's symptoms of depression and referred her to a therapist. Leslie dutifully went to therapy and took the Celexa; later she was switched to Zoloft in combination with a small dose of

Ritalin. Rather than focusing on her symptoms of anorexia, the therapist focused on Leslie's depression, not even considering the possibility that Ritalin would further subdue Leslie's appetite. During the next three years, Leslie's condition did not improve, even though more than six different antidepressants were prescribed in combination with mood stabilizers. Leslie continued to be depressed and unable to stop her patterns of restrictive eating. By the time I evaluated Leslie, her depression was deep and chronic, and she had missed out on the previous three years of her college experience.

Desperately concerned, Leslie's parents kept her home from school for a semester and brought her to me for a complete physical and nutritional assessment. Leslie was severely malnourished, with deficiencies of essential minerals and vitamins. After working closely with her physician and a nutritionist to restore her diet and nutritional status, Leslie finally began feeling better. As her depression lifted, she became able to discuss her eating disorder in therapy and to examine the issues of a past sexual trauma in a new and honest way.

A 2009 overview of progress in drug studies published in the *International Journal of Eating Disorders*, Dr. Scott Crow and colleagues stated: "Pharmacotherapy provides little benefit in the treatment of [anorexia nervosa] at present."

The longer a patient suffers with anorexia, the less likely she is to recover. When treatments do not work, when patients and families waste time and money, they can become demoralized and hopeless. The promise of recovery drifts further and further away.

Finding the proper medication for an individual does not, however, involve the trial-and-error approach so commonly seen in psychiatry today. Instead, an exciting new technological tool called an rEEG can help a psychiatrist choose the best medication for an individual based on the individual's brainwave patterns. Referenced-EEG can prevent patients from being subjected to endless possibilities of medication combinations.

Let's stop the guesswork. The recommendations outlined in the next section of the book will provide a framework for successfully treating anorexia: nutrition, medication based on rEEG, and therapy. When a patient is receiving the correct nutritional supplements and the proper medication, recovery is possible and health becomes a reality. The runaway train of irreversible health consequences comes to a stop.

Chapter Seven

Beyond Calorie Counts
and Meal Plans

Our dietary habits do more than affect us throughout the day; they influence our long-term health. In no uncertain terms, we are what we eat. However, an equally important and perhaps more significant corollary is that we are what we don't eat. When the body lacks certain nutrients, health, mood, brain chemistry, and even brain structure are affected. Nutritional deficiencies routinely cause physical and/or emotional problems that complicate the diagnosis and treatment of anorexia. And they can trigger symptoms of mental illness, delaying treatment and potentially causing serious harm to both body and mind.

There are several reasons why specific nutritional deficiencies in anorexia are often ignored. Chief among them is that most doctors lack nutritional knowledge. And, while textbooks present neat lists of symptoms caused by lack of specific nutrients, the real-world relationship between nutrient deficiencies and symptoms is often not clear—which is not surprising, considering how different we all are from each other.

In the mid-twentieth century, Roger Williams, PhD, described the concept of biochemical individuality, which is based on the idea that each person needs different levels of nutrients for optimal health and functioning and has a unique response to nutritional deficiencies. For example, in days past, sailors on long voyages were likely to develop scurvy, a disease triggered by a lack of vitamin C that caused unsavory symptoms such as bleeding from mucous membranes, depression, and even death. During the eighteenth century, sea-going Chaplain Richard Walter noted that the disease seemed to have as many different symptoms as people who suffered from it: "… for scarcely two persons have the same complaints, and where there is found some conformity in symptoms, the order of their appearance has been totally different."

In my clinical practice, I see tremendous individual variation in physical and psychological symptoms among people with the same nutritional deficiency. Take Susan, for example, a 43-year-old who suffered from debilitating panic attacks. Not understanding her symptoms and concerned about the possibility of a brain tumor, Susan's doctors hospitalized her on two separate occasions. Yet even after performing extensive tests, they were still unsure of what was wrong.

When I saw Susan, I noticed that her B12 levels were below 200 pg/mL (picograms per milliliter) (laboratory standards for normal levels are between 200 and 900 pg/mL), yet she had never displayed the fatigue, anemia, and nerve damage typically seen with a B12 deficiency. On the contrary, she was energetic. Yet, within a week of starting B12 injections, Susan was experiencing less anxiety, and in two months her debilitating panic attacks had completely disappeared!

Twenty-two-year-old Beth, who was also suffering from a B12 deficiency, had entirely different symptoms. She suffered from anorexia as well as fatigue and depression that were severe enough to warrant several visits to the hospital. Correcting the B12 deficiency finally relieved Beth of both the depression and the fatigue.

Both women suffered from vitamin B12 deficiency, and their symptoms improved with B12 supplementation. Yet these deficiencies manifested in ways that were quite different from what most doctors would expect, for neither woman experienced the nerve damage and anemia described in the textbooks. These two case histories highlight the fact that we are all biochemically unique, and that nutritional deficiencies can surface in unique and sometimes baffling ways that may make them hard to diagnose.

Before taking a look at how anorexia affects nutritional status, let's examine the stages of deficiency and the general effects that malnutrition has on mental health.

Stages of Nutrient Deficiency

If a nutrient deficiency is severe and prolonged, the classic symptoms of a deficiency disease will appear, and treatment can be prescribed based on these symptoms. That is, advanced cases of scurvy or pellagra can be recognized by doctors schooled in nutritionally related diseases, and replenishment of the missing nutrients can ensue.

But what happens when you are deficient for a shorter period of time—say, days rather than months? Or what if you are not severely deficient in a particular nutrient, just below average? Such situations are referred to as subclinical nutrient deficiencies.

Subclinical nutrient deficiencies can profoundly affect your health, even though the classic symptoms of the disorder may not be present. It is generally recognized that there are three stages of subclinical nutrient deficiency: preliminary, biochemical, and physiological.

In the preliminary deficiency stage, only a bare minimum of a given nutrient is present. Remarkably, more than 92 percent of Americans take in less than the minimum amount of vitamins necessary to prevent a vitamin deficiency disorder! Is it any wonder that we suffer from increasing complaints of fatigue, anxiety, insomnia, and depression?

The biochemical deficiency stage involves the depletion of vitamins and nutrients from the body's tissues. This deficiency stage is common in patients with anorexia. Routine blood work often reveals low iron or decreased ferritin, the protein in the blood that stores iron. Often, patients in this stage are not yet anemic and may not suffer from the consequences of iron deficiency such as fatigue. Yet iron is critical for proper brain function, and as levels drop, the stage is set for depression and fatigue.

In the physiological deficiency stage, physical and psychological symptoms may begin to appear as the body's stores of nutrients are depleted. The processes that depend on the missing nutrient no longer occur, or function is impaired. One of the nutrients that most Americans and many patients with anorexia are deficient in is magnesium. Magnesium has far-ranging effects, and as the body depletes its supply of magnesium, deficiency can result in fatigue, memory difficulties, anxiety, and depression.

Subclinical vitamin and mineral deficiencies are only beginning to be appreciated by the medical profession. Just bringing these levels up to normal is a great help, but arriving at "optimal nutrition" requires supplying the body with greater levels to ensure adequate nutritional intake.

Pellagra

One example of the importance of diet and nutrition on mental health is one of the classic vitamin deficiency disorders, pellagra. Pellagra is a vitamin B3 deficiency that was common in this country in the early 1900s. A brief history of pellagra is relevant to our search for a better understanding of anorexia nervosa.

Pellagra was given its name in 1771 from the Italian phrase for "rough skin." However, the affliction tormented individuals and populations for centuries before it was formally named at the end of the eighteenth century. There are a number of Biblical scholars who suggest that some of the torments afflicting Job were none other than symptoms of pellagra.

Those who are familiar with pellagra know it as the disease of the "four Ds"—dermatitis, diarrhea, dementia, and death—identifying pellagra's primary symptoms. Pellagrins—people suffering from pellagra—were plagued with skin lesions, intestinal distress, lethargy, and depression.

The disease first came to the focused attention of the American medical establishment in the earliest days of the twentieth century, when it reached epidemic proportions across the South.

The disease and its cause stymied doctors for decades. The only known constant was pellagra's long connection with corn. Not only was cornpone consumed in great quantities in the American South, but polenta was a staple in Italy, where the disease was common in the eighteenth and nineteenth centuries.

In 1915, Joseph Goldberger, a physician in the U.S. Public Health Service, discovered the cause of pellagra that had eluded everyone else. Most investigators assumed that pellagra resulted from something its sufferers ate. Goldberger realized that it was the result of something they didn't eat. He immediately urged that the Southern diet be modified to include fresh milk, meat, and eggs.

He could see that people who ate a more varied diet did not suffer from pellagra. But what he did not fully understand—and what he didn't have adequate tools to help his colleagues understand—was that the South was effectively suffering a famine. People were starving to death even when they consumed sufficient calories.

Ultimately, nicotinic acid (vitamin B3) deficiency was identified as the cause of pellagra. It took a while longer to fully appreciate corn's role in the disease. By the middle of the twentieth century researchers discovered that corn increased the body's vitamin B3 requirement, while milk reduced it. Even later research discovered that tryptophan, abundant in milk and turkey, fights the deficiency because the body can make niacin (vitamin B3) from tryptophan.

More than 30 years after Goldberger identified the cause, pellagra was essentially eliminated. Of course, those 30 years were filled with too much unnecessary suffering.

Pellagra and Mental Illness

During the height of pellagra in the South, one-quarter to one-half of Southern mental hospitals contained pellagrins who were mistaken to be schizophrenic. The similarities between the two disorders made it difficult for physicians to separate the two diagnoses.

The earliest symptoms of pellagra are similar to those found in common psychiatric disorders, including anxiety, depression, and fatigue. As pellagra progresses, the psychological symptoms grow in severity and resemble those of schizophrenia. Changes in perception, which gradually transitions to delusions and hallucinations, are hallmarks of pellagra.

These changes in thought, both in content (delusions) and processing (putting thoughts together), occur from early to late stages of the disorder. Changes in mood, perception, and thought are characteristic of both pellagra, a vitamin deficiency illness, and schizophrenia, a major psychiatric illness of unknown etiology. The similarity in psychological symptoms between the two disorders makes it virtually impossible to separate them based on mental state alone.

After learning that a deficiency in vitamin B3 was the cause of pellagra, physicians examined patients for possible pellagra by evaluating their response to vitamin B3. Any improvement in condition resulted in a diagnosis of pellagra rather than one of schizophrenia. Physicians, however, only supplied small amounts of vitamin B3. These amounts were too low for chronic sufferers of pellagra. Many chronic pellagrins require doses of more than 1 gram per day for several months before they see improvement. Compared with the current Recommended Daily Allowance for vitamin B3, that amount is 60 to 70 times the amount recommended for adult men and women, respectively. Dr. Abram Hoffer, a pioneer in understanding the relationship between nutrition and mental health, believes that many chronic pellagrins may have been misdiagnosed as schizophrenic because they were not receiving enough vitamin B3.

There is no clear way to differentiate between these two diseases. Symptoms are strikingly similar. Disease progression is similar. And both may respond to doses of vitamin B3. Yet, many, if not all, of the physicians who embarked on examining schizophrenic patients for possible pellagra were fearful of connecting nutritional deficiencies with mental illness.

Anorexia Nervosa: Self-imposed Famine

To the body and brain, not eating is not eating. Restricting essential nutrients clearly has physiological consequences. It doesn't matter if the cause is a severe drought, political upheaval, or a morbid fear of gaining weight which causes someone to restrict calories.

Deficient is deficient. The lack of nutrients required for proper brain function will result in symptoms!

Not surprisingly, once-rare diseases caused by nutritional deficiencies are now reported in patients with anorexia. Case studies of pellagra and scurvy in patients with anorexia nervosa continue to be reported in medical journals.

One of the earliest published cases of pellagra in patients with anorexia, appearing in the journal *Archives of Dermatology*, highlights the telltale dermatological effects of pellagra. The case involved a 20-year-old woman who was initially admitted to the hospital for severe weight loss. After receiving treatment for anorexia nervosa, the woman was later discharged. Several months after treatment, the woman began suffering from skin changes. She noticed that the backs of her hands and forearms were covered in a red rash. Exposure to sunlight would make her symptoms worse. Her physicians recognized the dermatological symptoms as the presence of pellagra. After treatment with 100 mg of vitamin B3 three times a day for three weeks, her rash disappeared.

Another case of pellagra in a patient with anorexia, published in the journal *European Child and Adolescent Psychiatry*, depicts the challenges of diagnosing vitamin deficiency illnesses in those suffering from anorexia nervosa. In 2003, a 14-year-old girl was admitted to The Child and Adolescent Psychiatry department of the Medical University of Warsaw with severe complications from anorexia nervosa. After careful examination, the doctors compiled a rather extensive list of her symptoms, including hypothermia, abnormal heart rate, decreased hemoglobin, decreased blood glucose levels, swelling in her lower limbs, redness of her skin, diarrhea, and shedding of her skin on the forearms, elbows, and the nape of her neck. In addition to her physical symptoms, she complained of fatigue, dizziness, and diminished concentration. With vitamin B3 therapy, her dermatological and gastrointestinal symptoms resolved.

Although it seems easy to diagnose vitamin deficiency illnesses in anorexia due to the extreme malnutrition, the reality is that it remains difficult to separate complications of anorexia from those of vitamin deficiency disorders. The sheer number of complications alone makes it difficult for many physicians to identify vitamin deficiency disorders from the effects of anorexia. Furthermore, there are numerous similarities between anorexia and vitamin deficiency disorders.

An examination of the symptoms of pellagra and anorexia finds a significant number of commonalities between the two diseases, in particular the psychological effects of both diseases: depressions, delusions, and restlessness.

Interestingly, the demographics of pellagra also mirror the same trend as that of anorexia. Research conducted during the twentieth century found that the number of cases of women suffering from pellagra was consistently double the cases of men; whereas in anorexia, the number of women suffering from the devastating illness outnumber men nine to one.

Most patients with anorexia nervosa do not have pellagra; however, they clearly have subclinical deficiencies of niacin and other nutrients that need to be replenished for sustained recovery.

Pellagra's Lessons

What are the lessons we can learn from the history of pellagra?

First, nutritional deficiencies contribute to a disease with primarily psychological symptoms.

Second, there is cultural and political resistance to recognizing that nutrition is fundamental to good health. Goldberger's great contribution was to establish that a balanced diet—or, in this case, a small amount of brewer's yeast—prevented pellagra.

Third, medicine has to understand that subclinical deficiencies of nutrients may have significant psychological and/or physical consequences that can be treated safely.

Malnutrition and Mental Health

It's clear that nutritional deficiencies can cause disease, but we also need to understand that they have profound psychological effects, even in the absence of disease. Vitamin and mineral deficiencies can affect brain health and mental function, influencing thoughts, feelings, and behavior. Nowhere is this more evident than in prenatal nutrient deficiencies and in children who suffer from malnutrition.

During the winter of 1944–1945, as World War II was approaching its final stages, the German Army blocked the delivery of food supplies to the Western Netherlands. Pregnant women, in particular, suffered during the "Dutch Hunger Winter," as daily rations were reduced to less than 1,000 calories per day. Much later, when the children carried *in utero* during this period reached adulthood, researchers analyzed the effects of these prenatal nutritional deficiencies. They found that prenatal exposure to severe maternal malnutrition during the first and second trimesters led to a two-fold increase in the risk of schizophrenia and a two to three-fold increased risk for antisocial personality disorder in adulthood.

Malnutrition also has profound effects during childhood. In the early 1980s, Janina Galler, MD, a leading researcher of childhood nutrition, conducted several malnutrition studies in Barbados. Life in Barbados—with its very high literacy rates, high standards for environmental sanitation and water supply, and good health care—closely resembled that of Western societies, making the study findings relevant to malnutrition seen in the U.S. Studies on Barbadian children showed that the IQ scores of boys and girls ages 8 to 11 with a history of malnutrition were significantly lower than those of their well-nourished peers. About 50 percent of the malnourished children had IQ scores below 90, the cutoff for normal or average intelligence. Among their healthier schoolmates, only 17 percent scored below 90.

Behavior is also affected in malnourished children. They are often described as "functionally isolated" from their surroundings because they tend to be apathetic and passive. In the classroom, malnourished children suffer from attention problems, reduced social skills, and emotional instability when compared with their well-nourished peers.

Induced Nutritional Deficiencies

Nutritional deficiencies do not result just from wartime conditions or economical circumstances. Nutritional deficiencies can be induced even by procedures that are meant to benefit our health, such as bariatric surgery.

As rates of obesity increase around the world, the number of bariatric surgeries has risen dramatically. Bariatric procedures can be divided into two categories: physical reduction of the size of the stomach through the implantation of a medical device (gastric banding) or bypassing a portion of the small intestine (gastric bypass surgery). Gastric banding leads to weight loss by limiting the amount of food intake, since the size of the stomach is reduced. Gastric bypass, which accounts for 80 percent of bariatric surgeries in the United States, not only restricts the amount of food intake, but also causes malabsorption of food and nutrients.

Nutritional complications are common after gastric bypass surgery. Deficiencies of fat-soluble vitamins (A, D, E, and K), vitamin B12, thiamine, folate, iron, calcium, and zinc are frequently seen. The most common nutritional deficiencies include deficiencies of B vitamins and zinc. Several studies found that roughly one-third of all bypass patients had vitamin B12 deficiencies two years following surgery. Zinc deficiencies are common following all forms of bariatric procedures; however, in a study of a particular form of bariatric surgery, nearly 50 percent of all patients were zinc deficient!

I have seen growing numbers of patients with significant nutritional deficiencies after bariatric surgery develop psychological symptoms, including depression, obsessive thoughts about food, and anorexia nervosa. The nutritional deficiencies induced by gastric bypass surgery have resulted in severe cases of refractory eating disorders where psychological intervention has provided limited benefits. This is an area that desperately needs to be researched further as the number of bariatric surgery procedures continue to increase.

Better Nutrition Equals Better Health

As frightening as it is to hear how nutritional deficiencies and malnutrition can harm psychological well-being, it is equally heartening to learn that proper nutrition has beneficial effects on mood and mental health.

A study of school-age children in Australia discovered that well-nourished children improved verbal learning and memory when their diets were fortified with multiple micronutrients in the form of a micronutrient drink containing iron, zinc, folate, vitamins A, B6, B12, and C.

The power of proper nutrition isn't just limited to children. Good nutrition benefits everyone. Sometimes simple changes in dietary habits or nutritional supplementation can lead to dramatic benefits. A classic study published in the *British Journal of Medicine* evaluated the effects of proper nutrition on the behavior of adult prisoners. The diets of 231 prisoners were supplemented with either a placebo or a combination of vitamins, minerals, and essential fatty acids. After about 20 weeks of supplementation, the prisoners who received nutrients were better behaved. Those who received vitamins, minerals, and essential fatty acids had a 35 percent reduction in disciplinary incidents and a 37 percent reduction in violence compared to their fellow inmates. All of these improvements were statistically significant. Providing prisoners with adequate amounts of nutrition led to better behavior! The public health implications of this study are enormous.

Carol, a 20-year-old struggling with anorexia, came to see me for help when her eating disorder was interfering with her ability to remain in college. She had struggled with anorexia since the age of 16 with increasing physical symptoms, including irritable bowel syndrome and heart arrhythmias. She initially was not forthcoming with her thoughts around her weight and was not as worried about her weight restriction as her parents were.

Carol, however, was quite concerned about her "list" of physical symptoms that had been annoying her for over a year. Carol described chronic insomnia, irritable bowel syndrome, muscle twitches, fatigue, headaches, and sensitivity to loud noises. As I explained to Carol that a common cause of these symptoms was nutritional deficiencies, especially magnesium deficiency, Carol was suddenly engaged. She listened intently as I helped her understand the role of magnesium in energy metabolism, muscle function, and stress.

For Carol, I recommended nutritional testing and started her on magnesium supplements. Carol, like many patients I see, wants information on nutritional health. She participated more actively in her recovery when given this information. Magnesium supplements helped Carol with her muscle twitches and headaches, and within a few weeks on follow-up visits, we discussed her nutritional testing and found other nutritional deficiencies that Carol was eager to understand. Carol is taking classes part-time, wants help with her eating disorder, and has been compliant with treatment.

We know from experience that what we eat affects us. Research teaches us that what we don't eat also affects us, sometimes in significant and long-lasting ways. There are significant implications and consequences to deficits of even a small handful of nutrients. Patients suffering from anorexia nervosa develop nutritional deficiencies with physical, emotional, and chemical consequences. In other words, very quickly, anorexia becomes a physical illness, not a mental illness.

Chapter Eight

How Diet and Nutrition Can Start, Worsen, or Stop Anorexia

My years of clinical experience in treating anorexia have made it abundantly clear to me that poor nutrition is a major contributing factor to the disease, one that can induce anorexia, sustain the course of the illness, and exacerbate existing symptoms of anorexia. Will an otherwise healthy adolescent develop anorexia if he or she repeatedly consumes the wrong diet? Probably not, but the risk is much higher in those who are genetically vulnerable with certain personality traits and who are suffering from depression, anxiety, or obsessive compulsive disorder—and that category includes a huge number of teens.

Restrictive eating and the skipping of meals affect the onset and/or exacerbation of anorexia in three definitive ways:

1. As adolescents grow and develop, the need for zinc increases. Diets low in calories and, particularly, low in meat, are almost always deficient in zinc. A lack of zinc decreases the appetite and increases the likelihood of meat avoidance, due to unpleasant taste sensations, initiating a cycle of symptoms consistent with anorexia nervosa. Both lack of appetite and meat avoidance can contribute to a further decrease in zinc intake, compounding the problem.
2. The water-soluble vitamins (particularly B1, B3, and vitamin C) must be ingested on a regular basis, as they are not stored in the body. When the diet is poor, deficiencies in these nutrients can arise fairly easily. As is the case with zinc, when these nutrients are deficient there can be a decrease in appetite that can contribute to a vicious circle of restrictive/chaotic eating, leading to further nutrient depletions, which then leads to increasingly restrictive or chaotic eating.
3. Restrictive eating and the skipping of meals can trigger binge eating, which is typically followed by intense guilt, self-loathing, and an increased resolve to restrict eating further, making nutrient depletion almost certain.

There is a subset of girls, young women, and young men in whom these nutritional deficiencies can create or exacerbate anxiety, depression, and the underlying temperamental traits of perfectionism and an obsessive-compulsive personality. When these are combined with co-existing depression and/or anxiety, vulnerability to an eating disorder is more likely.

Puberty: The Foundation of Mental Health is Laid

During puberty, the course of an adolescent's overall development is determined. Critical growth takes place at this stage of life: Adolescents add what will amount to be 20 percent of their adult height, 45 to 50 percent of their peak bone mineralization and skeletal mass, and 50 percent of their adult weight. Metabolism changes significantly to accommodate the synthesis of hormones and the rapid increase in body tissue. Changes also occur in systems regulating appetite and weight. The profound changes and tremendous growth that occur during puberty depend upon the nutrients obtained by dietary intake.

Good nutrition is also crucial to the developing brain of the adolescent. The brain is the most complex organ in the body, and although it accounts for only 2 percent of the body's weight, one-quarter of the body's energy is dedicated to fueling it. There are 100 billion nerve cells (neurons) in the brain, and each connects to more than 2,000 other neurons. More than 250 brain chemicals (neurotransmitters), substances that coordinate how we think, feel, and behave, have been identified.

It's a surprising and frightening fact that, on average, the age of onset for all mental illness is approximately 14. This means that by age 14, the foundation for mental illness can be set. Two important processes that occur during adolescence that may play a role in mental illness are pruning and myelination. As the brain grows from infancy to its adult state, it constantly refines itself. With every newly acquired skill, the brain cells make new connections to each other. But during the transition from childhood to adulthood, the brain decides which connections to keep and which to eliminate. Neurons that are used infrequently are pruned, or removed, leaving the most active ones to thrive. This process results in a more efficient, better organized brain.

Another important process that takes place within the brain beginning early in life and continuing through adolescence is myelination. Myelin is the fatty white coating around each neuron that adds a layer of protection and increases the speed at which nerve impulses move through the central nervous system.

Both pruning and myelination, which play important roles in integrating emotional processes, depend on an adequate amount of fat and protein in the diet, as well as key trace minerals and vitamins. One of the most important is vitamin B12, although all of the nutrients required to fuel the body's cells are required by the cells in the brain. But remember, the brain's need for energy is higher than the rest of the body: almost 25 percent of total metabolic energy is used by the brain. Deficiencies in the vitamins and minerals that create this metabolic energy may interfere with normal brain function and development before they produce outward physical symptoms.

My point is that the brain's need for adequate nutrients and energy is at an all-time high during adolescence, which is the same period during which kids are the least likely to get them. In fact, it's the period when they are more likely to eat more poorly than any other societal group.

How the Standard American Diet Contributes to Eating Disorders

Triple-decker bacon cheeseburgers with fries, pizza, cola beverages; the ice cream truck that rings its bell through leafy suburban streets: these are icons of American life. These images, however, are deceptively benign. These foods that typify what Americans eat may evoke nostalgia, but they endanger our lives and are undoubtedly contributing to the increase in eating disorders seen in the past several decades.

The Standard American Diet, all too appropriately abbreviated SAD, is high in factors that increase disease risk and low in factors that protect against obesity, hypertension, diabetes, high blood cholesterol, stroke, and cardiovascular disease. The SAD is:

- High in animal fats
- High in unhealthy saturated, hydrogenated, and trans fats
- High in sugar
- High in processed foods
- High in sodium
- Low in fiber
- Low in complex carbohydrates and whole grains
- Low in plant-based foods (fruits and vegetables)

One of the major culprits in the SAD is refined sugar. Refined sugar is responsible for empty calories without nutritional value. Studies have shown a correlation between sugar and many diseases and conditions—including premature aging, diabetes, cancer, suppressed immune systems, and disordered eating. A recent report by the American Heart Association (AHA) recommended drastic cuts in sugar consumption. Women, the report says, should eat no more than 100 calories of processed sugar daily; men should eat no more than 150 calories. Yet the average American consumes 355 calories from added sugar every day. According to the AHA, "Over the past 30 years, total calorie intake has increased by an average of 150 to 300 calories per day, and approximately 50 percent of this increase comes from liquid calories (primarily sugar-sweetened beverages)."

Countries consuming the opposite of the SAD (i.e., a diet low in animal fat and sugar, high in fiber and plant-based foods) such as Japan and the Mediterranean countries report much lower rates of cancer, coronary artery disease, and diabetes than the United States. They also have a lower incidence of disordered eating.

In *The End of Overeating: Taking Control of the Insatiable American Appetite*, Dr. David Kessler shows that foods high in sugar, salt, and fat activate the reward center of the brain, actually altering brain chemistry.

Frightening Facts About Teen Eating Habits

- A 2007 study found that teens reduced their intake of fruits and vegetables by almost one serving a day when they entered high school and by the same amount when they turned 18.
- Today, both girls and boys consume twice as much sweetened soda as milk.
- 95 percent of adolescent girls do not eat the recommended daily servings of fruit and vegetables, and between 1999 and 2004 their consumption of fruits and vegetables declined by one serving per day.
- In one survey, almost half of all teens surveyed reported eating no vegetables that day.
- 88 percent of adolescent girls get less calcium than most two-year-olds do, even though their calcium needs are three times higher.
- One in three teens eats fewer than three meals a week with their families, in spite of the fact that recent research has shown that the more often families eat together, the less likely kids are to smoke, drink alcohol, use drugs, be depressed, develop eating disorders, or contemplate suicide.

Most likely this occurs because fat and sugar trigger a release of dopamine, a "pleasure" neurotransmitter, and as dopamine increases, a cycle of reward is built into the brain circulatory system, causing an addictive reaction to these foods. In other words, eat fat and sugar, feel better. Soon it becomes a habit.

Changing to healthier food choices can protect against disordered eating. This shift includes consuming nutrient-dense whole foods which provide the necessary nutrients for synthesis of appropriate levels of neurotransmitters (such as dopamine and serotonin). These neurotransmitters play an important part in the hunger/satiety signals that tell an individual when to eat and when to stop; signals that are almost always faulty in those with eating disorders. Providing the brain with adequate nutrients is key to reestablishing proper levels of these nutrients, which can do much to prevent cravings, binge eating, and disordered eating.

Nutrition Guidelines for Adolescent Girls

Unhealthy eating patterns are the most frequently occurring chronic disease risk behavior in American kids between age 12 and age 17. Efforts to become conscious of just how unhealthy these eating choices are and to take steps to change them will help protect our children against disordered eating and allow them to develop to their fullest potential.

So what exactly constitutes a healthy diet for a teenage girl? The United States Department of Agriculture (USDA) issues nutritional guidelines every five years based on the latest nutrition and medical research. The current guidelines, released in 2005, recommend consumption of a variety of fruits, vegetables, grains, dairy products, fish, lean meat and poultry, beans/lentils, and healthy fats, while limiting the intake of saturated and trans fats, cholesterol, sugar, salt, and alcohol. Specifically:

- Less than 10 percent of calories should come from saturated fat (animal fats such as the fat on meat, or butter and cream).
- Less than 300 mg of cholesterol (the equivalent of about one egg) should be consumed per day.
- Trans fatty acids (trans fats, also known as partially hydrogenated fats) should be avoided as much as possible.
- Total fat intake should fall between 20 and 35 percent of total calories.
- Most fats should come from polyunsaturated and monounsaturated fats (healthy fats) such as those found in fish, nuts, and vegetable oils.

The USDA also estimates how many calories children and teens need to grow, stay healthy, and combat disease, based on their age, gender, and activity level. The guidelines that pertain to adolescent girls and young women are as follows:

Daily Calorie Guideline Based on Activity Levels

Gender	Age (Years)	Sedentary	Moderately Active (Equivalent of walking 1½ to 3 miles per day)	Active (Equivalent of walking 3 to 5 miles per day)
Female	9–13	1,600 cal	1,600–2,000 cal	1,800–2,000 cal
	14–18	1,800 cal	2,000 cal	2,400 cal
	19–30	2,000 cal	2,000–2,200 cal	2,400 cal

Source: Dietary Guidelines for Americans 2005

What Adolescent Girls Are Eating Today

Clearly, the foods and portions recommended by these guidelines are vastly different from what is typically consumed in the Standard American Diet. And the diets of teenagers are least nutritious of all. In theory, teens should be eating about 2½ cups of vegetables, 2 cups of fruits, 6 ounces of grains, 5½ ounces of protein like meat, eggs, or beans, and 3 cups of milk every day. In reality, American teens' diets are full of sugar, white flour, and added fats, and most don't consume anywhere near the recommended amounts of any of the food groups. If vegetables are eaten at all, they may be in the form of French fries or iceberg lettuce. Fruit servings often take the form of fruit juice. Yet one quarter of the day's calories (approximately 500 calories) come from sweets and sweeteners, like high-fructose corn syrup, that are found in nutrient-poor foods such as sugary sodas and juices, chips, and baked goods.

Because adolescents tend to fill up on junk at the expense of nutritious foods, they typically don't get sufficient vitamins and minerals. The National Research Council suggests recommended dietary allowances of vitamins and minerals that are critical to growth and development. The recommended amounts in these guidelines tend to be low; they were intended to prevent severe nutritional deficiency diseases rather than ensure optimal levels of nutrients in the diet. They also do not account for

Serving of Each Food Group and Serving Sizes

In addition, the USDA suggests recommended daily servings of the basic food groups. The following is based on a daily caloric intake of about 2,000 calories a day, an average amount for a young woman:

Food Groups Daily Intake for 2,000 Calories a Day

Fruits: A variety of fruits; 2 cups daily (four 1/2-cup servings)

Vegetables: A variety of vegetables, 2½ cups daily (five 1/2-cup servings). Make selections from all five vegetable subgroups (dark green, orange, dry beans or legumes, starchy vegetables, and other vegetables) several times a week.

Grains: 6 ounces of grain products (half from whole grains). 1 ounce of grain is equivalent to 1 slice of bread, 1 cup of cereal, or 1/2 cup of cooked rice, cooked pasta, or cooked cereal.

Oils: 6 teaspoons (2 tablespoons) of oils/fats daily (vegetable oil, low-fat mayonnaise, salad dressing)

Dairy Products: 3 cups of fat-free or low-fat milk or yogurt, or 3 servings of 1½ ounces cheese

Meat, Fish, and Poultry, Dry Beans, Eggs, and Nuts: 5½ ounces lean, low-fat or fat-free meats

Sugar: Foods and beverages with few added sugars or sweeteners

Salt: Less than 2,300 mg of sodium per day (about 1 teaspoon of salt)

Sources: USDA MyPyramid and US Dietary Guidelines 2005.

environmental and lifestyle factors that can destroy vitamins, or for individual biochemistry.

Vegetarianism and Anorexia

Your family sits down to dinner one evening and your 14-year-old daughter looks with disgust at the plate of chicken placed in front of her. "I am not eating that," she declares, seemingly out of the blue. "I've decided to be a vegetarian."

As a parent, you may be unsure how to respond. Is this decision impulsive? Is it likely to be short-lived? What if it isn't? Practical questions immediately pop into your mind: When did she decide this? Why?

What exactly does she plan to eat? How will her body get enough protein? And then a new thought pops up: "Should I be worried about her?" The answer to that question is: probably.

What is a Vegetarian?

Vegetarianism is defined as the practice of not eating meat, poultry or fish, or their by-products. However, some vegetarians consume eggs and/or dairy products, making the following distinctions necessary:

- *Vegans* do not consume any animal flesh (meat, poultry, fish, and seafood) or animal products (eggs, dairy, and honey), and they usually avoid wearing and using animal products such as leather, silk, wool, lanolin, and gelatin. All vegans are vegetarians, but not all vegetarians are vegans.
- *Lacto vegetarians* are vegans who consume milk and milk products.
- *Ovo-lacto vegetarians* are vegans who consume milk products and eggs.

It is a well-accepted fact that adults who follow a vegetarian diet are healthier than non-vegetarians. When eating a balanced diet that includes plant protein sources, adult vegetarians tend to weigh less, smoke fewer cigarettes, drink less alcohol, and exercise more than non-vegetarians. However, the health benefits seen in adults do not always extend to the 6 percent of U.S. teenagers who call themselves vegetarians. About 75 percent of adolescent vegetarians are girls, most are in middle school, and close to two-thirds of them claim to eat some chicken, fish, or red meat. Some of them do eat a variety of protein, fat, and carbohydrate, but others do not. And the latter group has been found to be less healthy than their non-vegetarian peers. In interviewing many adolescent patients, I have been accustomed to their honesty as they describe themselves as "fake vegetarians."

The "Vegetarian Excuse"

While most young vegetarians will profess ideological motivations for their vegetarianism, some stop eating meat as a way of experimenting with food restriction, creating food "rules," and exerting control over their food intake. The danger is that vegetarianism can be used to mask a budding eating disorder. Many of my preteen and teenage patients tell me they find it easier and less problematic to say they are vegetarian than admitting they don't eat meat because of the fat and calories it contains. Calling oneself a vegetarian is not only socially acceptable, it may even be admired. In short, becoming vegetarian may be an attractive option for teenagers who are trying to mask their concerns about eating high-fat foods.

For many adolescents, becoming vegetarian may also occur more naturally. Teenagers who are beginning to restrict their food intake sometimes don't even realize that their eating habits resemble those of a vegetarian. When I talk with them about the foods they are eating, they may initially deny being vegetarian. But when questioned further, they might report that they haven't eaten any meat products in two weeks. And when they did eat some meat, it was a small amount and only done to appease a family member.

Is Vegetarianism a Risk Factor for Anorexia?

This raises an important question: Does becoming a vegetarian increase the risk of developing anorexia? The answer is unclear. It has not yet been consistently demonstrated that being a vegetarian can cause the development of symptoms of anorexia, although the results of some studies are a bit alarming. For example, in Israel, researchers found that 56 percent of patients with anorexia had stopped eating meat one to six years before they developed the eating disorder, and many of them began avoiding meat at around age 11!

Research points to a clear association between anorexia and vegetarianism among those already in the throes of anorexia. Multiple studies have found that women with anorexia report an aversion to foods with a high protein content, such as red meat, fish, milk, and eggs. One group of researchers determined the prevalence of vegetarianism among patients with anorexia was approximately 50 percent; another group found it was 45 percent; while a third found that 76 percent of a sample of anorexic patients avoided both beef and poultry. When questioned, many patients with anorexia claimed to dislike the taste of meat and find it nauseating.

The prevalence of vegetarianism in anorexia is important because people who are both anorexic and vegetarian have poorer outcomes for recovery from the disease. In vegetarians, anorexia lasts longer and involves more weight loss, and there is a decreased rate of success in maintaining normal weight and normal eating patterns. In addition, vegetarian anorexics are more "weight phobic" than their non-vegetarian counterparts and more frequently abstain from eating.

Even in those who are not formally diagnosed with an eating disorder, being vegetarian has been associated with a number of troubling food-related behaviors. One large study done in Minnesota assessed the eating habits of more than 2,500 young adults, ages 15 to 23. Of the study subjects, 4 percent were current vegetarians, 11 percent were former vegetarians, and the rest were non-vegetarians. About 20 percent of the current vegetarians reported they had engaged in binge eating and felt out of control during the prior year. Some 26.8 percent of former vegetarians reported they engaged in extremely unhealthy weight-control behaviors (defined as purging and using laxatives, diuretics, and diet pills) during the previous year. In contrast, only 5 percent of non-vegetarians reported engaging in binge eating and feeling out of control.

Similarly, another study assessing the eating habits of college women found that vegetarians reported more unhealthy behaviors than non-vegetarians. A total of 36.7 percent of vegetarians scored high enough on the "unhealthy eating scale" to indicate that they were at risk of eating disorders, compared to 8.8 percent of non-vegetarians. The traits that showed a statistically significant increase in vegetarians were the taking of laxatives, exercising strenuously to burn off calories, and preoccupation with the desire to be thinner.

Nutritional Deficiencies in Teenage Vegetarians and How They Can Lead to Anorexia

Although troubling, the association between vegetarianism and anorexia is only part of the picture. The deficiencies of the key nutrients such as zinc, vitamin B12, and tryptophan that will likely result from the typical teenage diet, minus meat and other high-protein foods, can set the stage for psychiatric disease.

Poor Intake of High-Protein Foods. Studies have found that when teenagers decide to stop eating meat products, they do not consistently substitute other high-protein foods. In the aforementioned study reporting that 76 percent of a group of anorexic patients avoided beef and poultry, not one patient regularly substituted another protein source for meat, and good alternative sources of protein such as fish and soy-based products were eaten only infrequently.

A diet without a regular, adequate source of protein fails to provide the body with essential nutrients such as zinc, vitamin B12, and tryptophan. It can also lead to increased snacking on foods that are high in sugar and low in nutrients. While teenage vegetarian diets may contain sufficient calories thanks to plenty of high-sugar, high-fat, high-calorie foods, these foods typically don't meet the nutritional needs of a growing body. During adolescence, a time of accelerated physical growth and increased psychological and emotional stress, it becomes increasingly likely that deficiencies will occur when entire food groups or kinds of foods are restricted.

Unfortunately, many parents and professionals focus solely on encouraging the adolescent to ingest sufficient calories. They may not be overly concerned about nutrient deficiencies, especially if the adolescent has not lost a lot of weight and blood tests have not produced abnormal results. You should understand, however, that even without a dramatic weight loss, he or she may be malnourished. Early signs and symptoms of nutrient deficiencies—ranging from digestive disorders and fatigue to skin problems—can develop subtly and gradually: so gradually, in fact, that it may take years for some nutritional deficiencies to become clinically evident. Some of the most common deficiencies seen in teenage vegetarians are zinc, vitamin B12, and tryptophan, all of which are found in high-protein foods and may play critical roles in the development and/or progression of anorexia.

Zinc. Female vegetarians have been found to have measurably lower levels of zinc in their blood, urine, and hair compared to non-vegetarians. This makes sense when you consider that in the United States more than half of the zinc we ingest comes from animal sources; one-fourth comes from beef alone. So the zinc status of vegetarians is at risk from the start by virtue of the fact that they don't eat meat.

To make matters worse, the small amount of zinc that vegetarians do consume is not absorbed well. This means that even if vegetarian and non-vegetarian teenagers consume similar quantities of zinc (which, by the way, is almost always below recommended amounts), the vegetarians will not absorb zinc as effectively. A major reason why vegetarians don't absorb zinc well is that the plant foods highest in zinc, including legumes, whole grains, nuts and seeds, are also high in substances called phytates, which block zinc absorption. Consequently, it is estimated that vegetarians need to consume 50 percent more zinc per day than non-vegetarians to achieve the recommended dietary amount.

One study looking at the eating habits of vegetarians found that 50 percent of vegans, 21 percent of lacto vegetarians, and 14 percent of ovo-lacto vegetarians ingested less than one-third of the Recommended Daily Allowance (RDA) for zinc. (The RDA is 9 mg per day for ages 14 to 18, and 8 mg per day for adult women.) Another study found that 44 percent of vegetarian women ingested less than 6 mg of zinc per day.

Add vegetarianism to the mix, and zinc deficiency becomes even more likely in anorexia, because anorexics are less likely to consume meat or other foods that are high in zinc. In the Israeli study mentioned earlier, all of the patients with anorexia were found to be zinc deficient. And among anorexics, vegetarians have significantly lower dietary intakes of zinc than non-vegetarians. As will be discussed in future chapters, too little zinc in the diet can contribute to anorexia by promoting a decrease in appetite and sense of taste and smell, an aversion to meat, depression, anxiety, and nausea after meals.

Vitamin B12. Vitamin B12 is found primarily in meat products and, to a lesser extent, in eggs and milk products. It is also made by bacteria in the digestive tracts of animals. Because vegans do not eat these foods, they are especially at risk of developing a deficiency. While some plant sources do contain a slightly different form of vitamin B12, it is not the active form of the vitamin that is found in meat and is therefore not a reliable nutritional source.

Vitamin B12 is extremely important to the brain and the body in general, and a deficiency can cause a wide range of psychological problems. Among other things, a vitamin B12 deficiency can lead to decreased production and function of neurotransmitters, such as the serotonin, norepinephrine, and dopamine that are intricately involved in mood and mental health. Low levels of vitamin B12, then, can cause potentially severe psychological symptoms, including fatigue, depression, and anxiety.

In my practice, anxiety and panic have been the most dramatic symptoms of low B12 levels that I have witnessed. As B12 levels return to normal, anxiety consistently decreases.

Tryptophan. Amino acids are necessary for building new cells, making hormones, and repairing all of the parts of the body. Linked together in different combinations, they are also the building blocks of proteins. Amino acids are needed to make everything in the body—from brain cells to skin, from muscles to bone. Most relevant to anorexia, though, is the role amino acids play in psychological function. As precursors for most of the neurotransmitters in the brain, they are required for the production of substances such as serotonin, dopamine, and norepinephrine.

The amino acid tryptophan is a precursor for serotonin. It is also one of nine essential amino acids, which means that it must be obtained from food; it cannot be made within the body. Low dietary intake of tryptophan can cause inadequate serotonin synthesis in the brain, which has been associated with a depressed mood. Acutely ill anorexic patients with low caloric intakes have low levels of tryptophan and may suffer from decreased serotonin function, and therefore depression. In fact, many psychiatrists believe that the poor response to antidepressant medications in patients with anorexia is due to low serotonin levels.

Deficiencies in zinc, B12, and/or tryptophan can exacerbate the underlying symptoms of anorexia (e.g., decrease in appetite and sense of taste and smell, aversion to meat, depression, anxiety, fatigue, and nausea during refeeding), contributing to the onset and continuation of the disease and impairing recovery. If the recovering anorexic continues to feel anxious, fatigued, depressed, or revolted at the thought of eating meat or eating in general, it is more likely that she will slide back into anorexia and less likely that she will be able to maintain recovery.

Protecting the Health of Your Vegetarian Teen

So what should you do if your preteen or teenager declares one day that she/he is no longer going to eat meat? First and foremost, treat the decision to avoid a specific food group as a red flag. Both you and your teen's healthcare provider must address it seriously. Remember:

1. Becoming vegetarian may be an excuse to begin restricting food intake.
2. Vegetarianism is very common in anorexia.
3. Teenage vegetarian diets, in general, can be deficient in many nutrients.
4. Inadequate protein intake can lead to deficiencies of zinc, vitamin B12, and tryptophan—three nutrients that play a key role in mood and mental health.

Now, it is possible that your child may be just fine on a vegetarian diet. Due to the interplay of genetic makeup and environment, your teen may have a lesser biological need for certain nutrients. But it is also possible that she might have a greater biological need for nutrients such as zinc, B12, or tryptophan, which are concentrated in meat sources.

In Chapter Twenty-Seven you'll find practical advice about what to do when a child decides to become a vegetarian. Included are the questions you should ask your child about his or her decision. In addition, I have listed concerns you may want to share with your child when having a conversation about the choice. Discussing the importance of nutrients, and then devising and following a well-balanced, protein-sufficient vegetarian diet, can help prevent nutritional deficiencies and maintain physical and mental health.

Of course, if your teen's decision to become a vegetarian is accompanied by any overt behavioral changes that concern you—such as drastically reduced food intake, eating alone, or ritual behaviors around food—you must consult a mental health professional.

Chapter Nine

Anorexia, Genes and Nutrients

More than a few patients have told me that they are helpless victims of fate. "It's in my genes," they say. "My mother is depressive, my aunt is anorexic, and my brother can't walk up or down a staircase without counting every single step. It doesn't matter what I do now. Nothing will help me."

It's true that there is a connection between genes and anorexia. Studies of families and twins have indicated that genetics are involved in the development of the disease. Indeed, genetics may be responsible for as much as half the risk of suffering from anorexia, but as I pointed out in Chapter One, genetics is not destiny. You may have inherited genes that can predispose you to the disease, but those genes are not destined to control your life. That's because there is a difference between genetic presence and genetic expression. In other words, just having certain genes doesn't mean that those genes will automatically express themselves.

Genes Make Us Who We Are–Almost

Genes are the basic building blocks of everything we are. Found within every cell of the body, these incredibly long sequences of DNA (deoxyribonucleic acid) tell the cells what kind of cells they are, what proteins and other substances they should manufacture, and much more.

Thanks to his or her genetic makeup, each person is anatomically and biochemically unique, with his or her own individual ways of responding to life. This uniqueness frames the way that each of us perceives and interacts with the world. For instance, when a family sits down to enjoy dinner, each member is actually tasting a different dinner due to the unique distribution of taste receptors in the tongue.

This concept isn't anything new; it was known in the early 1930s that some people could not perceive certain tastes. By the 1990s, it was discovered that not only were some people taste-blind, but a few tasters—an estimated 25 percent—experienced taste with far greater intensity. Linda Bartoshuk and her colleagues at the Yale University School of Medicine described these intense tasters as "supertasters." Research by Bartoshuk found that these supertasters had a higher than average number of taste buds, leaving them better able to perceive fatty foods, bitter foods, and oral pain (such as from spicy food). This biochemical uniqueness informs how we taste each meal and differ in our taste preferences. Each family member will taste the same meal differently and like different components of the same meal.

A person with a larger stomach will eat more than another with a smaller stomach, and those with smaller bladders will inevitably need to get up and use the restroom sooner than those with larger bladders. Responses to stress also vary: when something goes terribly wrong, one person will break down and cry, another will get angry and seek revenge, another will try to learn from it, another will try to ignore it, and so on.

Genes are the body's blueprints, detailed instructions that create both body and mind, and frame the psychological outlook. But whereas the blueprint for a building is unchanging and must be followed to the tiniest specification, our DNA blueprint is only partially fixed. Some parts of it are unalterable—for example, the behavior of our blood vessels or size of our feet—but many parts are more like "suggestions" or "possibilities" than orders. The latter are highly malleable and quite responsive to the environment, to our emotions, and to what we eat.

Epigenetics–Beyond Genes

The idea that genes are both fixed and not fixed may seem strange until you consider that while a building's blueprint is finalized at some point, our genetic blueprint is not. It is a work in progress, constantly being rewritten. This is why the many genes that contribute to the appetite and body image can tell the body to eat an appropriate amount of food for years, and then change to instruct the appetite to disappear and the mind to recoil in horror at the thought of even an ounce of fat on the hips.

What is rewriting our genes? It's the epigenome, a word that means "in addition to the genes" or "above the genes." You can think of your genes as your computer hardware—the CPU, screen, keyboard, mouse, and printer—and your epigenome as the software that tells that hardware what to do by "switching" certain genes on or off. While the hardware never changes, the way it behaves is continually altered by the software.

To push the analogy even further, think of your "epigenome software" as constantly being updated, racing through versions 1, 2, 3, and so on at a rapid pace. Your epigenome software is a work in progress, continually being updated in response to your diet, stress levels, and all the other factors that make up your environment. Researchers from Duke University used laboratory mice to demonstrate one way in which this works. When they exposed female brown mice to a chemical called bisphenol A (BPA), which is found in plastic water bottles and other items, the chemical affected their genes and epigenome. Their offspring were born with yellow hair, putting them at greater risk for diabetes, obesity, and cancer. But when female mice were exposed to BPA and fed genistein, an active ingredient in soy and soy products, the effects of BPA were reversed and their offspring tended to have brown hair. This study showed that both BPA and genistein could change the way genes expressed themselves in mice and their offspring.

The same phenomenon occurs in humans. Take, for example, the large amount of fat in the typical American diet. When a high-fat diet is consumed during pregnancy, it increases the exposure of the fetus to fat and results in an increased risk of breast cancer in the child later in life. Thus, the mother's diet permanently alters the child's natural cancer-protective programming. Likewise, exposure to a diet high in refined sugars while in the womb can predispose a child to obesity and type 2 diabetes in adulthood.

Psychiatric disorders are also influenced by epigenetic changes, which can impact the structure of nerve cells, creation of new brain cells, plasticity of brain cells (ability of the brain to grow and change according to demand), and the amounts and actions of neurotransmitters such as serotonin and dopamine. All of these changes can alter a person's behavior.

Who rewrites your epigenetic software? To a large extent, you do. You do so every day by eating what you eat, responding to stress the way you do, and otherwise interacting with your environment in your own unique way. The results may affect not only you, but also your unborn children.

In fact, in *The Genie in Your Genes: Epigenetic Medicine and the New Biology of Consciousness*, Dawson Church, PhD, challenges the notion that genetics is destiny. Reversing the long-held theory that genes are an unalterable prescription that programs not only the color of our eyes but also the diseases we will develop, he argues that genes do not determine our fate. The environment—including our own attitudes, beliefs, life experiences, and behaviors, as well as the time and conditions in which we live—have a great influence over the expression of the genes we were born with. The "genie" Church alludes to is our newly discovered ability to change the blueprint of our genes—for ourselves and for the next generation.

Church bases his claims in the new field of epigenetics, which studies how the environment works to turn genes on and off or make their influence strong or weak. One of the pioneers of this new field is Dr. Lars Olov Bygren at the Karolinska Institute in Stockholm. In the 1980s, Bygren began to study the effect of years of famine in a remote area of Sweden during the nineteenth century. By early 2000, it was clear to him that the patterns of famine and feast not only powerfully affected the men who had undergone them, but also the genetic characteristics of the next generation. Those men who went from famine to feast within a single season, for instance, produced children who lived significantly shorter lives. Bygren's study revealed that these changes in gene activity did not alter the genetic code itself but were still passed down to the next generation.

This discovery at the root of epigenetics has profound implications. It overturns the old view that we are prisoners of our genes. The epigenome can change the expression of genes negatively or positively. Lifestyle choices like eating too much or not enough, or smoking, for instance, can put our own health at risk. It turns out that these behaviors can also predispose our children to disease and early death.

But this ability to influence genetic expression also has exciting and empowering implications. A healthy lifestyle can make a difference for ourselves and for our progeny. Epigenetics shows that even things we can't see—like beliefs, feelings, and attitudes—also play an important role in the epigenetic control of our genes, making possible actual changes in cell structure. Scientists are now learning to manipulate the epigenome to silence bad genes and spur on the good ones.

Genes and Anorexia

There is no doubt that anorexia nervosa has a strong genetic component: it runs in families and can be passed down from one generation to the next. People in families with eating disorders have 10 times the risk of developing an eating disorder themselves compared with people from families with normal eating behaviors. But as we've seen, genetic links are not necessarily destiny.

To develop an eating disorder, you must first inherit a certain set of genes, or certain mutations—accidental changes in the genes that occur during replication. There is not a single gene for anorexia; it's likely that there are many involved. Then, something in the environment must trigger activity in the genes, so they can become turned on by the epigenome software and express themselves. Nutrients, which provide the building blocks for genes, turn many genes on and off. Stress can also trigger the expression of genes involved in anorexia. We are still working to explore these complex interactions.

That's why anorexia is not strictly a psychological illness. Instead, it can be described as an "individual reaction" to the Standard American Diet. Look at it this way: in the majority of the population, eating the unhealthful American diet produces weight gain. As a result, we are in the throes of an epidemic of obesity, with more than two-thirds of our population being either overweight or obese. Anorexia and other eating disorders have risen in tandem with the obesity epidemic. While it may be partially attributed to our cultural idealization of thinness, anorexia may also represent a paradoxical reaction to the Standard American Diet. Anorexia may be a response to deficiencies in key vitamins and minerals, such as zinc, that are required for healthy psychological functioning.

That's why simply refeeding an anorexic patient to ensure consumption of a minimum number of daily calories is not the most effective treatment. Ensuring the proper intake of zinc and other vitamins and minerals, with a diet and supplement program specially designed for each individual patient, is a more effective way to ensure optimal brain function and psychological and physical health.

Kathy avoided treatment for her anorexia for nearly five years. In high school, she was a great athlete who skated competitively and danced. But she was also great at counting her calories and spending hours examining her body in the mirror. Her competition schedule dictated what she would eat. All forms of fat were shunned and the calories she consumed were rigidly connected to her competition schedule. When she competed she allowed herself 1,000 calories, and on practice days she limited her caloric intake to exactly 600 calories. According to government guidelines, the caloric intake for a moderately active 16-year-old is 2,000 calories per day.

Kathy wasn't alone in her struggle. As a child, Kathy's mother had also struggled with anorexia, and at age 46 she continued to worry obsessively about her weight. Although it was obvious to Kathy and everyone in the family, "nobody talked about it."

During her freshman year in college, Kathy developed a stomach virus and was unable to eat much of anything for almost five days. As she began feeling better, she was unable to return to her baseline caloric intake. She started losing weight very quickly and had difficulty completing school work. She began to isolate herself from friends and was unable to escape her obsessive thoughts that she was overweight and should lose a few more pounds. She never sought treatment until she was forced to take a medical leave from college.

As part of her treatment program, Kathy required five weeks of specialized residential treatment. She restored some weight, her mood improved, and she generally felt "better." But she remained 15 pounds under her ideal body weight, and she was now honest with her family about her obsessive worrying about her weight and restrictive food intake.

After the five weeks of treatment, Kathy returned to college with high hopes and an outpatient team experienced in treating eating disorders. She finished the semester, but never returned to college. Her eating disorder and relentless, obsessive worrying about weight gain interfered with all aspects of school and consumed her life. Her parents described her transformation as "frighteningly unreal." Every conversation related to some aspect of needing to lose weight or fears of gaining weight.

When I first saw Kathy two years after she left college, she explained to me that "everything helped but nothing worked."

Kathy, prompted by her parents, agreed to an intensive nutritional rehabilitation program. As you will learn in the following chapters, metabolic testing helps to determine the most appropriate nutritional supplements. Kathy agreed to start nutritional supplements as she understood there were only a few calories to "worry about." It's been one year since Kathy has been in any treatment program. She valiantly participates in nutritional therapy, takes her medications, and engages in psychotherapy. She continues to restore weight, and her obsessive thoughts, as Kathy describes them, "are quiet and at times can disappear for days."

We still have a lot to learn about the ways in which genes and nutrition interact and how stress factors in. This much we do know: We are not victims of our genes. There is no gene or combination of genes that dooms a person to suffer from anorexia. The proper use of zinc and other minerals and vitamins, as well as diet in general, can help overcome unfortunate genes and keep both mind and body healthy.

We'll look at using nutrition to guard against anorexia in later chapters.

Chapter Ten

Malorexia

The first half of this book put forth a new understanding of anorexia nervosa. Cultural and societal factors should no longer shoulder all of the blame; anorexia is not simply a desire to be thin taken to the extreme. Instead, it is a complex, multi-faceted disorder with genetic, psychological, biological, and neurochemical components. Individuals stop eating, and it is the subsequent malnutrition associated with self-starvation that ultimately contributes to the clinical symptoms observed as well as the difficult and lengthy recovery process. Treating only the psychological components of the illness without addressing the fact that the brain and body are malnourished is not enough. To ensure recovery, the malnourished brain needs to heal.

In anorexia, individuals consciously restrict their food intake to the point where they derail normal development and risk death.

This powerful denial of food is not well understood by psychiatrists and mental health care professionals. Current treatment and prolonged recovery processes filled with relapses testify to the fact that the model of anorexia that psychiatrists have been working with for more than 50 years is flawed. A new approach is clearly needed. But to know how to best approach an individual with anorexia, a more complete understanding of the disorder is required. This chapter will cover one critical piece of the puzzle that has not yet been mentioned: the role of intense anxiety in anorexia, and how pathological fear can influence the course of the illness.

Constant Anxiety

Every individual with anorexia nervosa struggles with anxiety. The anxiety is minimized or even disappears with restrictive eating. Many patients can readily describe the constant sense of pathological fear that envelops their lives. These feelings of panic have been likened to the emotion experienced by a parent who suddenly realizes he or she has lost a young child in a crowded area. Imagine the sudden sheer terror! But whereas most people experience anxiety as short-lived in certain predisposing situations, such as when delivering a speech or encountering an animal on the attack, individuals with anorexia experience pathological fear about their body, weight, food, and calories constantly—24 hours per day, 7 days each week.

Occasionally, medications such as the anti-anxiety benzodiazepines or antipsychotic medications can provide temporary relief from these overwhelming feelings. Dramatic or long-lasting relief from the panic and anxiety, however, is not likely with medications.

When I interview patients with anorexia and ask about their treatment goals, it is not surprising that they do not say that their goal is to eat. But they are all asking for relief. They articulate in different words that they want to be free from the anxiety and intrusive thoughts that control their lives. They want to stop feeling the extreme, life-threatening panic on an everyday basis. The pleas for help are desperate and gut-wrenching as patients share the discomfort of chronic anxiety, even though they cannot understand why we might be worried about their weight or nutritional health.

This pervasive, pathologic fear in anorexia has been described in the medical literature. In an article published in the *International Journal of Eating Disorders*, Michael Strober, PhD, clinical psychologist and the Director of the Eating Disorders Program at the Neuropsychiatric Institute at UCLA, addresses the issue:

"What differentiates the majority of young people who naturally register anxious distress over weight as puberty unfolds from the unfortunate few who inexplicably succumb to a fear of weight that is irrational, unrelenting, and disabling?"

One of the proposed hypotheses brought forth by Strober is the possibility that those with anorexia may have inherited factors that lead to the "'overexpression' of fear-based learning …, a far greater than normal acquisition of conditioned fear to weight, progressing rapidly thereafter to absolute, unrelenting morbid dread necessitating food avoidance."

These sufferers of anorexia may be more vulnerable to anxiety, and over time with subsequent nutritional deficiencies, the fear of food and weight gain is sustained and intensified by neurophysiological changes in the brain.

"Whatever it Takes"

Living with this constant anxiety, individuals will do or try anything they can to flee it. Unfortunately, the escape routes they usually choose are hazardous and often deadly.

In an effort to redirect and allay their anxiety, individuals with anorexia most often engage in the following three activities:

1. Substance abuse
2. Exercise addiction
3. Further food restriction

Unfortunately, these behaviors only serve to exacerbate the underlying disorder and confound practitioners.

Jennifer is a 37-year-old woman who has struggled with eating disorders since her teens. Her description of her feelings of constant and intense panic offer valuable insight to understanding anorexia:

"The first thing you need to understand about me is that I have to restrict what I eat. I don't have a choice, because the feeling of panic is so overwhelming, I have to do something to make it stop. From the outside, I seem to be in complete control of my life. To be in control – that's the point, isn't it?

"The trouble is, I almost always feel like I am spinning out of control with panic that feels crazy, like life-or-death. I reached a point where I would do whatever it took not to feel that way. For me, that meant restricting what I ate and exercising compulsively. As a teenager, I became a vegetarian. That allowed me to become very restrictive about my eating and still maintain a very acceptable—even moral and noble—front.

"Eventually my parents took me to the doctor when my period stopped. Nobody in my family believed in 'therapy,' so I was on my own pretending to be in treatment. My anorexia eventually went underground; no one knew.

"I was 19 when I entered my first marathon, and 25 when I participated in my first triathlon. I had just given birth to my daughter six months before! But instead of seeing my dedicated exercise regime as an indication of sickness, I was praised for my exercise routine.

"My tight control of my diet is also envied by my friends and colleagues. They constantly comment about wanting to be like me and being able to do what I do. What a joke! If they could only live inside my head, they would see a feeling of panic that is so overwhelming and so incomprehensible that I do whatever it takes to not feel that way."

Substance Abuse and Anorexia

Individuals with pathological fear are consumed with anxiety and incessant panic that threatens to erupt. Not counting the ubiquitous restricting of food, alcohol abuse is a common way that patients with anorexia find relief. It is estimated that between 12 and 18 percent of those with anorexia abuse or are dependent upon alcohol. While most anorexics begin abusing alcohol after the onset of their eating disorder, some are found to have a previous history of substance abuse.

The association between eating disorders and substance abuse is surprising to many. About half of individuals with an eating disorder abuse or are dependent upon alcohol and drugs. In contrast, approximately 9 percent of the general population abuses alcohol or illicit drugs. More than one-third of people with substance dependence report having some form of eating disorder. In addition, having a family history of substance abuse doesn't help anorexics. Individuals with a first-degree relative who is an alcoholic have a worse clinical course of their eating disorder, and experience a greater number of abnormal thoughts and behaviors, such as greater body dissatisfaction and a greater drive for thinness.

Most concerning, the presence of alcohol abuse after being discharged from a hospital or treatment program negatively affects a patient's clinical outcome in a significant way. Not only do women who abuse alcohol take longer to recover from their anorexia, but abusing alcohol also puts them at an increased risk of dying from their eating disorder. One study published in the *Archives of General Psychiatry* found that alcohol use, following treatment for an eating disorder, is one of the most consistent predictors of mortality.

Exercise Addiction

I recall a haunting image many years ago during my medical school education when I would exercise in a small gym located in a nearby hotel. The first time I entered the space, my attention was drawn to an emaciated woman furiously exercising on a piece of equipment in the corner of the room. I would soon come to learn that she was a regular fixture. Every time I went to the gym, whether in the morning or evening, weekday or weekend, there she was on that same machine, intensely focused without any noticeable signs of stopping. It was more than eight years before I fully understood her illness and the pathological anxiety that must have been responsible for relentlessly propelling her arms and legs. Many of us have witnessed the compulsive street walkers, the frail, gaunt individuals who power walk day and night with little joy or meaning in their rhythms.

Excessive exercise in individuals with anorexia is a highly reinforcing behavior: the more frequent and intense the workouts, the calmer one feels. Anorexics often exercise beyond what is considered healthy, to the point that the regimen can become harmful to the body. In many ways, an exercise addiction can be likened to an alcohol or drug addiction—so much so, that a group of researchers took a scale for measuring substance dependence and modified it into one that measured exercise dependence. Interviewing individuals with anorexia about their exercise habits, they found that about half of the individuals with anorexia surveyed reported behavior over the past month that was consistent with an unhealthy addiction to exercise.

Students away from home have unmonitored and unlimited access to their school gyms, so it's not surprising that the staff of some college athletic facilities restrict compulsive exercisers from using the gym due to health concerns.

Understanding the Pathological Fear

The vicious cycle of eating disorders has its roots in genetics and grows through childhood and adolescence. Genetically determined temperament and personality traits, such as being anxious, obsessive, or a perfectionist can become amplified in adolescence, when pathological eating often begins. Disordered eating leads to neurobiological changes in the brain that can alter brain function, increasing feelings such as depression, rigid thinking, and anxiety. To relieve the feelings of pervasive anxiety, individuals with anorexia do anything they can. Commonly, they further restrict food intake or abuse alcohol or exercise. These behaviors can quiet the mind, so the individual continues to engage in them. Unfortunately, long-term restricted eating leads to further nutrient deficiencies and more extensive changes in brain function, and the downward spiral continues.

In addition to characteristic childhood traits, individuals with anorexia frequently have anxiety disorders predating the onset of their eating disorder. One research group found anxiety disorders, including overanxious disorder and obsessive-compulsive disorder, to be present in 60 percent of a group of women with anorexia. Further, in 90 percent of those cases the anxiety disorder was present before the eating disorder developed. The exception to this finding was panic disorder, which tended to develop after the onset of the eating disorder.

Having a history of anxiety adversely affects the clinical outcome of an individual with an eating disorder. For instance, children who were described as being more anxious or fearful and then later developed anorexia were found to have a lower body mass index (i.e., they lost more weight) during the course of their anorexia.

Examining brain function with functional MRI has identified areas of the brain that seem to be activated by an anorexic's intense fear of food and calorie intake. The parts of the brain affected regulate fear as well as the body's automatic response to fearful situations. This automatic reaction of the body is known as the "fight-or-flight" response, and it is usually triggered when the body goes on sudden high alert. The brain is bathed in adrenaline, rational thought is clouded, and the body's muscles are tensed for action. The brain's ability to absorb and use this learned fear behavior may be due to zinc. A study published in the journal *Proceedings of the National Academy of Sciences*, has implicated that zinc may play a role in the transmission of information during fear learning. Zinc may regulate how fear is interpreted by the brain.

Picture a fly trapped on a windowsill relentlessly trying to escape, hurling itself against a pane of glass, over and over again, in an effort to overcome feelings of being cornered. These are the feelings that people with anorexia experience that compel them to engage in their maladaptive coping strategies.

An Approach to Anxiety: What Can Be Done?

To begin to understand the mind of an anorexic, imagine a moment of panic that you have experienced, and recall the feelings of overwhelming dread. While those feelings eventually dissipated for you, they do not disappear as easily in individuals with anorexia. Only compensatory behaviors, such as increased food restriction, excessive exercise, and substance abuse—all of which can cause further harm to the body—can make the anxiety temporarily wane. Individuals with anorexia cannot simply be talked out of their panic.

Yet, there is hope! I believe the correct medications and aggressive nutritional therapies can treat the pathological fear in anorexia. I have witnessed individuals progress from a constant state of panic to the point where their anxiety is no longer the driving force behind their illness.

Proper treatment, including both medication and restorative nutritional support, is necessary to quell a patient's anxiety. Without addressing both of these areas, the effects of starvation and malnourishment cannot be reversed, brain chemistry cannot be corrected, and patients are doomed to tragic outcomes.

While all who treat anorexia agree that disordered thinking about food, eating, and body image are core clinical symptoms, not all professionals understand that malnourishment of the body and brain lies at the root of the problem. To convey the importance of self-starvation and malnutrition as the underlying mechanism in anorexia, I suggest a new term: Malorexia—perhaps a new diagnosis?

The term malorexia incorporates the Latin root "mal," which clearly evokes the sense of feeling bad. It is a reminder that "bad" nutrition and "bad" intestinal absorption are inherent in an illness of starvation. I would describe malorexia this way: It is a complicated illness of restrictive eating and self-starvation initiated by multiple factors that contribute to severe malnutrition and consequent biochemical disturbances in the brain. When the brain does not receive essential nutrients such as amino acids, zinc, fatty acids and B vitamins, it cannot function normally. Malorexia—a distant relative of vitamin deficiency diseases such as scurvy and pellagra—is the clinical result of any pathway that leads to the restriction of essential nutrients.

Once an individual stops eating and becomes malnourished, one of the subsequent effects in the brain is a marked pervasive anxiety. In other words, people with malorexia have a disorder of pathological fear. These feelings of overwhelming panic and anxiety are so powerful that they not only take on a life of their own, but they can also determine an individual's behavior.

The next section of this book describes in detail how to ensure that an individual embarks on the most effective path to recovery, including how a relatively new tool called rEEG can determine the most appropriate psychiatric medication for a given individual. In addition, these chapters cover all of the essential nutrients needed for optimal function of the body and brain, as well as the nutritional supplements critical for individuals with anorexia. By incorporating the recommendations outlined in the upcoming chapters, you can help facilitate a smoother recovery process for yourself, your child, or another loved one.

Feeding the starving brain the nutrients it requires will help break the starvation cycle and quiet the overwhelming thoughts of fear and anxiety. Implementing the right psychiatric medications and the proper nutritional support can bring freedom from anxiety and relief from intrusive thoughts.

Emily, now 35 years old, had struggled with anorexia since the age of 16. In our sessions she narrated a long history of restrictive eating, obsessive food rituals, and repetitive thoughts about her weight and her body.

For more than a decade, she had been in and out of various eating-disorder treatment programs. After she graduated from college she held a job for awhile, but then had to go on disability and live at home with her parents because her eating disorder flared up again.

As I listened to Emily, I envisioned her on a treadmill of obsessive thoughts. She worried about the past, ruminating about what she had done, what she hadn't done, and what she should have done. When she wasn't hashing over the past, she worried about the future—about her job, her family, her friends, her weight, her appearance. Emily was unable to live in the present. She told me that she had only felt free of the thoughts that imprisoned her for a total of about three months during the past 17 years.

Unfortunately, Emily had discovered that alcohol brought her relief from the self-blaming monotonous grooves in which her mind ran. After a few drinks she could give herself over to living in the moment. Trying to replicate this rare sensation, Emily began to drink three or four glasses of wine every evening after restricting calories throughout the day. In the mornings, the obsessive thoughts returned with ever-increasing shame and guilt.

When Emily came to me for treatment, I ordered an rEEG. Based on the results, I prescribed two medications, Depakote and an MAOI antidepressant. She began attending Alcoholics Anonymous (AA) and committed herself to using nutritional supplements and following a healthy diet. She was placed on a nutritional program of essential fatty acids, B12, zinc, magnesium, and amino acids.

Emily is back at work and has not been hospitalized for more than two years. Although she still worries about the future, she now feels in control of her own thoughts. She says proudly, "I am not a puppet to obsessions any longer." Nutritional restoration and medication targeted to Emily's particular brain chemistry through rEEG gave her enough relief from her dark and obsessive thoughts to progress in therapy, return to her job, and, most importantly, regain a sense of power in her own life.

Chapter Eleven

The Plan:
A New Approach to Anorexia

New understandings in genetics, neurobiology, and neuroimaging support the idea that anorexia is a complex, biologically based mental illness. It is not merely a lifestyle choice due to cultural or parental pressures. Instead, the illness stems from biological and chemical disturbances in the brain.

The plan I have developed for treating anorexia is not a "one-size-fits-all" treatment plan. The five steps below comprise focused, effective interventions that should be initiated after a comprehensive evaluation by a professional who is experienced in treating eating disorders. Following my plan *will* optimize both physical and psychological health for you, your child, or loved one.

The first three aspects of my approach to anorexia involve evaluating and addressing specific conditions that may sustain the destructive symptoms of anorexia and prolong the course of the illness. A medication component as well as an individual's nutritional status is also addressed in the last two aspects of my approach. The plan includes:

- Testing for and correcting zinc levels in the body.
- Testing for elevated levels of urinary peptides.
- Testing for celiac disease.
- Using rEEG to identify the most beneficial psychiatric medications addresses the medication component.
- Testing for and correcting underlying nutritional deficiencies involves an overall assessment of an individual's nutritional status.

Step 1: Testing For and Correcting Zinc Levels

Testing for a zinc deficiency involves a simple taste test, but the benefits of correcting low levels of zinc in the body are enormous. Studies worldwide have shown that the mineral zinc likely has a significant role in the development of anorexia, as it alone can cause altered taste perception and a decrease in appetite, both of which can lead to decreased food intake, weight loss, and depression.

Being a mineral, zinc is not made by the body, but rather is acquired through eating food that contains zinc. Unfortunately, foods that adolescents are likely to eat—such as pasta—are low in zinc and can actually prevent the body from absorbing zinc from the foods it is most present in, such as meat and fish.

Without adequate zinc, general health—as well as appetite regulation and psychological function—will suffer. Fortunately, if a person is found to need it, zinc supplementation is widely available and well tolerated.

Step 2: Testing For and Correcting Elevated Levels of Urinary Peptides

Underlying digestive problems can compound the illness of anorexia, and can even prevent full recovery. It's important to identify and address these as part of treating anorexia. Testing for substances called urinary peptides via a simple urine test is necessary, because the presence of abnormally high levels of peptides indicates that the individual has a deficient or inactive digestive enzyme called dipeptidyl peptidase IV.

Without adequate functioning of this digestive enzyme, a person's body cannot completely digest foods that contain dairy and/or wheat proteins (called casein and gluten, respectively). Incompletely digested casein and gluten proteins are harmful because they can directly affect the brain; they can trigger a number of psychiatric symptoms, including obsessive thoughts. Not only is this obsessive thinking about food, meals, and one's body inherent in anorexia, but it is one of the factors that often contributes to relapse and prevents a sustained recovery.

If a person has elevated levels of these peptides in the urine, treatment—which includes supplemental digestive enzymes as well as eliminating casein and/or gluten from the diet—can be tremendously successful.

Step 3: Testing for Celiac Disease

Testing for celiac disease involves a blood test; occasionally, a tiny biopsy of the small intestine is required for diagnosis. I include it here because identifying and successfully managing celiac disease in patients with anorexia can dramatically improve the long-term clinical outcome of the eating disorder.

Celiac disease is an autoimmune disorder. Autoimmune disorders are conditions in which the body actually causes damage to itself. Whenever an individual with celiac disease eats foods containing a protein called gluten, the body attacks itself, potentially causing widespread and irreversible damage. Some gastrointestinal symptoms people can experience if they have celiac disease include abdominal pain, diarrhea, constipation, bloating, and weight loss.

Unfortunately, people may have undiagnosed celiac disease for years!

Once diagnosed, management of celiac disease involves completely eliminating gluten (found in wheat and other grains) from the diet and restoring nutritional deficiencies.

Step 4: Using Referenced-EEG to Identify the most Beneficial Psychiatric Medications

Although my approach to anorexia focuses on nutritional factors, the correct psychiatric medication can markedly decrease a patient's clinical symptoms, which can then allow the individual to participate more actively in the recovery process. Yet, as I have previously stated, studies demonstrating medication successes in treating anorexia have been underwhelming. Given all of the psychiatric medications available, the combinations a patient can be put on are endless, and there is still no guarantee that a patient will feel better!

The new tool I recommend, called rEEG, eliminates the guesswork involved in choosing medications. Used for more than 10 years to hone medication selection in patients with anorexia, rEEG measures individuals' brainwaves non-invasively and compares them to a known database. This information can be used to determine which medication, or combination of medications, will work best given the way the individual's brain functions.

Step 5: Correcting Underlying Nutritional Deficiencies

When people do not eat a well-balanced diet that includes proteins, whole grains, fruits, and vegetables, they may not be getting the essential nutrients their bodies require for healthy growth and normal function. Consider the amount and types of foods consumed by an individual with anorexia. Imagine all of the vitamins, minerals, amino acids, and essential fatty acids that are not getting into the person's body!

Underlying nutritional deficiencies can not only cause medical complications, but also serious psychological ones. For example, a deficiency of the mineral magnesium is commonly associated with anxiety, insomnia, and constipation. Vitamin B and C deficiencies can result in symptoms of depression, fatigue, and decreased appetite. A lack of sufficient fats in the diet, leading to a deficiency in essential fatty acids, can be associated with psychiatric conditions such as depression, attention-deficit hyperactivity disorder, and bipolar disorder.

Fortunately, most nutrient deficiencies can be identified through blood and urine laboratory tests. Once a person's specific nutritional needs have been determined, a plan can be devised to restore them to optimal levels through supplementation. Most patients with anorexia do not mind taking nutritional supplements, as they contain few calories. The effects of supplements alone can be significant. When taking them, patients subjectively feel better—more focused and less anxious—and can become better partners in the recovery process.

Toward Peace of Mind and Better Health

My goal is to restore physical health and peace of mind to patients who are suffering from anorexia nervosa. In the chapters that follow, you will learn both specific and general ways to stop the deteriorating progression of the physical, mental, and emotional devastation seen in the disorder. Fundamentally, my approach is about brain health: When provided with critical amounts of essential nutrients, vitamins, and minerals, both the brain and the body will function better. This is truly the key to recovering from anorexia without the fear of relapse.

Hannah's story is an example of the plan in action and its amazing ability to help those suffering from anorexia.

I have treated Hannah, a 29-year-old patient, for almost two years. When she arrived at my office for her initial appointment, she was severely emaciated. Claiming that she had struggled with disordered eating for her entire adult life, she described a long history of obsessive thinking and compulsive rituals that occupied her days.

Hannah now realizes her mother and sister also had eating disorders. Her sister binged and purged in college. At the dinner table during her childhood, she remembers that her mother counted calories and recorded her meals.

When Hannah began to restrict her eating as a young adult, she lost the ability to control her diet. "I would be lost in the grocery store. I spent hours walking up and down the aisles, reading the ingredients on every label. I didn't know what to buy. I knew that all the other shoppers were looking at me, disgusted by how fat I was."

After a comprehensive nutritional evaluation and rEEG guided medication choices, Hannah is confident that she has recovered. She attributes her healing to three essential elements: restoration of healthy nutrition, the right medications as determined by rEEG, and non-judgmental advice and support from her therapist, family, and and friends. "I was so malnourished that I had lost all perspective," Hannah explains. "I consider myself an intelligent person. Yet I looked in the mirror every day, and I never saw my eating disorder." The nutritional supplements helped Hannah see and think more clearly. Based on the results of an rEEG, Hannah began taking a combination of two medications, an antidepressant and an anti-convulsant. These drugs would never have been an obvious choice for treating anorexia, but Hannah got better. "The rEEG," she continues, "saved me years of more failed drug trials."

Proud to be recovering from anorexia and OCD, Hannah feels a sense of mission to speak to others about her experience. "Part of the disease is secrecy," she explains. "I want others to know that recovery is possible at any stage. As a society we need to be sure that people with anorexia get the personalized care they need. It breaks my heart that people with my disorder continue to suffer because they can't find the help they need. Treatment for this disorder is about beating the clock," she concludes.

Chapter Twelve

The Link to Zinc

A citrus fruit grower in Florida was despondent. The orange trees in his grove had again failed to bear any fruit. Perplexed as to why, the frustrated orange grower decided to cut his losses and sell his sickly grove. To prepare for the sale, he nailed several "For Sale" signs on the trees, making sure the signs were visible to drivers on the highway. Yet despite the signs, no one showed up to inquire about purchasing his grove.

The following season, however, brought an unexpected change of fortune. Flowers and fruit appeared on every tree that bore a "For Sale" sign. Why? Unbeknownst to the citrus grower, the trees had been suffering from a deficiency of the mineral zinc. The nails that held the signs in place were coated with zinc. Absorbing the mineral, the trees were restored to health. This true story, reported in 1967 in *Mother Earth: Journal of the Soil Association*, reveals the profound importance of the micronutrient zinc.

This chapter, as well as the following two, will cover the connection between the mineral zinc and anorexia. To begin, I will discuss in general terms the role of zinc in the body and share relevant scientific studies that lay the foundation for understanding its role in anorexia.

Essential to Overall Health

Long before the Florida grower's amazing discovery in his own orange grove, scientists realized that zinc is an essential nutrient for all living organisms. Found in every tissue and every cell in the human body, zinc affects biological processes ranging from cell growth to DNA synthesis. It's a necessary part of more than 200 enzymes, which are substances that make certain chemical reactions possible and increase the speed of others. All of the major enzymes in the gastrointestinal (GI) tract depend on zinc. These enzymes help facilitate the breakdown of fats, proteins, carbohydrates, sucrose, and lactose, and increase the activity of other digestive enzymes in the pancreas and small intestines. Zinc is crucial to immune system function, and it promotes wound healing, bone development, and growth. In addition, it accelerates the process of skin cell renewal, contributing to the health of skin and hair.

One of the most interesting, albeit least discussed, roles of zinc is its ability to regulate genes. Zinc can bind to proteins that directly interact with a person's genes, determining whether a gene becomes turned on and activated, or turned off and inactivated.

Zinc and Brain Function

Zinc is especially important to the central nervous system. Chemical complexes known as "zinc fingers" maintain the protein structures of the system. Zinc stimulates the production of brain compounds called neurotransmitters, which are essential chemicals that relay signals and regulate mood. It plays a part in making myelin, the white matter coating the nerves that helps them to conduct impulses between the brain and other parts of the body. Zinc is also a factor in brain growth and the transporting of hormones and growth factors.

Zinc Deficiency

The first case of human zinc deficiency was documented in 1961 in Shiraz, Iran, and involved a 21-year-old man whose physical body resembled that of a 10-year-old. When taking his history, his doctor learned that the man ate almost nothing other than whole-wheat bread. The doctor knew that although whole-wheat bread does contain some zinc, it also contains phytates, compounds that bind up zinc and prevent it from being absorbed by the body. Once the man's diet was supplemented with absorbable zinc, he began to grow normally, and eventually attained average adult height and normal sexual development. His cure was as dramatic as the transformation of the citrus grove.

Severe zinc deficiencies can result from a combination of nutrient-poor diets and high levels of stress, both of which are now common in today's westernized countries. Many early, subtle signs can indicate low zinc levels in the body. Generally, the first sign is a diminished sense of taste and smell; food does not taste "normal." As the zinc deficiency progresses, it leads to other symptoms: increased sensitivity to pain; nausea, bloating, and other GI problems; and eventually a delay in growth and sexual development. In addition to these physical effects, zinc deficiency profoundly influences mood and psychological well-being and can contribute to apathy, anxiety, depression, lethargy, and impaired learning and memory.

Symptoms of Both Anorexia Nervosa and Zinc Deficiency

- Decreased appetite and meat avoidance
- Decreased taste and smell
- Nausea and bloating during refeeding
- Insomnia and poor sleep habits
- Depression
- Attention difficulties
- Increased vulnerability to stress

Zinc and Anorexia Nervosa

Some symptoms of a zinc deficiency bear a strong similarity to the symptoms of anorexia nervosa. In both conditions, there is a diminished sense of taste and smell, a decreased appetite, avoidance of meat, nausea and bloating during refeeding, insomnia and poor sleep habits, depression, and attention difficulties.

The striking similarities between the symptoms of anorexia and zinc deficiency have led a number of researchers to delve deeper into the idea of using zinc supplements as a part of treating anorexia. In fact, more than 125 years ago in a residential facility in London, women who had anorexia hysteria (now called anorexia nervosa) were treated with a diet that was rich in oysters, a good source of zinc. These women recovered quickly. Despite this finding, though, there was little study of using zinc to treat eating disorders until 1979, when Dr. Rita Bakan of the British Columbia Institute of Technology observed that anorexia and zinc deficiency share many of the same characteristics, and that those with the highest risk for both disorders are adolescents and young women. She began to recommend zinc supplements for anorexia, and since that time, the results of numerous case studies and clinical trials published in prestigious medical journals have supported Dr. Bakan's recommendation.

Today there are many reports in the medical literature showing that at least half of those who suffer from anorexia nervosa have a measurable zinc deficiency, as well as a diminished capacity to absorb zinc from foods and supplements.

Case Studies

Case studies are written reports in which researchers describe an individual's course of illness and specific treatment. Because one person's response to a treatment could be coincidence or due to individual biochemistry, case studies are not considered conclusive proof that a treatment works. They do, however, suggest avenues for further study.

The first case of successful zinc supplementation was reported in the journal *The Lancet* in 1984 by Dr. Derek Bryce-Smith. A 13-year-old girl whose weight had dropped to 69.5 pounds was diagnosed with anorexia nervosa and found to have abnormally reduced taste sensitivity on the Zinc Taste Test (ZTT), indicating a zinc deficiency. (See Chapter Fourteen for more on this test.) In addition to her regular treatment, her physician gave her a total of 45 mg of zinc per day in liquid form, approximately three times the amount recommended in 1984. Within two weeks, the patient's mood and appetite had improved dramatically, and after 12 weeks, her weight had increased to 84.4 pounds. The doctors continued the zinc supplementation for 10 months, and her weight rose to 97.1 pounds, which was normal for her height and age. The patient's mood, demeanor, and appetite all remained normal during the 10 months of zinc supplementation.

When this same patient then experienced significant stress from academic pressures, her zinc deficiency recurred and her weight decreased; she had a relapse of her eating disorder. When zinc supplementation was prescribed again, her symptoms rapidly improved. This single case demonstrated that:

- This patient with anorexia nervosa had measurable reduced taste sensitivity that indicated the presence of a zinc deficiency.
- When receiving liquid zinc supplementation, she became happier, ate more, and gained weight.
- When she had increased stress in her life, she had a relapse of her anorexia and was again found to have a zinc deficiency.

A case study reported in 1989 by Alexander Schauss, PhD, and Carolyn Costin, MA, MEd, MFCC, tells of a 26-year-old woman with an 11-year history of anorexia nervosa who responded well to zinc supplementation. The 5-foot 8-inch patient, who survived primarily on popcorn, weighed only 91.5 pounds when she was referred to the treatment team. She complained of always feeling cold and tired, and she had reduced taste sensitivity. Four days after being given supplemental liquid zinc, her symptoms began to improve. She began to eat foods other than popcorn! After two weeks, her mood and sleep improved. After a month, her weight had increased to 102 pounds, and within four months she had returned to a normal weight. Schauss and Costin detail this patient and other cases in the 1989 booklet *Zinc and Eating Disorders*, a publication documenting the role zinc plays in treating anorexia and bulimia.

Another case study, this one reported in a Japanese medical journal, involved a 16-year-old girl with anorexia nervosa who was hospitalized due to vomiting, abdominal pain, and diarrhea. During her first week of hospitalization, she continued to lose weight until she was only 58 percent of her ideal body weight. She complained that she did not enjoy eating, declaring that food was tasteless. Hearing her complaints, her doctors measured zinc levels in her blood and performed a functional test of zinc deficiency called the alkaline phosphatase test. Alkaline phosphatase is a zinc-dependent enzyme in the liver; a low level can indicate low zinc levels. Both tests were abnormally low. Believing that her zinc deficiency was responsible for her lack of taste and anorexia, her doctors immediately began treating her with intravenous zinc. Astonishingly, all of her digestive problems disappeared after only the second day of treatment. Gradually, she began to enjoy her meals. After a week of receiving zinc intravenously, she was switched to oral zinc supplements. Over the course of the next two months, she regained weight until she was at a normal weight for her height. While her immediate success was due to intravenous zinc (a mode of delivery rarely used in this country), her improvement continued even on oral zinc supplementation. Physicians attempting to understand and treat anorexia nervosa should take note of this patient's dramatic recovery!

Clinical Trials of Zinc Supplementation in Patients with Anorexia

In comparison to case reports, clinical trials—and, in particular, randomized, double-blind, placebo-controlled trials—provide a stronger scientific argument for or against using a treatment. In these studies, patients are randomly placed in groups. One group receives the treatment under investigation; the other receives a placebo or an inactive version of the treatment, often a sugar pill that looks like the drug. In double-blind studies, neither the subjects nor the researchers know who is receiving the active treatment and who is receiving the placebo until the study has ended. These medical studies are best for obtaining objective, unbiased results.

To date, six clinical trials have been conducted to determine the effectiveness of zinc supplementation in treating anorexia nervosa. All were done in the 1980s and 1990s. Four were randomized, double-blind, placebo-controlled trials, and two studies were open-label trials, meaning that both researchers and patients knew that the patients were receiving zinc. A summary of each study follows:

Study #1: Zinc Deficiency in Anorexia Nervosa

Authors: Rebecca L. Katz, Carl L. Keen, Iris F. Litt, and colleagues

Journal: *Journal of Adolescent Health Care* 1987; volume 8: pages 400-406.

This randomized, double-blind, placebo-controlled trial was the first to assess zinc supplementation in patients with anorexia. Fourteen adolescent patients with anorexia nervosa between 14 and 19 years of age, and 20 healthy-weight control subjects who were similar to the patients in age, sex, and race were randomly assigned to receive either 220 mg of zinc sulfate (containing 50 mg of elemental zinc) or a placebo for six months. All of the anorexic subjects also received "standard care" for the eating disorder, consisting of psychotherapy, behavioral modification, and nutritional rehabilitation. The researchers assessed the patients' mood, appetite, and ability to taste food, and they took blood and urine samples several times over the course of the study to determine zinc levels.

At the beginning of the study, most of the patients with anorexia showed delayed sexual development and had no menstrual periods. Half had experienced hair loss, 66 percent had skin abnormalities, and, in general, most had impaired ability to identify different tastes as compared to control subjects. The average zinc intake of the anorexics was 7.7 mg a day, which was below the current recommended daily dose of 9 mg for adolescents.

Thirteen members of the anorexic group completed the study. After six months of zinc supplementation, they were significantly less depressed and less anxious than they had been initially, and they had gained more weight and height than those in the control group. They also had an improved sense of taste, a reversal of skin abnormalities, and they showed evidence of appropriate sexual development.

Study #2: Oral Zinc Supplementation in Anorexia Nervosa

Author: S. Safai-Kutti

Journal: *Acta Psychiatry Scandinavia* 1990: volume 82, Supplement 361, pages 14-17.

In this Swedish study, 20 women with anorexia nervosa, ages 14 to 26, were given daily oral doses of 45-90 mg of zinc sulfate. This was an "open label" trial.

After 24 months of zinc therapy, 17 patients had increased their body weight by more than 15 percent, and one participant increased her weight by 57 percent. Another patient experienced a 24 percent increase in weight after just three months of zinc supplementation. None lost weight or developed bulimia after receiving zinc, and 13 patients began having menstrual periods.

Study #3: Assessment of Zinc Status and Oral Supplementation in Anorexia Nervosa

Author: Neil I. Ward

Journal: *Journal of Nutritional Medicine* 1990; volume 1: pages 171-177.

In this study, samples of blood, urine, and hair from 15 women with anorexia nervosa and 15 controls were analyzed for zinc and other minerals. The eating-disorder patients were all between 13 and 24 years of age and had been ill for an average of three years. Their diet consisted of mostly vegetables, salads, fruits, and a small amount of carbohydrates, resulting in a dietary zinc consumption of less than 2 mg a day.

Members of the two groups (those who had anorexia and those who did not) received either a placebo or zinc supplementation (15 mg of zinc in one of four different forms: sulfate, orotate, gluconate, or citrate). Each participant in the three-month study received one tablet in the morning and one in the evening of their assigned supplement.

At the beginning of the study, those with anorexia had lower levels of zinc in their blood, urine, and hair than those in the control group. These differences were statistically significant, which means they were most likely due to the disease, rather than chance. In both patients with anorexia and in healthy comparison subjects, zinc supplementation led to increases in blood levels of zinc within days (showing zinc absorption) followed by increases in urinary zinc (showing excretion of zinc). Low levels of urinary zinc suggest zinc deficiency as the body can't afford to lose any zinc; conversely, increases in urinary zinc reflect adequate amounts of zinc in the body.

Patients with anorexia reported improvements in appetite and taste sensitivity after only three days of supplementation, and their weight markedly increased over the course of the study. The zinc absorption in the study varied depending on the formulation. Zinc citrate was best absorbed, followed by zinc gluconate, zinc orotate, and zinc sulfate. Due to the small number of patients enrolled in the trial, however, more research is required to determine definitively which form of zinc is best absorbed.

Study #4: Zinc Status Before and After Zinc Supplementation of Eating Disorder Patients

Authors: C.J. McClain, M.A. Stuart, B. Vivian and colleagues

Journal: *Journal of the American College of Nutrition* 1992; volume 11: pages 694–700.

Thirty-three patients with eating disorders (15 with anorexia, 18 with bulimia) and 12 healthy control subjects were involved in a randomized, double-blind, placebo-controlled zinc study. Blood and urinary levels of zinc were determined both before and after zinc supplementation. All participants in the study underwent four weeks of supplementation with either a placebo or zinc (zinc acetate given three times a day in 25 mg doses for a day's total of 75 mg). The four weeks of supplementation occurred concurrently with hospitalization and eating-disorder treatment (refeeding) for all of the patients with eating disorders.

At the beginning of the study, the patients with anorexia nervosa had a reportedly low dietary zinc intake, an average of 6.5 mg daily, well below the then daily recommended 12 mg. They also had significantly lower levels of urinary zinc, suggesting that their bodies were in a zinc-deficient state and attempting to hold on to as much zinc as possible. Those who received zinc supplements over the course of four weeks showed significant improvements in both blood and urinary zinc levels compared with those who didn't receive the supplements. At the end of the study, those receiving zinc were no longer zinc-deficient and showed signs of improvement in their eating disorders. The patients with anorexia who received the placebo treatment had less weight gain.

Surprisingly, patients with anorexia who received the placebo rather than zinc supplementation showed decreased urinary levels of zinc over the course of the study. The researchers found that even with the recommended amount of zinc in their diet as part of refeeding, the anorexic patients left the hospital with lower zinc status than when they entered the treatment program!

This reveals the heightened demand for zinc—higher even than the RDA—in patients with anorexia. Once these patients begin refeeding, they need increased amounts of zinc. Aggressive refeeding without supplementing with zinc may further aggravate zinc deficiency, impairing the recovery process and increasing the risk of relapse.

Study #5: Zinc Deficiency and Childhood-Onset Anorexia Nervosa

Authors: Bryan Lask, Abe Fosson, Ursula Rolfe and Shanthi Thomas

Journal: *Journal of Clinical Psychiatry* 1993; volume 54: pages 63–66.

This 12-week double-blind, placebo-controlled study involved 26 children with anorexia nervosa (ages 9 to 14 years old) who were admitted to a specialized eating-disorders program at the Hospital for Sick Children in London, England. The patients were divided into two groups: One received standard treatment (psychotherapy, family therapy, and refeeding), while the other received standard treatment plus zinc supplementation. The latter group was subdivided into two subgroups: the first received a placebo for six weeks, while the second received 50 mg of oral zinc sulfate supplements every day. The groups were then switched to the other treatment for the remaining six weeks.

Zinc deficiency was common among the patients in the study and was closely linked to the degree of malnutrition. During the 12 weeks spent in the hospital, the blood zinc levels in all of the children rose as they began to eat and gain weight. Thus, the researchers concluded that low zinc levels are the result of self-starvation and are rapidly reversible without zinc supplementation.

However, it's important to note that the researchers in this study measured blood plasma levels rather than urinary levels of zinc. Plasma levels of zinc are unreliable for diagnosing deficiencies. Plasma zinc levels often remain normal in chronic, mild zinc deficiency. Blood zinc levels can fluctuate throughout the day, and there are many factors that can alter zinc levels in the blood, including the amount of protein present in the blood, acute infections, stress, the time of day blood is taken (how long after a meal), pregnancy, liver disease, malignancies, and pernicious anemia (a type of anemia caused by vitamin B12 deficiency).

What's more, the study involved very ill children, most of whom could not complete the study. Of the seven anorexic patients who received zinc supplementation, four dropped out due to illness. The study results were based on only three patients.

Study #6: Controlled Trial of Zinc Supplementation in Anorexia Nervosa

Author: Carl Birmingham, Elliot M. Goldner and Rita Bakan

Journal: *International Journal of Eating Disorders* 1994: volume 15; pages 251–255.

This randomized, double-blind, placebo-controlled study, conducted in Canada, involved 35 young women between 15 and 30 years old who were hospitalized with anorexia nervosa. Each day, 16 of them were given 100 mg of zinc gluconate, while 19 were given a placebo until they achieved a 10 percent increase in their body mass index (BMI) on two consecutive weigh-ins. All of the patients also received "routine treatment" for anorexia consisting of counseling, meal supervision and refeeding.

Patients who received zinc supplementation had double the rate of weight gain as compared to those who did not receive zinc. The zinc-supplemented patients gained enough weight to reach the 10 percent increase in their BMI in 25 days, versus 32 days for those who did not receive zinc.

What Do These Studies Tell Us?

While more research will help clarify the relationship between zinc deficiency and anorexia, five of the six studies summarized above show that zinc supplementation improved treatment outcomes for patients with anorexia nervosa. Furthermore, none of the study participants reported major side effects or symptoms due to any form of zinc. This suggests that not only are zinc supplements effective, they are also safe and well tolerated.

Based on this evidence, the federal health agencies of Canada, Australia, and New Zealand now recommend zinc supplementation for the treatment of anorexia nervosa. Unfortunately, relevant health organizations in the United States—including the American Psychiatric Association and the American Dietetic Association—have not followed suit, and their lack of endorsement has prevented the widespread practice of zinc supplementation in anorexia treatment.

Only one of the studies described, conducted by Lask and colleagues, found no benefit from zinc supplementation. However, as mentioned, (unreliable) zinc blood levels were measured, the study was conducted in very ill children, and only three patients completed the study. Three patients do not justify extrapolating conclusions to a larger population. Yet this is the study that many physicians invoke when claiming zinc is not an effective treatment for anorexia nervosa. I am not sure why they don't consider the other available research. The preponderance of data suggests a relationship between zinc and anorexia nervosa.

Here is what we can learn from these research studies about zinc deficiency and anorexia nervosa:

- There appears to be a relationship between zinc and anorexia.
- Zinc seems to either cause or sustain the illness of anorexia.
- Zinc is a safe supplement with minimal side effects.
- Additional research is desperately needed.

Summary of Research Trials of Zinc Supplementation for Anorexia Nervosa

Lead Author and Date of Publication
Katz 1987

Daily Dosage
220 mg of zinc sulfate

Number of Patients
14 with anorexia, 20 healthy-weight controls; ages 14–19 years-old

Type of Study
6-month, double-blind, placebo-controlled, randomized trial

Compared with placebo, zinc supplementation led to:
• Significantly less depression and anxiety
• Greater weight gain
• Improved taste function
• More rapid sexual development
• Resolution of skin problems

Lead Author and Date of Publication
Safai-Kutti 1990

Daily Dosage
45-90 mg of zinc sulfate

Number of Patients
20 patients; ages 14–26 years old

Type of Study
Open-label trial

Compared with placebo, zinc supplementation led to:
- 17 patients increased their weight by more than 15 percent
- 1 patient increased weight by 57 percent and another by 24 percent
- None lost weight
- Menstruation returned in 13 patients

Lead Author and Date of Publication
Ward 1990

Daily Dosage
15 mg of zinc sulfate, zinc orotate, zinc gluconate, zinc citrate, or placebo

Number of Patients
15 patients and 15 healthy control subjects
Placebo-controlled comparative study

Compared with placebo, zinc supplementation led to:
- Increased zinc levels in the blood and urine
- Increased weight over the course of the study
- Rapid improvements in taste sensitivity
- Zinc absorption varied depending on the supplement given

Lead Author and Date of Publication
McClain 1992

Daily Dosage
75 mg of zinc acetate

Number of Patients
15 with anorexia nervosa, 18 with bulimia nervosa
and 12 control subjects 14–36 years old

Type of Study
Randomized, placebo-controlled, double-blind study

Compared with placebo, zinc supplementation led to:
- Increased urine and blood zinc levels in all patients receiving zinc
  supplements

Lead Author and Date of Publication
Lask 1993

Daily Dosage
50 mg of zinc sulfate

Number of Patients
26 hospitalized children 9–14 years old
12-week, double-blind, placebo-controlled crossover study

Compared with placebo, zinc supplementation led to:
- Zinc deficiency was common
- Zinc levels in the blood rose whether patients received zinc supplements or not
- No significant difference was seen in weight gain between the zinc supplement and placebo groups
- BUT only three of seven subjects receiving zinc completed the study and were included in the data analysis

---

Lead Author and Date of Publication
Birmingham 1994

Daily Dosage
100 mg zinc gluconate

Number of Patients
35 with anorexia ages 15–30 years-old

Type of Study
Double-blind, placebo-controlled, randomized trial

Compared with placebo, zinc supplementation led to:
- Patients receiving zinc had double the daily rate of weight gain as those who received a placebo

Chapter Thirteen

The Functions of Zinc

The previous chapter established that there is a connection between anorexia and zinc—a connection that was discovered decades ago but continues to be ignored by health professionals treating anorexia. This chapter moves beyond a discussion of zinc's general involvement in the eating disorder to an examination of the specific role it plays in symptoms commonly associated with anorexia: osteoporosis, appetite changes, digestive problems, depression, attention deficit hyperactivity disorder (ADHD), and insomnia.

Although a zinc deficiency has wide-ranging symptoms, there is no obvious deficiency disease stemming from low zinc levels, making it difficult for doctors and therapists to easily recognize a zinc deficiency. This contrasts with other vitamins and minerals. For example, people who lack sufficient vitamin C will develop scurvy, with its characteristic anemia, bleeding gums, and loose teeth. A severe lack of the B vitamin niacin causes pellagra, which can be identified by the appearance of the 4Ds: dermatitis, diarrhea, dementia, and possibly death. A lack of zinc, though, can cause diverse problems, including loss of appetite, weakened resistance to infections, slow wound healing, slowed growth, delayed sexual maturation, weight loss, changes in taste sensation, apathy, and depression. But it doesn't trigger a major disease. And, because the symptoms of zinc deficiency can also be caused by many other physical and/or psychological ailments, zinc deficiency is generally not suspected as a possible cause.

Making matters worse, it is difficult to get an accurate measure of a person's zinc status because the mineral is so widely distributed throughout the body. Its levels in specific parts of the body are carefully regulated. For example, the body will pull zinc from the cells to ensure that blood levels remain adequate, even if it leaves the cells without adequate zinc stores. This means that a patient may have perfectly normal results on a blood test for zinc, but still suffer the effects of zinc deficiency.

It's easy to see why the zinc-anorexia connection is almost completely ignored. Doctors are slow to recognize the signs and symptoms of a mild or moderate deficiency, and they lack the tools to detect it even if they do suspect it is present. Yet most individuals with anorexia do have a chronic zinc deficiency. And, as you will read later in Chapter Twenty-Six, a zinc deficiency contributes to the high rates of treatment failure and increased risk for relapse seen in anorexia.

The Role of Zinc in Physical Growth

Zinc is an essential nutrient for health and growth due to its involvement in many enzymes and physiological processes. A zinc deficiency can disrupt biological functions such as gene expression and protein synthesis, leading to abnormalities in skeletal growth and maturation as well as cognition.

Zinc is necessary for growth and development throughout infancy, childhood, and adolescence. A zinc deficiency can impair growth by disrupting thyroid function. The thyroid gland produces a hormone that regulates calcium levels in the blood, which helps ensure that calcium is not leached from the bone at a higher rate than it's deposited.

Without enough zinc in the diet, infants' growth may be stunted. One country in which this is very evident is Ethiopia, where more than 50 percent of the infants have hindered growth. In a study published in the medical journal *The Lancet*, researchers attempted to augment the development of infants by giving them zinc supplementation for six months. The 184 infants in the study were physically healthy with the exception that 90 of them were abnormally small for their age. The infants were randomly assigned to either consume a placebo or a 10-mg zinc supplement per day, six days a week for six months. Zinc supplementation had a significant impact on growth rate and weight gain in the abnormally small infants; over the course of the study they grew 7 cm and increased their body weight by 80 percent. In contrast, the placebo group only grew an average of 3 cm and had a 20 percent increase in weight.

Zinc deficiency also affects stature during adolescence, a time when most teens gain 15 percent of their adult height and 45 percent of their peak adult bone mass. Adolescent girls with higher levels of zinc grow taller and have higher bone mineral densities than those with lower zinc levels. Having low zinc levels during puberty can cause short stature, delayed sexual maturation, and poor bone mineralization.

Osteoporosis

Zinc is critical not only for normal bone growth and body development, but also for maintaining bone health throughout an individual's life. Calcium's importance in helping build strong bones is well known, but it isn't the only mineral essential for bone health; zinc is also crucial. It is necessary for the proper function of the enzyme alkaline phosphatase, which deposits calcium into the long bones of the limbs. Zinc also enhances the effects of vitamin D, an active promoter of bone formation and mineralization. Consequently, a zinc deficiency during adolescence can lead to slower bone growth, lower bone mass, and weaker bones—just when the bones are supposed to be growing denser and stronger! If an adolescent does not eat foods rich in minerals, sufficient bone mass is not developed at this critical developmental juncture. This can set the stage for osteoporosis, a disease in which the bones become demineralized, weak, brittle, and highly susceptible to fractures.

Although osteoporosis primarily affects the elderly, young women with anorexia are also at risk. Several studies have concluded that low bone mineral density, a precursor to osteoporosis, occurs at alarming rates in patients with anorexia. It has been reported that 50 percent of patients with anorexia who have stopped menstruating for at least 20 months experience low bone mineral density. If menstruation has stopped for at least 24 months, 38 percent have been found to develop the most severe form of bone mineral loss: osteoporosis.

The low bone mineral density commonly found in anorexia has severe consequences. Compared with their healthy counterparts, women with anorexia have a seven times greater than normal fracture risk. The high risk of bone breaks continues later in life. Anorexics have a 57 percent cumulative risk for fractures at the spine, hip and wrist, even 40 years after their initial eating disorder diagnosis.

These women suffering from anorexia are not only consuming too few bone-building nutrients, but their low body weight upsets the body's delicate hormonal balance. The result is too little estrogen, which is necessary for strong bones, and too much adrenal hormone, which causes bone loss.

Zinc and Appetite Regulation

Appetite regulation is a complicated area of research. Scientists continue to scrutinize the hormones, neurotransmitters, and peptides involved in what makes us hungry and feel full. It appears that peptides (small proteins) play a major role in appetite regulation.

Zinc has been found to have an effect on many of the hormones and peptides that are involved in the complex process of appetite regulation, most notably, cholecystokinin-8 (CCK). CCK is a gut hormone that sends signals directly to the brain when we feel full. CCK also induces physical changes: It slows the rate at which food leaves the stomach, stimulates the release of bile from the gall bladder to help break down fats, boosts secretion of digestive enzymes, and increases small intestine motility, which speeds the process along in the gastrointestinal tract. The upshot is that CCK helps you feel full and stop eating, while your digestive system turns its attention to digesting the food.

When partially-digested protein and fats from the stomach arrive in the duodenum, which is the first section of the small intestine, CCK is released by the small intestine and begins sending signals to the pancreas and gall bladder. Some studies have shown that CCK levels are up to three times higher in anorexics than in healthy people; higher CCK levels also last significantly longer. In one study published in *Life Sciences*, CCK levels in healthy people returned to normal within 30 minutes of the hormone's release into the small intestines, while in people with anorexia, they remained elevated for at least 100 minutes. Why is this important? This prolonged secretion of CCK makes people with anorexia actually feel full sooner and for a longer period of time. In other words, they do not have as much of an appetite.

These abnormalities with CCK levels in anorexia may result from low zinc. Zinc is necessary for the proper function of the enzymes that block the effects of CCK and restore hunger. One such "let me be hungry again" enzyme is called aminopeptidase A (APA), which inactivates CCK. When zinc levels are low, APA is also low. This allows CCK levels to rise. Satiety is both enhanced and prolonged, a common feeling experienced by those suffering from anorexia nervosa.

Another example of zinc's effect on appetite involves a "communications molecule" in the brain called neuropeptide Y (NPY), which signals hunger. Studies with animals have shown that one of NPY's functions is to increase the desire to eat, and that blocking NPY decreases appetite. NPY, produced within cells in the brain, is only effective when it is released from the very cells that produce it. Without adequate levels of zinc, the brain may not be able to release enough NPY, and the desire to eat may drop. As shown in a 2002 study published in *The Journal of Nutrition*, a lack of zinc prevents NPY from being released in the brain, effectively preventing NPY from making a person feel hungry.

CCK and NPY are not the only substances that influence appetite. Another peptide shown to be important for increasing appetite is the opioid peptide dynorphin. Dynorphin cannot function properly in the brain without zinc and other nutrients. Dynorphin, a potent stimulator of feeding, only appears to be effective in the presence of zinc. This was seen in a study published in the journal *Physiology & Behavior* in which zinc-deficient animals did not increase their food intake when they were given an injection of dynorphin. In the situation of a zinc deficiency, dynorphin does not have an effect and will not stimulate feeding.

While researchers have examined these peptides that influence appetite, they have failed to appreciate the fact that a zinc deficiency can decrease their effects.

Zinc's Effect on Taste and Digestion

People with anorexia frequently complain that food is tasteless, and they report that they mix strong-tasting condiments like mustard, pepper, or Tabasco sauce with foods that might not blend with these flavors. However, these complaints are generally dismissed by health professionals who think an individual's inability to taste is "all in her head." Few professionals even consider that there might be something actually wrong with the taste mechanism in patients with anorexia.

The reality is that anorexics may have a decreased sense of taste because they are zinc deficient.

Taste is closely related to the function of gustin, a zinc-dependent protein present in saliva that plays an important role in the development of mature taste buds. Without enough zinc, gustin does not function very well. The sense of taste is impaired. Diminished taste may also be due to structural changes of the taste buds. A study conducted in laboratory animals found that when animals had a zinc deficiency, the number and size of their taste buds decreased.

In my clinical experience, I have seen time and time again that when I treat patients with anorexia with zinc supplements, they quickly regain their sense of taste.

Zinc plays a vital role in digestion by making it possible for certain digestive enzymes to break down food into its constituent parts. Common zinc-dependent digestive enzymes include proteases (which break down proteins) such as trypsin, chymotrypsin, and carboxypeptidase; lipases (which break down fats) such as pancreatic lipase and lipoprotein lipase; and enzymes that break down sugars such as maltase, sucrase, and amylase. The nausea and abdominal distension often seen in patients during refeeding may actually be the result of a zinc deficiency! Digestion is impaired without adequate digestive enzymes. When zinc supplements

Zinc-Dependent Digestive Enzymes

Enzyme	Facilitates Digestion of
Trypsin	Protein
Chymotrypsin	Protein
Elastase	Protein
Carboxypeptidase	Protein
Lipase	Fat
Amylase	Polysaccharides
Maltase	Maltose
Sucrase	Sucrose
Lactase	Lactose
Pepsin	Protein

and digestive enzymes are included in the treatment regimen, patients commonly experience less nausea and discomfort during and after meals.

Zinc and Depression

Depression is common in anorexia nervosa; as many as 65 percent of individuals struggling with anorexia will develop depression at some point in their lives. Let's explore how depression may be the result of a zinc deficiency.

Clinical research has shown that those diagnosed with major depression have significantly lower levels of zinc (12 to 16 percent lower) compared to people who are not depressed. Further, the lower the level of zinc, the more severe the depression. Of particular interest, a recent study published in 2009 in the journal *Biological Trace Element Research* found that the young women they identified as being depressed had lower than normal levels of zinc. All of these women had lower blood zinc levels and much less dietary zinc compared to their healthy counterparts.

Other researchers have taken a different approach to studying the role of zinc in mental illness by evaluating possible antidepressant effects of zinc supplementation. A study published in the *European Journal of Clinical Nutrition* found that zinc supplementation had a positive effect on mood in normal young women. For 10 weeks, 31 healthy young women between the ages of 18 and 21 were randomly assigned to take either a multivitamin alone or a multivitamin in conjunction with 7 mg of zinc daily. At the end of the study, the women who consumed zinc with their multivitamin reported feeling less angry and hostile. They also felt less depressed!

Zinc supplementation has also been found to augment the effects of antidepressant medications. The *Journal of Affective Disorders* published a study showing that when people took a zinc supplement in addition to taking their usual antidepressant, their depression improved more quickly. Every day over the course of 12 weeks, 60 depressed patients took their antidepressant medication (in this case, imipramine) as well as either 25 mg of zinc or an inactive placebo pill. The depressed patients who took the combination of zinc supplementation and imipramine felt markedly happier and less depressed, sooner!

The antidepressant and anti-anxiety effects of zinc have also been seen in adolescent girls with anorexia. A study published in the *Journal of Adolescent Health* described these effects. Fourteen patients with anorexia took zinc supplements for six months while receiving standard care for their eating disorder. By the end of the study, their taste sensation had improved and their skin abnormalities had cleared up. They also reported feeling significantly less depressed and anxious as compared to how they had felt at the start of the study.

So how does zinc affect mood? It is possible that zinc's mood-elevating properties are linked to its ability to help maintain important neurotransmitters in the brain. But another important theory that has been proposed involves a protein found in the brain called brain-derived neurotrophic factor (BDNF). BDNF, which is found in areas of the brain associated with learning and memory, stimulates the growth and development of neurons. As mentioned in Chapter Two, BDNF levels are significantly decreased in patients with anorexia nervosa. Studies have also linked low levels of BDNF to depression, suggesting that adequate levels of the brain protein are necessary to prevent depressed moods.

We don't fully understand the links between BDNF, mood, and antidepressant medications, but it appears that certain antidepressants work in part by protecting BDNF in the brain and preventing its levels from falling too low. The low BDNF levels in anorexia and depression may be related to zinc deficiency. Some theorize that zinc functions the same way as antidepressants, helping to ward off or reverse depression by ensuring that BDNF remains at the proper level.

Zinc and ADHD

Zinc deficiency also appears to be implicated in ADHD. Several studies have found that children and adolescents with ADHD have lower levels of zinc in their blood, hair, urine, and nails than other children. In addition, two trials have shown that zinc supplementation significantly reduced symptoms of hyperactivity and impulsivity in children and adolescents.

Researchers have also speculated that zinc supplementation may enhance the benefits of stimulant medications commonly used to treat ADHD. A study published in the journal *BMC Psychiatry* examined the effect of adding zinc supplementation to methylphenidate (the stimulant medication Ritalin) treatment. Forty-four children who were diagnosed as having ADHD all received methylphenidate as well as either a placebo or zinc sulfate (55 mg per day). After six weeks of treatment, the childrens' behavior was reassessed by their teachers and parents. The children who received zinc in combination with Ritalin had fewer ADHD symptoms as compared to the children who only took Ritalin alone.

Insomnia: Is It Zinc Related?

Many patients with anorexia have trouble sleeping, which has most often been attributed to their having low levels of melatonin. Melatonin is a hormone that the brain manufactures in response to darkness to help people to fall asleep. Guess what? Zinc is required for the synthesis of melatonin! In studies, it has been shown that animals who are deprived of zinc subsequently demonstrate low levels of melatonin. Further, melatonin production has been found to increase when zinc supplementation is given.

Chapter Fourteen

Zinc Deficiency and How to Avoid It

The previous two chapters established that low levels of zinc are frequently seen in individuals with anorexia and are associated with many of its common symptoms. Also discussed was the fact that people can become zinc-deficient by eating a diet devoid of meat products. But that can't be all there is to developing a zinc deficiency, can it? No, it's only the tip of the iceberg.

A number of cumulative factors or conditions can increase an individual's susceptibility to becoming zinc-deficient. But it is a zinc deficiency in a genetically vulnerable person at puberty that puts a person most at risk for developing anorexia. Imagine a precariously built tower of blocks; the blocks themselves are the factors that can cause a zinc deficiency. When the final block—puberty—is placed on top, it all comes crashing down. Precisely at puberty is when eating disorder genes are triggered to precipitate anorexia.

Let's first discuss the conditions that can cause a depletion of zinc:

- Puberty
- Stress
- Vegetarianism and dietary factors
- Environmental toxins
- Estrogen/birth control pills
- Increased exercise
- Anorexia

Puberty

Puberty involves a period of rapid growth and an increase in sex hormones. It occurs at a time when an individual is transitioning physically, socially, and psychologically from being a child to becoming an adult. In girls, estrogen hormones are responsible for many of the body's changes, and will affect the brain, bones, muscle, skin, breasts, and reproductive organs. Consequently, dramatic physical and emotional changes occur. During puberty, adolescents gain 20 percent of their adult height, 45 to 50 percent of their peak bone mass, and 50 percent of their adult weight and skeletal mass. Hormones also cause neurodevelopmental changes in the brain. Pruning, or the loss of neurons, takes place, as does myelination, which occurs when a protective sheath is formed around nerve cells, ensuring their growth and ability to mature.

Many of these processes cannot occur normally without the presence of zinc. Zinc is required not only for myelination of nerve cells, but also for bone and skeletal growth. As the body uses increasing amounts of zinc to facilitate this growth, zinc stores begin to drop. The problem is only compounded further by co-occurring emotional demands. Stress, as will be discussed next, additionally increases zinc needs in the body. With all of these heightened demands, the zinc supply in the body continues to be depleted.

The official RDA for zinc is 8 mg per day for children, and 9 mg per day for adolescents, but experts believe this is too low given the increased physiological demand. Yet, even using this value, only about 20 percent of adolescent girls meet the daily requirement for zinc. That means that unless an individual consciously increases her zinc intake through foods or via supplements, she will likely lose zinc during puberty, elevating her risk for anorexia.

Early puberty deserves a quick mention. In this country, girls are entering puberty younger than ever. Hormonal changes, which can be present before any physical changes have emerged, can begin as early as age 8! Because of this, it is not unusual for me to see girls as young as 9 and 10 who are beginning to manifest signs of an eating disorder. In fact, a study in the journal *Hormones and Behavior* found that both male and female college students who reported going through puberty earlier than their peers had more eating disorder behaviors, including binge eating and concerns about body, shape, and weight.

Stress

A second risk factor is stress. Stress can take many forms. The body is under stress physically during the accelerated growth of bones and muscles during puberty. Individuals can become stressed emotionally, for example, when starting a new school or experiencing a family trauma. During all types of stress—whether involving the bones or the brain—the body uses zinc. Without replenished stores, however, the body's zinc stores drop. This subsequent zinc deficiency, unfortunately, can then lower the body's ability to adapt to further stressful situations—the stress continues—and the zinc deficiency continues.

One study, involving zinc-deficient rats that were stressed by being put in a confined space, showed that having a zinc deficiency causes a decrease in proteins in the brain that are normally protective against stress. Without as many of these beneficial proteins, the body cannot adapt as well to a stressful situation. A vicious cycle results: Zinc deficiency increases vulnerability to stress, and stress, in turn, can lead to zinc deficiency.

One reason that adolescent girls may be more susceptible than boys or adults to developing an eating disorder is that zinc levels in young girls are affected by stress more dramatically compared to the other groups. While it is unclear why young girls are more physiologically sensitive to periods of stress, it is important to recognize that they are. This may be why anorexia so often develops at significant times in one's life, such as the onset of puberty, leaving for college, when parents divorce, or after being abused sexually or physically.

Vegetarianism and Dietary Factors

Vegetarianism, too, can heighten susceptibility to zinc deficiency. The story of my patient Mallory illustrates how adopting a vegetarian lifestyle can put a young girl at risk for anorexia.

According to her parents, Mallory was always a sensitive and gentle child. When something upsetting happened—even a small thing—she would become inconsolable. For instance, at age 6, she cried for a full day after her goldfish died.

At age 9 she decided to become a vegetarian. Her mother worked hard to prepare healthy meals for her that she ate; these seemed to provide her with enough energy.

Mallory thought she was just being a good friend when, at age 14, she agreed to go on a diet with her friend Cindi. Although Mallory didn't need to lose weight, Cindi had always been slightly overweight and had had difficulty sticking to a diet. Mallory was convinced she could help Cindi change her eating habits, and the two began what they called the "four-week diet." While Cindi struggled with the diet from the start, Mallory found dieting easy.

With each passing day, refraining from eating became easier for Mallory. Over the course of 12 months, Mallory lost 25 pounds. I was called to treat her after she was admitted to the hospital with a dangerously low heart rate of 40 beats per minute.

Testing revealed that Mallory had abnormally low levels of zinc. I immediately began to treat her with zinc supplements and a comprehensive nutritional program. Slowly, she began to improve. As her normal weight and health returned, her mother said with joy and relief, "I have my daughter back."

Mallory's situation can teach us two important things. First, it's important to understand that it doesn't matter why people restrict their eating and food intake—what matters is that they do. As a result of limited food intake, individuals are more likely to develop a zinc deficiency.

But you might be saying, "My child eats a lot. Do I still need to worry about her developing a zinc deficiency or being zinc-deficient?" Unfortunately, the answer is yes.

As covered in detail in Chapter Eight, the typical dietary choices of adolescents are far from ideal. The Standard American Diet lacks foods rich in zinc. Many foods that are popular with adolescents, such as pasta and bread, inhibit zinc absorption. Meat is the primary source of zinc in the American diet. More than half the zinc in the American diet comes from animal foods; a quarter of it comes from beef alone. Adolescent girls typically do not consume adequate amounts of meat or foods rich in zinc.

The second thing we learn from Mallory is that being a vegetarian places someone in a higher risk category for developing a zinc deficiency with anorexia, even if the person is not obsessed with body image or with becoming thinner.

Not eating meat predisposes an individual to developing a zinc deficiency. Although adult vegetarians are healthier than adults who regularly eat meat, teenage vegetarians are actually less healthy than teenage non-vegetarians—especially when it comes to zinc. They typically consume less zinc than their meat-eating counterparts.

In a study of the dietary habits of vegetarians, it was discovered that 50 percent of vegans, 21 percent of lacto-vegetarians (those who consume milk), and 14 percent of lacto-ovo vegetarians (those who consume milk and eggs) took in less than one-third of the daily requirement for zinc. Complicating matters is that vegetarians commonly consume foods that are high in phytates. Phytates are found in cereal grains, legumes, and nuts; they prevent zinc from being properly absorbed in the body by directly binding to zinc. Several studies comparing zinc absorption in people on high-phytate diets to zinc absorption in those on low-phytate diets have found that people on high-phytate diets absorb significantly less zinc from their GI tract.

The connection between vegetarianism, low zinc levels, and anorexia has been explored in scientific research. In studies of vegetarians and eating-disorder patients, it was found that vegetarians with anorexia had a significantly lower intake of zinc than non-vegetarian anorexics. In 2002, researcher Pia Tannhauser, formerly of the Clinic for Research and Treatment of Eating Disorders at Rambam Medical Center in Israel, noticed that among a group of 45 young women and schoolgirls with anorexia, 96 percent avoided beef, and 75 percent avoided both beef and poultry. More than half of them had not eaten meat for a year before the onset of anorexia. Many had begun abstaining from meat at around the age of 11, and for as long as 6 years before being diagnosed. All of these girls had a zinc deficiency, and because they had avoided meat from such an early age, their zinc deficiencies likely developed well before the onset of puberty.

Tragically, a zinc deficiency can make teenagers start avoiding meat—the very food that could help them rebuild the zinc stores in their bodies. As mentioned in Chapter Thirteen, having a zinc deficiency can cause an individual to have an altered sense of smell and taste. Often, this results in a physical aversion to the smell and taste of meat. Feeling nauseated when smelling or tasting meat can lead to avoiding it, which then serves to worsen a zinc deficiency.

Tannhauser asserts that having a zinc deficiency in childhood also causes more extensive complications; it can permanently influence the development of a young girl's personality, and predispose her to eating-disordered thinking about her body and food.

Environmental Toxins

Environmental toxins also heighten vulnerability to zinc deficiency. BPA is a synthetic chemical found primarily in hard plastics, the linings of cans, and in many household containers and bottles. A growing number of health concerns have been raised over the past few years about the safety of these containers. In the body, BPA can bind to estrogen-related receptors, having an effect similar to the hormone estrogen.

Initially, it was thought that BPA would leach from containers and bottles into foods and beverages only when heated. Now, however, scientists think that everyday use (as in those plastic water bottles we all carry) can lead to harmful effects. There appears to be reason for concern. BPA was found in the urine of 93 percent of a large population sampled, and it has been thought to contribute to reproductive cancers, fertility problems, and endocrine-related disorders. Some states have banned the use of BPA in manufacturing reusable food containers, and infant formula and baby food cans and jars. Stores such as CVS and Walmart have agreed to stop selling products that contain BPA. In addition, consumers have been cautioned not to use containers or bottles labeled with the Society of the Plastics Industry recycling code numbers 3, 6, or 7, as they may contain traces of BPA.

How does this toxic chemical relate to anorexia? BPA can affect zinc availability and levels in the body. It binds to zinc and prevents its absorption, and also disrupts zinc-dependent metabolic pathways. High BPA concentrations in the body can result in lower zinc levels.

BPA is one of the most prevalent environmental toxins affecting zinc, but other chemicals can also deplete the body of zinc. These include nonylphenol (found in cleaning products) and benzophenones (found in sunblock, perfume, soap, and printer toner).

Estrogen and Birth Control Pills

Estrogen, too, has been implicated in zinc deficiency. Having higher than normal levels of circulating estrogen hormones has been shown to be associated with more eating disorder symptoms, such as body dissatisfaction and binge eating. Why is this important? Well, the most popular contraceptive in the United States is birth control (or oral contraceptive) pills. Approximately two million teenagers ages 15 to 19 take these estrogen-containing pills to prevent pregnancy, regulate their menstrual cycle, relieve menstrual disorders, or treat acne.

Unfortunately, these pills can contribute to a zinc deficiency. Studies have shown that women on birth control pills are more likely to have lower levels of circulating zinc in their blood than women who do not take these pills. Estrogen contributes to a zinc deficiency by decreasing zinc absorption, increasing zinc excretion, and interfering in the use of zinc by different parts of the body. Excess estrogen also causes an increase in copper levels, which may worsen depression, a symptom of zinc deficiency.

Exercise

In addition, intense exercise can make people more susceptible to becoming zinc deficient. During strenuous exercise, zinc is released from body tissues and cells into the blood. Zinc blood tests performed immediately after a person exercises may demonstrate normal, or even elevated, levels of zinc. However, the body then loses zinc as it is excreted from the body through sweat or, after a few hours, in urine. Zinc stores subsequently become low, needing to be replenished. Yet, instead of being encouraged to eat meat, athletes are often urged to eat carbohydrates. High in phytates and low in zinc, high-fiber carbohydrates only contribute to the problem.

Girls with anorexia are known for the excessive exercise regimens they rigidly adhere to in order to lose or maintain a low weight. They may play multiple sports, run long distances, or engage in gymnastics or dance. But even girls without an eating disorder can become zinc deficient over time if their diet doesn't compensate for the zinc they lose after frequent and strenuous workouts.

Anorexia as a *Cause* of Zinc Deficiency

While it's true that a zinc deficiency may cause anorexia to develop, the eating disorder itself can further contribute to low levels of the mineral in the body. In an interesting study, Irish researchers compared zinc absorption in two groups: women with anorexia and healthy volunteers. The researchers gave all of the women a meal consisting of ham, bread and butter, tea and orange juice, plus a 50-mg zinc supplement.

Blood samples were taken before the meal as well as at several intervals afterward. As expected, pre-meal zinc levels were slightly lower in the patients with anorexia compared to the healthy volunteers. Blood levels taken after the meals, however, revealed a disturbance in zinc absorption. For four hours after the meal, zinc levels continued to be measurably lower in the women with anorexia. In other words, despite being given a meal with meat and a zinc supplement, the women with anorexia were unable to adequately absorb the zinc.

Genetics Are Triggered at Puberty

If an adolescent who has a genetic predisposition to developing an eating disorder—the perfectionistic, obsessive temperament described in Chapter Two—eats a healthy diet full of nutrient-laden foods, is not under undue stress, and does not develop a zinc deficiency, she has a better chance of escaping the clutches of anorexia when she hits puberty. On the other hand, suppose this same adolescent has a vegetarian or poor diet, takes birth control pills, exercises frequently, has just suffered an emotional trauma, and develops a zinc deficiency. When she reaches puberty and her eating disorder genes become "activated," her risk of developing anorexia is likely much greater.

Having some or all of the zinc-depleting conditions enumerated earlier inherently puts an individual at risk for developing anorexia. But during puberty—which further depletes zinc stores because of the body's increased zinc requirements—she is more vulnerable to developing the initial symptoms of anorexia following food restriction.

This understanding that eating disorder genes are activated during puberty stems from studies involving twin pairs. Looking at eating-disorder behaviors in identical twins, who share the same genes, and fraternal twins, who only share some of the same DNA, can help determine how strong the genetic component is. Behaviors such as weight preoccupation and body dissatisfaction were noted at ages 11, 14, and 18 in 386 pairs of twins. The researchers found that in children who demonstrated eating disorders before puberty at age 11, there was a negligible genetic component. In contrast, assessing those same individuals with eating disorders at ages 14 and 18, they found the role of genetic factors to be significantly greater (almost 50 percent). This time, from pre-puberty to post-puberty, is when genetic factors for developing anorexia emerge.

How Much Zinc Is Enough?

Because a low zinc status is linked to anorexia in so many ways, and because so many factors can contribute to a zinc deficiency, it is critical for individuals with anorexia or at risk for developing anorexia to maintain an adequate zinc status. Zinc can be ingested either through foods in the diet or through supplements.

The Food and Nutrition Board of the Institute of Medicine has established the most recent set of dietary guidelines, which are known as the Dietary Reference Intakes (DRI). The DRI is composed of a number of measurements. One of them, the RDA, provides nutritional recommendations for daily intake. However, the RDA is based on a few small studies that estimated how much zinc an average person absorbs when consuming a healthy diet, and how much is needed to offset what's lost during normal metabolic processes. Thus, the RDA for zinc for girls aged 9 to 13 is currently 8 mg; for those aged 14 to 18, it increases to 9 mg.

I believe these recommendations are conservative, and particularly inadequate for those with anorexia nervosa, who are not only zinc-deficient due to low dietary intake, but often absorb zinc poorly. For adults, supplementation with zinc up to 30 mg per day and for adolescents 15 mg per day is safe and easily tolerated. I strongly recommend working with a health professional skilled in nutrition to determine individual needs. Talk to your pediatrician before supplementing any children under the age of 12.

Measuring Zinc Levels

Before you and your healthcare professional can figure out whether or not zinc supplementation is necessary, you will need to first determine the individual's zinc status. Zinc can be found in a person's blood, urine, saliva, hair, and nails; clinical studies have used all of these for testing zinc status. Unfortunately, there is no reliable test that measures zinc that is circulating or stored in the body, and certainly nothing that can detect mild to moderate zinc deficiencies. Only when a zinc deficiency becomes severe is it easy to identify through laboratory testing.

Blood tests are the most common way to measure zinc levels; however, the results are not the most accurate. Results can be in the normal range, even in people later found to be deficient. Blood tests aren't good at detecting small changes in zinc status that can result from infection, chronic inflammation, or because the individual has just exercised or eaten. Urinary tests are more reliable indicators of zinc deficiency. A low level of zinc in the urine is a sign that the body is attempting to hold onto zinc and not excrete it, because it doesn't have enough.

The best method for assessing zinc status is the ZTT. Developed in the 1980s by Dr. Derek Bryce-Smith, it involves giving an individual a taste of zinc sulfate solution (2 teaspoons or roughly 10 mL of liquid zinc) and observing the response. Approximately 2 teaspoons of the solution is swirled in the mouth for a total of 10 seconds before it is swallowed or discarded. Those who are zinc deficient will detect no taste (Category 1) or very little taste (Category 2), while those with sufficient amounts of zinc will experience a bitter or metallic taste. A mildly bitter taste is considered a Category 3 response, and a strongly bitter taste is considered a Category 4 response.

The ZTT has been validated through use on thousands of patients. In three studies involving more than 700 healthy volunteers, Alexander Schauss, PhD, (one of the first authors to write about zinc and anorexia) found that most people fell into categories 2, 3, or 4. Only 1 to 2.5 percent were category 1 responders. In contrast, in a separate study of nine people with anorexia, 100 percent were classified as Category 1 responders.

The ZTT can be conducted at home by everyone in the family (which can be a good way to get patients with anorexia to participate). Instructions

The Zinc Taste Test

Instructions: Avoid consumption of any fluids or foods, cigarette smoking, or exposure to cigarette smoke for one hour prior to taking the test. Swirl 1 teaspoon of the zinc solution in the mouth for 10 seconds. Then spit it out or swallow it. Record the taste according to the descriptions in the chart below.

Responses

- Category 1: Has no taste or tastes like water.
- Category 2: Has no taste at first, but after a few seconds has a dry, mineral, bicarbonate, "furry," or sweet taste.
- Category 3: Has a definite but not strongly unpleasant taste at first, which tends to intensify over time.
- Category 4: Has an immediate unpleasant strong or metallic taste. The taste may linger for 1/2 hour or more.

Interpreting the Results

- A Category 1 or 2 response indicates a zinc deficiency that will likely benefit from zinc supplementation.
- A Category 3 or 4 response suggests zinc status is adequate. Supplementation of zinc should be integrated as part of a preventative nutritional strategy.

for taking the test are provided in this chapter. It must be noted that not all brands of liquid zinc are reliable for the ZTT. I recommend zinc sulfate monohydrate, a solution of 4 mg per tsp.

After Assessing Zinc Levels

Please follow the guidelines on the ZTT above. ZTT solution (zinc sulfate monohydrate) three times per day for 2 weeks. During the first two weeks, take zinc with digestive enzymes and probiotics. I only recommend using the ZTT zinc until you find the taste too strong. Eventually, as you replenish zinc, you will notice a stronger taste. The variability in how long it takes can range from weeks to months.

If the ZTT results in a 3 or 4, a multivitamin that contains at least 15 mg of zinc should be adequate.

Although it is safe to supplement with zinc at home, I believe that it is best as part of a comprehensive nutritional and medical treatment plan. Anorexia is a complex and serious medical illness; not all people with anorexia are zinc-deficient, and not all will respond to zinc supplementation.

Dietary Sources of Zinc

Dietary sources of nutrients are almost always better absorbed than supplements and naturally are found together with other important synergistic minerals. Zinc is found in many foods. Particularly rich sources of zinc include seafood, fish, poultry, and meat. The following chart lists good sources of zinc and the amount found in a typical serving. As you can see, oysters offer much more zinc than any other food.

Dietary Sources of Zinc	
Food	**Amount of Zinc Per Serving**
Apples (raw with skin)	0.06 mg per 1 apple
Bagel (plain, sesame, poppy, or onion)	1.35 mg per 3½-inch bagel
Bananas (raw)	0.23 mg per 1 cup
Beef, ground (85 percent lean)	5.36 mg per 3 ounces
Breakfast cereal (fortified)	3.8 mg per 3/4 cup
Broccoli (boiled without salt)	0.70 mg per 1 cup
Cheese (cheddar, mozzarella)	0.9 mg per 1 ounce
Chicken breast (roasted, no skin)	0.9 mg per 1/2 breast
Chicken leg (roasted)	2.7 mg per leg
Cucumber (raw with peel)	0.21 mg per 1 cup
Egg (scrambled)	0.61 mg per 1 large egg
Flounder or sole (cooked)	0.5 mg per 3 ounces
Lobster (cooked)	2.5 mg per 3 ounces
Milk	0.9 mg per 1 cup
Oatmeal (instant)	0.8 mg per 1 packet

Food	Amount of Zinc Per Serving
Orange juice	0.12 mg per 1 cup
Oysters	76.7 mg per 6 medium
Peas (boiled)	0.8 mg per 1/2 cup
Salad with chicken and tossed vegetables (without dressing)	0.89 mg per 1-1½ cups
Yogurt (fruit, low fat)	1.6 mg per 1 cup

Source: http://www.nal.usda.gov/fnic/foodcomp/Data/SR20/nutrlist/ sr20w309.pdf. US Department of Agriculture.

Can You Get Too Much Zinc?

Although too little zinc can lead to a dangerous deficiency, too much zinc in the body can also present a problem. Balance is the key to the body's biochemistry. Luckily, zinc toxicity rarely occurs, but it *is* possible to overdose on zinc. Signs of an acute overdose include dizziness, lethargy, nausea, and vomiting. Taking too much zinc (i.e., daily doses higher than 100 mg) for prolonged periods of time can damage the pancreas and liver, as well as interfere with the absorption of other minerals such as copper and iron. Having a ratio of too much zinc relative to copper in the body can lead to lower levels of the "good" cholesterol HDL, anemia, and a weakened immune system.

Zinc toxicity is not common, but is important to understand. In one case, a physician was concerned about his enlarged prostate. Believing that a zinc deficiency might be contributing to this problem, he began to take zinc supplements. He took 150 mg of zinc each day, and gradually his prostate decreased in size. He continued this regimen for more than a year as a preventative measure. Later on, when his prostate once again grew enlarged, he increased his zinc dosage to 300 mg a day. But this time,

Signs and Symptoms of Zinc Toxicity

- Nausea
- Vomiting
- Diarrhea
- Abdominal pain
- Rapid heartbeat
- Lethargy
- Light-headedness
- Difficulty with fine finger movement

his condition worsened. He was diagnosed with a prostate infection and began to take antibiotics along with the zinc. Still, no improvement. Later, the physician was told that his exceedingly high zinc levels may have weakened his immune system and compromised his ability to fight off the infection. Immediately, he discontinued taking the zinc supplements; he slowly began to improve.

Another case of zinc toxicity involved a high school basketball player who began taking zinc to treat a chronic skin condition. According to Dr. Mark B. Salzman, who described this case, the teenager was frustrated with skin breakouts and reasoned that since his usual dose of zinc wasn't working, he should increase it. Unfortunately, the athlete soon began suffering from chronic fatigue, and he had to drag himself to games and practices. Diagnosed with severe anemia and a low white blood cell count, he was advised to stop taking zinc. Four months later, the boy felt more energetic.

The most common causes of zinc toxicity involve denture cream! *The New York Times* recently reported the case of a 64-year-old woman whose neurological problems were traced to her denture cream. Constantly fatigued, she began experiencing problems with movement and balance. Her legs were weak and had poor sensation. Her doctors were baffled, testing her for cancer, a B12 deficiency, and West Nile virus, until they noticed some strange test results. Although her copper levels were virtually nonexistent, her zinc levels were more than twice the normal amount. (Remember, zinc depletes the body's copper stores.) But what explained the high levels of zinc? After much investigation, it was discovered that the woman made up for her ill-fitting dentures by using much more than the recommended amount of denture adhesive. One of the key ingredients in her denture adhesive was zinc. Instead of using one tube a month, she was using about 24! Once she began using a zinc-free brand of denture cream, her fatigue faded away.

As these cases demonstrate, taking a dose of zinc far in excess of the RDA can lead to severe side effects. Be cautious when using vitamin or mineral supplements as they can affect the balance of other micronutrients in the body.

Chapter Fifteen

Casomorphin and Gliadorphin: Little-Known Link to Anorexia

When 24-year-old college student Claudia first came to see me, she had a 12-year history of anorexia and suffered from depression and obsessive compulsive disorder. She had been seeing an outpatient eating-disorders therapist, but she was still unable to structure her meals and gain weight. Then the dean of her college, concerned about her eating disorder, asked her to take a medical leave.

Claudia's eating habits were quite unusual. While she severely restricted her food, since the age of 16 she had eaten up to five pounds of flour mixed in water every day! She could not remember why she first began to eat flour, but it had something to do with the fact that flour never needed refrigeration. Although Claudia liked the taste of flour, the best part about eating flour, according to Claudia, was its effect on her mind: it was soothing and calmed her anxiety.

Flour mixed in water "tranquilized my racing thoughts," Claudia described. She discussed not being able to control the obsessional thoughts around calorie counting and her weight, but her sense of panic was quelled by her flour shake.

Although it may be hard to believe, the flour that Claudia had eaten on a daily basis for almost a decade affected her brain much like a drug. And like a drug, these effects became so addictive that Claudia simply couldn't stop eating it. Although her flour intake is now down to about 1 to 2 pounds a day, she still finds it a better mood stabilizer than any medication prescribed for her.

In Claudia's case, the food affecting her brain was wheat. But eating dairy products—such as milk, yogurt and cheese—can also affect the brain the same way as the potent drugs morphine, oxycodone, or heroin. And while the majority of the population will not be affected by eating foods containing wheat or dairy, there is a subset who are vulnerable. And it's very likely that they don't know about their intolerance or how their intolerance may be contributing to an eating disorder.

This chapter describes what happens in the body when wheat and dairy foods are ingested, how this process can affect psychological functioning, and how specific food intolerances may be responsible for anxiety, fatigue, and obsessive compulsive symptoms seen in some people with anorexia nervosa. Scientific research in this area is scarce, but the handful of studies that exist seem to support what I have noted in my clinical practice; that the intense, intrusive, obsessive thoughts so common in anorexia may be due to incomplete digestion of casein (from dairy products) and/or gluten (from wheat).

Digesting Wheat and Dairy Products:
The Process and the Problem

Wheat and dairy intolerances may have adverse effects on the body and brain because they weren't consumed by humans until about 10,000 years ago, which is relatively recent on the evolutionary timeline. The human body needs time to adapt to completely new kinds of foods, and some people may never tolerate them adequately. For hundreds of thousands of years, humans subsisted exclusively on wild plants, fish, animals, and insects. So it's not too surprising that when wheat and dairy foods first made an appearance in Europe, many who ate them became ill—and some even died. Thus, even though we tend to think of milk, cheese, bread, and pasta as dietary staples, many modern people remain unable to digest these foods properly.

Casein, Gluten and Dipeptidyl Peptidase IV

Casein is one of the main proteins in dairy products, and gluten is the major protein in wheat and other grains like rye and barley. Enzymes in the digestive system, specifically dipeptidyl peptidase (DDP) IV or DPP IV, break down the casein and gluten into peptides, which are shorter proteins made up of amino acid chains. The peptides are then absorbed through the small intestine, enter the bloodstream, and circulate throughout the body, where they perform a variety of duties, including assisting in the production of hormones and brain neurotransmitters.

When DPP IV is in short supply or is ineffective, the body cannot "snip" casein or gluten into small enough peptides. This incomplete protein breakdown results in large peptides. If the large peptide is a byproduct of incomplete casein digestion, it is called casomorphin. If it is a byproduct of gluten, the large peptide is called gliadorphin. As their names imply, these peptides are actually morphine-like analogs that have powerful effects on brain chemistry.

Inadequate Production of DPP IV

Although the reasons for decreased levels of DPP IV aren't completely understood, adequate production seems to be dependent on ingesting sufficient nutrients, including zinc. With severely restricted food intake, as in anorexia, there may be too few nutrients to produce enough DPP IV. In addition, pesticides, yeast in the digestive tract, certain antibiotics, and substances like gelatin and mercury have been found to deactivate DPP IV.

Psychological Effects of Casomorphin and Gliadorphin

Although casomorphin and gliadorphin are large peptides, they are absorbed into the bloodstream and can wreak havoc in the body and brain in two ways. First, the immune system perceives them as foreign and attacks by initiating an inflammatory response in the body. This creates a biochemical cascade of chemicals that can contribute to everything from depression to allergies. Second, these peptides travel through the blood and into the cerebral spinal fluid surrounding the brain, where they affect the brain much like morphine and other opiates. Because of this, casomorphin and gliadorphin are also called opioid peptides.

Opioid peptides are powerful, affecting digestion and muscle activation in the body and mimicking the effects of narcotics in the brain. In general, this class of substances dictates how we experience pain and sedation, although they do not affect everyone in the same way. For instance, morphine might slow one person's heart rate while dangerously increasing another's. Or it may produce euphoria in one individual and anxiety in another.

How can there be such drastic differences in people's response to the same substance? As you learned in Chapter Seven, this comes down to biochemical individuality. The unique genetic and biochemical make-up of each individual affects their responses to different nutrients, their need for nutrients, their reactions to medications, and their reactions to everyday stressors.

Abnormally high levels of the opioid peptides casomorphin and gliadorphin can also affect people in different ways. Some may find themselves exhibiting the symptoms of obsessive-compulsive disorder: thinking the same thoughts over and over again and performing the same action or ritual repeatedly to try to quell anxiety. Others may experience feelings of calmness or euphoria, much like exercise-induced endorphins or alcohol. But when they stop eating these foods, they may feel anxious and depressed. This can draw them into addictive cravings for dairy or wheat.

Let me share two stories to illustrate.

Emma is a 14-year-old adolescent who was referred to me for a medication consultation for incapacitating obsessive-compulsive disorder (OCD) and recent onset of restrictive eating with food phobias. Emma had developed elaborate rituals about what foods she could or could not eat, what bowls could be used for each food, and the exact time of each meal. Over the course of six months of increasingly compulsive behavior, Emma's weight started dropping significantly and she became concerned that she was "too fat." At this point, Emma weighed only 86 pounds.

Emma had already tried two antidepressant medications prior to meeting with me. On Prozac, Emma had experienced suicidal thoughts. With Paxil, she became agitated and unable to sleep. Her parents sought my consultation for a "non-medical" solution to Emma's problems.

Although I could not promise a solution without medication, I did recommend complete nutritional testing, including screening for the urinary peptides casomorphin and gliadorphin.

Emma had elevated levels of casomorphin and normal levels of gliadorphin in her urine. In response to this, I recommended DPP IV enzyme supplements and a reduction in dairy consumption. Although it was initially difficult for Emma to decrease her dairy intake, she was compliant with her enzymes. After a few months, everyone, including Emma, reported clear improvement in her food rituals and attempts with weight restoration. For the first time in a year, Emma had encouraging results.

Emma, however, didn't see that her decreased dairy consumption and supplemental enzymes were connected to her compulsive behavior around food until she had a sleepover at a friend's house. Having unlimited cake, ice cream, and milk without her enzymes made Emma a believer. For the next few days afterward, Emma noticed a dramatic increase in obsessive worries about her food and intrusive thoughts about being too fat.

Kathleen had anorexia throughout adolescence and into college. In college her symptoms only grew worse as she started purging her meals and drinking excessively. With her illness getting out of hand, Kathleen never completed college. Her life since then essentially revolved around mental health treatment. She was hospitalized multiple times for her eating-disorder and substance-abuse problems from the ages of 22 to 30.

At 32, Kathleen stopped abusing alcohol and started working again as a real estate agent. Off the alcohol, Kathleen struggled with intrusive thoughts concerning how she looked, her weight, and body. Each morning she changed her clothes anywhere from 10 to 15 times, worrying that people at work would think she was fat. If she happened to eat more than she thought she should, she experienced an angry, loud self-deprecating "voice" telling her that she was bad.

Kathleen, like Emma, tested positive for casomorphin. Kathleen was able to completely eliminate dairy and was motivated for nutritional therapies to help "prevent her eating disorder from winning again."

Over the course of two months without medication, but on a dairy-free diet, Kathleen described the loud "voice" that she once heard after eating as a "soft whisper."

Kathleen was a bright, charming, energetic young lady who had been caught in the grips of anorexia and substance abuse since the age of 16. A simple nutritional test changed her life.

Is Anorexia Made Worse by Casomorphin and Gliadorphin?

My interest in casomorphin and gliadorphin as possible contributors to a complex array of symptoms of anorexia began when I read a Swedish study published in the journal *Eating and Weight Disorders* that compared urinary peptide levels among three groups: patients with anorexia, patients with bulimia, and healthy control subjects. When the body contains high amounts of proteins they are often excreted in the urine, hence the term urinary peptides. The researchers in the study found that people with anorexia—especially those whose illness involved severe starvation—had significantly higher levels of peptides in their urine than both the control group and the group of patients with bulimia. Patients with eating disorders, in particular anorexia, are known to have abnormalities in many systems regulated by their brain—the endocrine system and the central and peripheral nervous system—that may lead to increased levels of neuroactive peptides. Although the researchers did not identify the urinary peptides, the researchers concluded that the peptides they found may have a role in the brain. They speculated that increased levels of neuropeptides—peptides that can act on the brain such as casomorphin and gliadorphin—might contribute to the characteristics and chronic course of anorexia.

Urinary Peptides and Obsessive-Compulsive Disorder

How can increased levels of urinary peptides contribute to anorexia? The most obvious route would be through the promotion of obsessive thoughts, which I have found over many years may result from high levels

---

of casomorphin or gliadorphin. Intrusive and obsessive thoughts and rituals concerning food and eating are commonly observed in patients with eating disorders; in fact, up to 21 percent of patients with anorexia also suffer from OCD according to a study published in the *International Journal of Eating Disorders*. And in many cases, the symptoms of OCD predate the onset of the eating disorder.

For the past 10 years I have evaluated casomorphin and gliadorphin urinary peptide levels of patients with anorexia who:

- Had severe, obsessive thoughts about their bodies, food, dieting, or exercise that seemed to control their lives and actions.
- Craved and consumed excessive amounts of dairy or wheat products.
- Reported intense feelings of sedation or calm after ingesting dairy or wheat products.

Over the years, I have treated hundreds of patients with anorexia and OCD who have had elevated levels of casomorphin and gliadorphin. When these peptides are eliminated, either through dietary restriction or providing supplemental DPP IV enzymes, improvement in symptoms is clear and often dramatic.

Low Levels of DPP IV in Those with Eating Disorders

Further indications that casomorphin and gliadorphin may play a part in anorexia can be found in a European study published in the journal *Nutrition* that compared the activity of the enzyme DPP IV in anorexics, bulimics, and healthy control subjects. The researchers found that DPP IV, which is necessary for the breakdown of casomorphin and gliadorphin, was significantly lower in patients with anorexia and bulimia than in healthy control subjects. Further, lower levels of DPP IV activity were associated with an increase in disturbed eating behaviors and depression.

Normalizing Casomorphin and Gliadorphin Levels Helps Treat Anorexia

The association between opioid peptides and eating disorders has only recently come to light, and there is no evidence to suggest that elevated casomorphin and gliadorphin levels can actually cause anorexia.

However, I have found that bringing casomorphin and gliadorphin levels back down to normal can be very helpful in treating patients. In some cases, it is the hurdle they need to leap over before they can make significant progress in their recovery.

For example, an 8-year-old patient of mine, Andrea, was just 6 when her obsessive and compulsive symptoms first manifested. Consumed with angry thoughts about a wide range of subjects, she tried to ward off her anxiety by praying constantly and washing her hands compulsively. She continuously craved milk and worried about being fat, although she was underweight for her age. Preoccupied with "not being good enough," she was also worried that other family members and friends would become sick.

After a lab test of her urine revealed that she had an abnormally high level of casomorphin, her diet was modified to eliminate dairy products and she was prescribed a DPP IV enzyme supplement. With this treatment, her symptoms rapidly improved. Her craving for milk decreased, and so did her OCD and anxiety. She no longer constantly worried about being overweight. She was able to benefit from psychotherapy and family interventions. "She is like a different girl," said her mother. "We had almost forgotten what her smile looked like."

This intervention for Andrea and many other younger patients I have treated for OCD and body image distortions provide clear evidence that biomedical testing such as urinary peptides may provide an approach for preventing a more significant eating disorder or the development of anorexia.

Finding a "Lost" Child

Christy was only 5 years old when her obsessive thoughts and compulsions began. By the age of 9, she was obsessed with the idea that she was contaminating the universe, and, because of that, she was unable to throw away any paper. She hoarded paper in her bedroom and was unable to stop herself from cleaning. At times she cleaned the same table for hours. With such unremitting and debilitating symptoms, she was unable to attend school.

At the same time, Christy started developing obsessions about being overweight, even though her weight fell in the normal range.

Many medication trials failed. Celexa increased her agitation, and Prozac triggered more aggressive thoughts of self-harm—to the point where she actually tried to hurt herself.

Christy's distraught parents contacted me, and I recommended complete nutritional testing, including a urinary peptide analysis. Her level of casomorphin was found to be significantly elevated.

I advised her family to gradually reduce her dairy intake and try to avoid all foods with casein. In addition, I prescribed an enzyme supplement with DPP IV to help Christy's body break down any casein that she might inadvertently ingest.

Over the course of a few months, without any medication, Christy's behavior improved. She stopped hoarding trash, and her obsessive thoughts decreased. Her obessional thoughts about being overweight were completely gone. After six months she never spoke about her weight again.

Expressing relief, her parents said, "It feels like we found our lost child."

"I Was A Professional Patient"

Jackie was a 25-year-old woman who had been struggling for almost 10 years with an eating disorder involving restricting food intake and, recently, purging her medication. She also suffered from OCD with obsessive list making, counting calories, arranging clothes and shoes, and worrying that she had done something wrong.

She described her life from age 16 to 20 as a nightmare. "I was a professional patient, going from one treatment provider to another," she said. Over the years, her medicine cabinet accumulated at least 12 different psychiatric medications, none of which worked.

Hospitalized numerous times for the treatment of severe malnutrition, her college studies were constantly interrupted. In the hospital, her obsessive thoughts were so loud and incessant that she would not eat. At those times, she would have to be fed via a nasogastric (NG) feeding tube. Her physicians tried medications addressing her anxiety, depression, and lack of concentration, without much success.

Jackie averaged three hospitalizations per year between the ages of 21 and 25, each ranging from 18 to 28 days. Her symptoms and hospitalizations made it impossible for her to maintain steady employment.

By the time Jackie came to see me, she was desperate. In addition to initiating nutritional support and tapering her medications, I performed an rEEG to get a clearer idea of which medications might be best for her neurochemistry.

After honing her medications using the rEEG results, Jackie's mood improved. She remained out of the hospital for two years and returned to full-time work. Meal times, however, were still problematic; she continued to obsess about food. Her OCD continued to impair her day to day functioning.

What was wrong?

After testing her urine, I had the answer. Jackie had abnormally elevated levels of casomorphin; she was not fully digesting the casein in the food she ate. By removing dairy products from her diet and adding a supplemental DPP IV enzyme, Jackie's obsessive thoughts finally decreased. "The difference is dramatic," according to Jackie.

For the first time in many, many years, Jackie now feels that her eating disorder is under control.

Testing and Treatment for Anorexia

The urinary peptide test that I recommend for all of my patients with anorexia can be ordered by any licensed healthcare professional. Check with your health insurance carrier whether your plan will cover it; some do, but many do not. Even if the laboratory test is not covered, however, I believe this test to absolutely necessary for obtaining crucial information that can directly impact treatment.

It is important to note that if the test results do not demonstrate elevated levels of casomorphin or gliadorphin in the urine, I do not advocate removing any major food groups from a patient's diet. Dairy products, for example, are an excellent source of protein, vitamins, and minerals necessary for healthy development and growth, and should not be discarded without good reason.

On the other hand, if the test results demonstrate abnormally elevated casomorphin and/or gliadorphin levels in the urine, eliminating foods from the diet that contain casein and/or gluten may be warranted, with supervision from a nutritionist or healthcare professional.

Common Foods That May Contain Casein

- Milk
- Yogurt
- Ice cream
- Cheese

- Baked goods
- Granola bars
- Cookies and crackers

For additional information, please see the Resource Section.

Common Foods That May Contain Gluten

- Bread
- Muffins
- Pretzels
- Crackers

- Couscous
- Pasta
- Pizza

For additional information, please see the Resources Section.

If you have ever tried to avoid dairy or wheat products, you'll know that the task can be overwhelming, especially at first. Long, confusing ingredient labels must be carefully scrutinized. Eating out can be challenging. Children and teenagers may reject the taste of gluten-free bread, pasta, and baked goods. If dairy products are avoided, an alternative source of calcium must be incorporated into the diet. Visiting a clinical nutritionist or registered dietitian can be invaluable in helping to solve these issues. National organizations dedicated to food allergies or celiac disease can be good resources (see Resource Section) and may offer practical advice as well as specific product ideas.

Following a dairy-free or wheat-free diet may be difficult and, at times, not recommended. For some patients, I have worked with their nutritionists in decreasing casein intake but not eliminating dairy products completely. I have found that adding additional DPP IV enzyme supplements are helpful for these patients.

Sarah is a good example. She was stabilized on medications guided by her rEEG and had just returned to work part time. She was following her meal plan, and for the first time in years she felt motivated towards recovery. Sarah was both hopeful and optimistic.

However, she continued to weigh herself three times a day, change her clothes multiple times in the morning, and had intrusive thoughts about her weight, thinking she was "too fat." For the first time in many years, Sarah understood that these behaviors were irrational, yet she continued to struggle with obsessional thoughts and compulsive behaviors.

By simply decreasing her dairy consumption and adding DPP IV supplements, her thoughts slowly, over the course of two months, changed. The daily irrational obsessions decreased to the occasional obsessional thought about her weight and appearance. "I feel free," she exclaimed in a recent phone call. "I now realize how abnormal my thoughts were."

If urinary peptides are elevated, I recommend DPP IV enzyme supplements with meals and any snacks that have casein or gluten as part of a comprehensive treatment plan. This helps make diet modifications more tolerable, as patients can still occasionally eat casein- or gluten-containing foods without experiencing a spike in their OCD or anxiety symptoms. I also recommend that patients take probiotics—live microorganisms that improve intestinal microbial balance—that are specifically designed to aid in the digestion of casein and gluten in the GI tract.

Nobody can predict the exact dosage of DPP IV required to adequately digest casein or gluten. Due to biochemical individuality, there is some trial period of determining the correct dose. I currently recommend a DPP IV enzyme with approximately 50,000 HUT (HUT is a standardized unit of protease activity) per serving and have patients take 1 to 4 with each meal.

Anorexia relapses are common and are often due to rigid thinking and obsessional thoughts. By making the proper dietary changes and bringing opioid peptide levels back down to the normal range, intrusive thoughts and compulsive behaviors surrounding food and eating can be reduced and, in some cases, even stopped completely.

Chapter Sixteen

Digestive Health:
The Foundation of Recovery

Recovery from anorexia nervosa is dependent on a healthy digestive system, and chronic digestive trouble is one of the factors that perpetuates restrictive eating behaviors. Bloating, abdominal distention, fullness, constipation, acid reflux, and just plain indigestion are common in anorexia, and if these factors are not addressed effectively, recovery is hindered, progress is slow, and relapse is imminent.

In this chapter, you'll learn ways to improve digestion, eat with fewer unpleasant symptoms, and heal a formerly cranky digestive tract. But first, let's take a look at how the digestive system works.

The Digestive System: A Well-Oiled Machine

You can think of your digestive system as a well-oiled machine made up of a series of long, muscular tubes designed to break down food, absorb its nutrients, and push it on down the line until there is nothing left but waste, which is expelled. The process of digestion takes place in a series of phases, the first involving simply the sight, smell, or thought of food.

Phase 1: Brain Activation

When seeing a plate of food, smelling its aroma, and thinking about that first bite, parts of the brain become activated and send signals to the digestive system. For some people, this can cause agitation, aggression, or anxiety, beginning a cycle of worrying, obsessions, and escalating panic. This translates to a complicated cascade of chemical reactions referred to as the stress response, designed to help the body stand and fight or run from danger. In the process, it "turns off" digestion. It's no wonder the anorexic feels sick at the thought of food!

Phase 2: Chewing and Swallowing

Chewing lubricates the food by combining it with saliva, reducing the size of the food particles, and mixing in the digestive enzymes salivary amylase, which breaks down starch, and lingual lipase, which breaks down fat. Both of these enzymes are dependent on the mineral zinc. Gustin, a polypeptide present in saliva that's responsible for the "mouth-watering" taste and smell of food, is also zinc dependent. Thus, if zinc levels are low—as is often the case in anorexia—digestion is hampered from the start, and there is a decreased ability to smell and taste food, which decreases the ability to make saliva, a key substance in the digestion process.

In fact, gustin, also known as carbonic anhydrase, is the sense organ found on the external edge of all single-celled organisms. This cell edge is exposed directly to the new external environment, and without gustin, the cell cannot sense this environment.

One study, published in the *Proceedings of the National Academy of Sciences* journal, demonstrates the direct relationship between zinc and gustin. Within the saliva, zinc concentrations were found to be directly proportional to the amount of gustin present. Patients with low levels of zinc in their saliva had decreased amounts of gustin. After zinc supplementation, lasting a little over a week, one patient who suffered from a decreased sense of taste showed a 150 percent increase in saliva zinc levels. This was also associated with an increase in gustin. As both the patient's zinc and gustin levels increased, the patient's sense of taste returned to normal.

As described in Chapter Fourteen, the ZTT is the best way to assess for a zinc deficiency. A small amount of a zinc sulfate solution (zinc sulfate monohydrate) is consumed, and your response is measured based on a scale. Those who are zinc-deficient note either no taste (a Category 1 on the scale) or very little taste (Category 2). A bitter or metallic taste indicates sufficient amounts of zinc (Category 3 for mild taste versus a Category 4 for stronger taste).

Phase 3: Digestion in the Stomach

After food is swallowed, it travels down the esophagus and into the stomach, thanks to rhythmic contractions of the ring-like muscles in the esophagus. This rhythmic movement, called peristalsis, propels the food through the entire digestive tract. It also keeps it from being pushed backwards (up the esophagus) by pushing in only one direction, toward the stomach. Once the food arrives in the stomach, the physical distention of the organ triggers the secretion of digestive enzymes and gastric acid. The stomach chemically and mechanically transforms the food into a liquid mixture referred to as chyme, which is made up of partially digested food, water, digestive enzymes and hydrochloric acid.

Hydrochloric acid (HCl) is so powerful and concentrated that a single drop is capable of burning a hole through a piece of wood. Luckily, the stomach lining is well protected from its corrosive effects by a thick layer of mucus that contains the neutralizer sodium bicarbonate. The extremely acidic nature of HCl is absolutely necessary for proper digestion, as it aids in:

- Absorbing minerals
- Absorbing vitamin B12
- Resisting infection
- Communicating satiety to the brain
- Breaking down protein

One of hydrochloric acid's key roles is to convert a substance called pepsinogen into pepsin, an enzyme that breaks protein into smaller particles called polypeptides. Without pepsin, protein simply cannot be digested.

A decrease in production of HCl impairs the absorption of nutrients, interferes with satiety signals, and hinders digestion, causing food sensitivities, flatulence, bloating, and pain or discomfort after eating. In other words, having adequate amounts of hydrochloric acid is good for digestion.

Gastroesophogeal reflux disease (GERD), better known as acid reflux disease, is often blamed on excess HCl. After eating spicy or greasy, fatty foods, many Americans experience heartburn, the painful burning sensation in the esophagus and the major symptom of GERD. Rather than avoid these foods, ads advocate that a simple pill will make the heartburn fade away. Prilosec, Tums, Maalox, and Nexium are household names, thanks to the bombardment of ads aimed at the millions of people who suffer from heartburn or GERD. Medication for GERD alone accounts for more than 60 million prescriptions per year.

The popularity of antacids and other medication aimed at lowering or neutralizing the acid in the stomach overshadows an important fact: HCl is necessary for proper digestion. Decreased production of HCl impairs the absorption of nutrients. That means that antacids, by lowering the amount of HCl in the stomach, can impair the body's ability to absorb vitamins and minerals! Low acid levels can even cause symptoms similar to GERD. Common symptoms of low stomach acid are anemia, a lack of energy, tooth decay, gum disease, food sensitivities, flatulence, bloating, and pain or discomfort after eating. The very medications that are supposed to help eliminate your symptoms can actually prolong them and cause other health problems, i.e., nutritional deficiencies.

Patients with anorexia are routinely prescribed antacids to counter-act indigestion and gas during refeeding. Although they already suffer from chronic malnutrition, their nutritional deficiencies are exacerbated with the use of antacids. The low stomach acid leads to the malabsorption of minerals (such as magnesium and zinc) and vitamins (including vitamin C and the B vitamins). What's more, if there are inadequate amounts of micronutrients such as zinc, as in the case of patients with anorexia, the stomach isn't able to produce enough hydrochloric acid to properly digest food!

Despite the potential harm antacids can cause your body, it's important to taper yourself off antacids gradually rather than stopping all at once. An important first step is to improve your digestion by taking the proper digestive enzymes and avoiding foods that may upset your stomach, such as coffee, aspirin, soft drinks, and alcohol. Once your digestive symptoms are under control, you can talk to your physician about changing your prescription medication for over-the-counter antacids. Over-the-counter antacids, such as Tagamet, are not as strong as their prescription counterparts. To slowly ease your body back to its normal production of acid, gradually decrease the dose of over-the-counter antacid until you no longer require any.

The simple facts are that HCl is necessary for proper digestion of many essential nutrients, and antacids interfere with adequate acid production. Zinc deficiency is another mechanism for interfering with adequate hydrochloric acid synthesis.

Phase 4: Digestion in the Intestines

When digestion in the stomach has been completed, the chyme is slowly pushed into the small intestine. Once it has arrived, the pancreas releases sodium bicarbonate to neutralize the acid, as the intestines don't have a protective mucus layer. The bulk of digestion of proteins, fats, and carbohydrates occurs in the small intestine. Partially digested protein is cleaved into single amino acids. Bile released from the gallbladder breaks fat into smaller droplets, and pancreatic enzymes break these droplets into monoglycerides and fatty acids. Carbohydrates are broken down into smaller molecules called disaccharides, and even smaller fragments called monosaccharides. These simplified forms of protein, fat, and carbohydrate are absorbed through the walls of finger-like projections in the lining of the small intestine and transported into the bloodstream. The absorption of most vitamins and minerals also occurs in the small intestine.

As you can see, the health of the small intestine is a critical determining factor in nutrient absorption. Restoring the health of the intestinal tract is a crucial part of recovery from anorexia, for even if an anorexic eats sufficient amounts of nutrients, if the body can't absorb them, the disease process will continue.

Restoring Digestive Health

I take a two-pronged approach to restoring the intestinal health of my patients: digestive enzymes and probiotics.

Digestive Enzymes

Digestive enzymes are assembled from amino acids as well as essential minerals like zinc, copper, and magnesium, all of which are obtained from food. These enzymes need to be synthesized from raw materials. There are three major types:

- **Food enzymes:** These are found in raw foods, plant or animal.
- **Digestive enzymes:** Secreted by the body, these fall into one of three categories:
  - Amylases – to break down carbohydrates
  - Proteases – to break down proteins
  - Lipases – to break down fats
- **Metabolic enzymes:** These support all the body organs and systems by performing various chemical reactions within the body cells. Without them, life would cease to exist.

Production of all digestive enzymes is dependent upon the presence of sufficient amounts of nutrients such as B vitamins, vitamin C, zinc, sodium, and protein. A lack of these nutrients leads to decreased production of digestive enzymes, and those that are produced may function poorly. This leads to a vicious circle: Poor nutrition causes inefficient digestion, which leads to poor absorption of the nutrients that are ingested, which leads to even more inefficient digestion.

Clearly it's necessary to stop this downward spiral, and a good digestive enzyme supplement can help. The benefits include:

- Restoration of optimal gastrointestinal function and digestive comfort.
- Minimization of carbohydrate intolerance.

- Help in protecting the gut from inflammation.
- Help in the support of a healthy gut flora balance.

Digestive Enzyme Supplements

Digestive enzyme supplements are made from either animal or plant sources. Enzymes extracted from animal sources include oxbile, trypsin, chymotrypsin, rennin, pepsin, and pancreatin. Many of the enzymes found in digestive enzyme supplements, however, are derived from plant sources, in particular the *Aspergillus* fungi family. Common digestive enzymes from plant sources are protease, lipase, amylase, and cellulase. Digestive enzymes from plants can also include bromelain from pineapple and papain from papaya.

The supplemental enzyme combination used should be a broad-spectrum type that helps digest carbohydrates, proteins, and fats. It should include carbohydrate- and sugar-specific enzymes (such as amylase), vegetable- and fiber-specific enzymes (such as cellulase), protein- and peptide-specific enzymes (such as protease), and fat-specific enzymes (such as lipase).

The purified, pharmaceutical-grade ingredients in the supplement should also be reported in units specified by the Food Chemical Codex (FCC) or by the U.S. Pharmacopoeia (USP). The presence of FCC and USP units indicate that the enzymes in the supplement have been rigorously tested by the USP, creating an easy standard for assessing and comparing the efficacy and potency of enzymes. FCC and USP units are widely recognized and highly regarded.

As with many supplements, the amount of digestive enzymes that each individual should take varies due to differences in diet, lifestyle, and biochemical individuality. Therefore, the best approach is to follow the directions accompanying the digestive enzymes and work with a health professional knowledgeable in nutritional medicine. The dose can be adjusted upward or downward to achieve the best response. It's also important to consider the size of your meal when taking digestive enzymes. Digestive enzymes, taken either at the beginning of a meal or during the meal, should reflect the amount of food you will be eating; more enzymes should be taken with a larger meal and correspondingly less should be taken with a smaller meal.

Each individual responds differently to the same set of digestive enzymes. Some may notice improvements in digestion and GI function immediately after taking digestive enzymes and others may not see improvements for several days or even a few weeks. Therefore, it's important to continue the digestive enzymes for a few weeks before adjusting the dose.

Probiotics

Healthy digestion is dependent upon the more than 400 different strains of bacteria that dwell within the intestines. The vast majority of these organisms are friendly bacteria that protect the digestive system from illness and infection, break down food, and synthesize nutrients. However, there are also "unfriendly" bacteria (pathogens) that cause disease, allergies, and inflammation. As long as the friendly bacteria outnumber the unfriendly kind, the digestive system should remain relatively healthy. But when unfriendly bacteria are allowed to proliferate, they produce chemicals that inflame and damage the gut. Depression, fatigue, excessive gas, bloating, constipation, diarrhea, and poor absorption of nutrients can ensue. If the lining of the intestinal tract continues to deteriorate, there may be allergic reactions and disruption of the immune response.

A variety of factors can diminish friendly bacteria, including:

- Alcohol ingestion, excessive
- Antibiotics
- Birth control pills
- Deficiencies in zinc, B vitamins, and essential fatty acids
- Diet high in refined sugar
- Infections
- Laxative abuse
- Poor nutrition in general
- Radiation
- Steroid use
- Stress

When the unfriendly bacteria start to take over, it becomes necessary to repopulate the gut with the friendly kind, which can be done with probiotics.

Probiotics are foods or supplements that contain plentiful amounts of live friendly bacteria. Examples of foods containing probiotics include yogurt, kefir, and other fermented milk products, and fermented foods such as sauerkraut, kimchi, tempeh, miso, and kombucha.

Although there is limited research using probiotics in the treatment of anorexia, I believe that a probiotic supplement is a key component for sustained recovery. Patients find immediate relief in chronic GI problems and improvement in symptoms of bloating, abdomen distention, and constipation.

The benefits of probiotics have been known for centuries. Cultures all over the world have used specific foods as a probiotic to enhance digestion. Yogurt, kefir, and other fermented milk products contain *Lactobacillus* bacteria, as do other fermented foods such as sauerkraut, kimchi, tempeh, miso, and kombucha which have been used by various cultures. Many of these cultures still use fermented foods and milk as part of their daily diets.

The use of probiotics in psychiatry also has interesting historical roots dating back hundreds of years.

The first reports of using probiotic supplements for depression occurred over a century ago. In 1910, Dr. George Porter Phillips reported that live bacteria supplements improved symptoms of depression in adults with melancholia. A few years later, in 1923, a medical journal published an article concluding that "acidophilus milk is recommended in the treatment of psychosis as a means to physical betterment."

Understanding how probiotics work first requires that you understand how your intestinal tract works alongside the microorganisms that are so important.

Your Intestinal Structure and Flora

The long tube that makes up your intestines is a structural wonder which, when healthy, does a great job of extracting nutrition from the food you eat. The inner lining of this tube is composed of folds and finger-like projections called villi. If completely unfolded and laid out flat on a surface, the intestinal tract would cover an area the size of a tennis court. In other words, the folds and villi create a large surface area inside of the intestines. With such a large surface area, food moving along the intestines comes into constant contact with the villi, maximizing the amount of nutrients extracted from food. The epithelial cells lining the villi, called enterocytes, have even smaller finger-like protrusions appropriately named microvilli. The microvillar surface, also known as the "brush border" because of its brushlike appearance, is extremely important to digestion. It is this surface that absorbs nutrients from food.

Although these cells are critical to digestion, they don't live very long and are replaced every three to six days. The constant replacement of cells is important to a healthy digestive system. If your digestive system is ill, once changes are made to restore its health, it will only take a matter of one to two weeks to start seeing improvements.

The microvilli lining the intestines work alongside trillions of microbes, an environment called the gut or intestinal flora. This term refers to the populations of microorganisms that reside in your intestines and help you digest your food.

These health-promoting microorganisms perform a host of useful functions, including digesting nutrients, metabolizing carcinogens, and creating a barrier against pathogens. For example, short-chain fatty acids are produced by bacterial fermentation of carbohydrates and proteins; the intestinal epithelial cells depend on short-chain fatty acids as an energy source. Furthermore, products of intestinal bacterial flora stimulate the immune system to maintain its readiness to protect against foreign viruses and bacteria.

The microvilli work best when they have these beneficial bacteria available to help with the digestion of food. As food comes into the intestines, it is broken down into smaller particles and digested by these bacteria. The nutrients from the food, including vitamins and minerals, are released and absorbed.

Probiotics and Anorexia

I have found that probiotics, in food or supplement form, can offer considerable relief from bloating, abdominal distention, and constipation. Although there is limited research on the use of probiotics in the treatment of anorexia, one study published in the *European Journal of Nutrition* examined the effects of adding yogurt containing *Lactobacillus bulgaricus* and *Streptococcus thermophilus* to the refeeding treatment of patients with anorexia nervosa. The patients were divided into groups and underwent the standard refeeding treatment, coupled with a nutritional program, psychotherapy, and any medications prescribed by their physicians. The only difference was that one group also received three servings of yogurt a day, while the other group received skim milk with an equivalent nutritional content.

After 10 weeks, patients who consumed yogurt showed an increase in the production of immunological markers that are also used to monitor nutritional status. The authors suggested that yogurt may improve the nutritional status of patients suffering from anorexia nervosa.

Probiotics and Mental Health

Psychological improvement may be another benefit of probiotics. Periods of stress can decrease the amount of beneficial bacteria such as *Lactobacillis* and *Bifidobacteria*, and this can lead to increased levels of inflammation and chemicals called cytokines. These pro-inflammatory cytokines have been shown to induce depression.

A research study on probiotics and depression published in the *Journal of Psychiatric Research* found that supplementation with *Bifidobacteria infantis* led to a lower inflammatory response and an increase in the amount of tryptophan, a precursor of serotonin, which is involved in mood regulation. This particular strain was concluded to have antidepressant properties in animals under stress. Although this study was conducted in lab animals, scientists believe the mechanism is similar in humans.

Many other studies have shown that probiotics have clear effects on mood. One study reported that live bacteria supplements improved symptoms of depression in adults with melancholia.

In a study published in the *European Journal of Clinical Nutrition*, 124 people consumed either a yogurt drink or a placebo each day for a three-week period. Participants who consumed the yogurt drink, and had previously rated their mood as poor, reported feeling happier.

In a fascinating double-blind, placebo-controlled study published in 2009, probiotic supplements were shown to decrease anxiety in those with chronic fatigue syndrome, which shares many symptoms with anorexia nervosa, including persistent and relapsing fatigue, headaches, GI complaints, anxiety, and depression. Those who took a daily probiotic supplement for two months containing 24 billion colony-forming units (cfus) of two bacterial strains decreased their symptoms of anxiety.

Probiotics and the Gastrointestinal Tract

Multiple health benefits of probiotic supplements have been documented by scientists around the world. The vast majority of the research has been with chronic GI dysfunction.

As we have discussed, GI problems are some of the most common complaints for patients with anorexia. In spite of this, most practitioners have used antacids and laxatives in the same indiscriminate trial-and-error approach that has been used for psychiatric medications. There have been very few studies on why chronic digestive and GI problems persist in patients with anorexia nervosa. Fortunately, as you better understand the role of probiotics in GI health, you will begin to see there is a lot that can be done.

Recent research has shown that probiotic supplements improve chronic GI conditions such as irritable bowel syndrome (IBS) and colitis.

A recent study led by Dr. Stefano Guandalini of the University of Chicago proved the effectiveness of probiotics in the treatment of IBS in pediatric patients. The well-controlled study spanned seven pediatric GI centers in the United States, Italy, and India, with 59 pediatric IBS patients participating in 12 weeks of treatment. The patients were randomly divided into two groups. For the first six weeks, one group was assigned a probiotic agent while the other received a placebo. At the end of six weeks, the groups switched treatment for six more weeks. At the completion of the study, patients were assessed for gastrointestinal symptoms, including abdominal pain or discomfort and bloating via a questionnaire. The probiotic agent was significantly more effective than the placebo at alleviating symptoms of gastrointestinal distress in the IBS patients.

Probiotic Supplementation

Probiotics can help restore the friendly bacteria to the digestive tract, which in turn will reduce GI discomfort and decrease inflammation. While incorporating foods containing live bacteria into the diet is beneficial, supplementation with probiotics is much more effective. According to *Consumer Reports*, as few as 1 in 1,000 bacteria from Dannon Activia yogurt, a food source of probiotics, survives the journey to the intestines through the corrosive stomach acid. That means that out of the 3 billion *Bifidus regularis* bacteria found in a 4 ounce serving of yogurt, only 3 million make it to the intestine!

I have found that supplementation with bacteria numbering in the billions is necessary for restoring healthy GI function to patients with anorexia. Initially, I recommend probiotic supplements containing at least two key strains of bacteria, including *L. acidophilus* and *B. bifidum*, with 10 to 15 billion cfu, two to three times per day between or before meals. After six months, a lower cfu amount, 3 to 5 billion, is sufficient.

A good probiotic supplement will have a special coating, an enteric coating, to protect the capsule as it travels through the stomach acid. This enteric coating is composed of gelatin and pectin, which eventually dissolves in the intestine, ensures that the bacteria survive their journey through your stomach acid to your intestines where they are needed.

Be wary of the manufacture date and the storage conditions of probiotic supplements that are sold. According to a report from Consumer-Lab.com, many probiotic supplements do not contain the amount of live bacteria that is listed on their labels at the time of purchase. They may have as little as 10 to 58 percent of the amount of bacteria listed on the product label at the time of purchase.

Once a probiotic regimen is begun, the good bacteria optimize the digestive terrain and immune functions as they move through the digestive tract and form colonies along the intestinal walls. As these beneficial microbes multiply, they compete with the harmful microbes living there. The probiotic microbes will crowd out these harmful organisms while establishing themselves throughout the digestive tract. The result should be a great improvement in digestive health.

Chapter Seventeen

Optimal Nutritional Support: Essential Fatty Acids

The role of dietary fat and essential fatty acids (EFAs) in maintaining mental and physical health cannot be underestimated. Although dietary fats have been much maligned over the years, scientists have clearly determined that essential fats are necessary for good health. Dietary fat plays such a critical role in your body's maintenance that excluding them from your diet has a major impact on your mental and physical health. There are many physicians and nutritionists who believe that omega-3 fatty acid deficiency is the most common nutrient deficiency today.

However, most of us continue to associate fat with a list of foods to avoid—"bad" food—that will result in weight gain. Yet, this is absolutely false. Not all fats are alike. Not all fats are bad food.

The medical community has successfully convinced the American public that fat is bad. This nutritional myth has left many Americans deficient in key omega-3 fats by creating a culture with severe limitation of all kinds of fats. Patients with anorexia nervosa, in particular, are caught in a nutritional nightmare by avoiding all fats, sometimes for years. Fatty acid levels need to be restored for sustained recovery from anorexia and other eating disorders.

Every membrane of every cell in your body is made from fat. Likewise, each cell in the body relies on EFAs for a variety of functions, including the manufacture and repair of cell membranes, the prevention of damage to the cell membrane, and the intake of nutrients and removal of harmful waste products through the cell membrane. Fat helps protect and maintain the structural integrity of the cell. Without proper fat intake, your cells are like a house with crumbling walls and a roof about to cave in.

Even more crucial is the role of fatty acids in the brain, in particular regarding brain function, growth, and development. This is reflected in the composition of the brain. About 60 percent of the dry weight of your brain is fat, mainly the omega-3 fatty acid DHA.

Dietary fats come in three different forms:

- **Saturated** fats are solid at room temperature. Saturated fats are commonly found in butter, lard, tallow, and coconut and palm oils.
- **Monounsaturated** fats tend to be liquid at room temperature, but solidify when refrigerated. Monounsaturated fats are found in olive oil, sesame oil, peanut oil, and nuts such as macadamias, cashews, and pecans.
- **Polyunsaturated** fats are liquid even when refrigerated. These fats can come from vegetables oils, flax seeds, cod liver oil, and cold-water fish.

A healthy body with sufficient amounts of vitamins, minerals, and amino acids can make many of the fatty acids that it needs. However, there are two classes of "essential" polyunsaturated fatty acids that the body cannot produce: omega-3 and omega-6 fatty acids.

There are three major types of omega-3 fatty acids:

- Alpha-Linolenic acid (ALA)
- Eicosapentaenoic acid (EPA)
- Docosahexaenoic acid (DHA)

Both EPA and DHA can be created from the parent fatty acid ALA, but the conversion rates are low, and direct consumption of EPA and DHA result in higher levels within the body.

Major types of omega-6 fatty acids include:

- Linoleic acid (LA), from which the body can make gamma-Linolenic acid (GLA)
- Arachidonic acid (AA)

Essential Fatty Acids and Anorexia Nervosa

Patients with anorexia have an immense fear of gaining weight and this leads them to essentially avoid all forms of dietary fat. Over a short time this significantly affects levels of EFAs. Two different research teams confirmed that this prolonged avoidance results in EFA deficiencies in the cell membranes of many patients suffering with anorexia. As you recall, every cell membrane of the human body is composed of fat. Those suffering from anorexia nervosa had abnormal fat contents in their cell membranes, indicating that they were suffering from EFA deficiencies.

Not surprisingly, multiple complications of anorexia are related to EFA deficiencies. EFAs are involved in many metabolic processes; therefore, deficiencies in EFAs have a wide range of effects. EFA deficiencies have been associated with constipation, elevated cholesterol, dry skin, vulnerability to osteoporosis, depression, suicide, and increased risk of cardiac death. Suicide and cardiac death are some of the most common causes of mortality in anorexia, and both are associated with omega-3 fatty acid deficiencies.

Despite the occurrence of EFA deficiencies among patients with anorexia and the severe consequences associated with deficiency, current treatment models rarely address this problem. According to Agnes Ayton, MD, an adolescent and child psychiatrist at the eating disorders clinic at Huntercombe Stafford Hospital, these omega-3 deficiencies may contribute to mood problems commonly seen during refeeding treatment and may increase the risk of relapse.

Ayton published a case report in the journal *European Psychiatry*, in which she describes the treatment of a severely malnourished patient with anorexia using the omega-3 fatty acid EPA. The 15-year-old patient entered the hospital emaciated, with dry skin and hair, and was extremely anxious and depressed. Like many patients with anorexia, she had an immense fear of eating. When initially hospitalized, she received several months of traditional treatment, including psychotherapy, psycho-education, dietary advice, and naso-gastric feeding. None of these treatments helped, as she relapsed once she left the hospital. Once readmitted to the hospital, ethyl-EPA was added to her diet. After three months of treatment with 1,000 mg of ethyl-EPA per day and a daily multivitamin, her anxiety and depression lifted and there was improvement in her weight. After six months of treatment, she enrolled in a college course and started working.

In another study published in the journal *Prostaglandins, Leukotrienes and Essential Fatty Acids*, Ayton and colleagues further explored the relationship between omega-3 fatty acids and anorexia during refeeding. Ayton and her colleagues reported on seven patients with anorexia nervosa who were supplemented with daily doses of ethyl-EPA (E-EPA), a purified form of an omega-3 fatty acid. Each of the seven patients received 1000 mg of E-EPA per day in addition to standard treatment. None of the patients was prescribed psychotropic medication during the three-month study.

There was a significant improvement in mood as well as overall health among the seven patients after the first six to eight weeks of treatment. Ayton and her colleagues characterized four of the patients as "partially improved" and three patients as "fully recovered" after three months of treatment. After eight weeks, all of the seven patients reported decreased anxiety and preoccupation with food. The patients were able to restore weight, and some of the patients who were experiencing delayed growth before the start of the trial experienced significant growth during the supplementation period.

Patients who stopped the E-EPA treatment after the study ended experienced a reversal of all these improvements. Two to three months after abandoning fatty acid supplementation, they experienced deterioration of mood, weight, and growth. The timing of this deterioration likely coincided with the rate of EFA depletion from the body.

Ayton and her colleagues concluded that ethyl-EPA supplementation may be beneficial for patients with anorexia nervosa, particularly during refeeding.

Omega-3 Fatty Acids and Weight Loss

Weight loss and the restrictive eating patterns in anorexia nervosa result in the drastic depletion in omega-3 fats. As the most metabolically active fats, omega-3 are the most quickly burned for energy during weight loss. When this happens insulin is poorly regulated and metabolism slows.

Without adequate omega-3 intake during periods of weight loss, patients regain weight more quickly. A common concern I hear from patients is that "I can only eat very little without gaining weight." Again, we typically understand this problem as "eating disorder behavior" and fear of weight gain. Sometimes it is, however, the nutritional deficiencies of trace minerals and EFAs that have created metabolic chaos and slowed metabolism. Easy weight gain is the result of this restricted eating pattern, which perpetuates a viscious cycle that traps one in the chronic relapsing world of anorexia.

Although it may appear counterintuitive, eating the right fats can actually facilitate weight loss. In fact, omega-3 supplements are actually associated with improved weight loss. How can this be? A study published in the *American Journal of Clinical Nutrition* found that people who consumed fish oil supplements and walked briskly over the course of 12 weeks (three times a week for 45 minutes) lost more weight and body fat than any of the other groups in the study. Those who exercised and did not take omega-3 supplements did not lose as much weight or body fat as the people who supplemented their diets with fish oil.

It can be difficult at times to convince a patient with anorexia to consume supplements that include the words "fatty acids" even though a fish oil capsule typically has about 10 calories. Basic education of the role of EFAs in metabolism can be extremely helpful and empowering to patients.

Stella was in and out of treatment programs for anorexia nervosa during the ages of 16 to 20. By the age of 21 she returned to college and started eating a "normal" diet. Although trying to watch her intake of high fat foods, Stella proceeded to gain 40 pounds above her ideal body weight in less than a year.

Stella understood the danger of restricting her caloric intake and made tremendous progress in therapy, yet she was now struggling with actually being overweight. Stella tried an endless array of diets, trainers, spas and fasts, but she was unable to lose the weight she gained. Despite almost two years of eating a normal "healthy diet" prescribed by professionals, despite being considered as "recovered" from anorexia nervosa, despite participating in therapy, and despite doing all the right things, Stella was suffering. She started to relapse into the old behaviors and thought patterns of anorexia nervosa.

Her parents sought my consultation after Stella essentially stopped eating in a desperate attempt to lose weight. After my initial consultation with Stella and her family, it was clear that Stella was suffering, yet what was most striking to me was her apparent state of malnutrition.

Besides concerns about weight gain with many weight loss attempts and the chronic depression, Stella described the following list of symptoms: always thirsty, fatigue, dry skin, migraines, frequent urination, and allergies. Classic symptoms of EFA deficiency!

Stella was consuming fish on a regular basis, took a multivitamin, and loved vegetables. She had not been underweight for more than two years, yet Stella had EFA deficiencies and, upon further nutritional testing, she was found to be low in vitamin B12, zinc, and iron.

After four weeks and 4 grams of purified fish oil per day, iron, zinc, and B12 supplements, Stella returned to the office. When I asked her how she was doing, Stella replied, "I don't notice anything. Maybe I lost 3 pounds." When I asked her about her excessive thirst, dry skin, frequent urination, and insomnia, she defensively shrugged, saying "Well, those things are all gone."

I used this opportunity to educate Stella about nutritional therapies and how treating the underlying cause of a problem may take time, but will solve a contributing factor to her slow metabolism following years of anorexia nervosa.

I have known Stella and her family for many years now. She eventually lost more than 30 pounds, completed college, and now works helping others with mental health problems.

The nutritional deficiencies of anorexia can persist long after a patient reaches "normal weight" and recovery is declared. EFA deficiencies can persist for long periods of time, and I believe this contributes to the vulnerability to mood and anxiety disorders, and weight gain which can result in distorted eating and compensatory purging behaviors. A long list of physical problems, including allergies, arthritis, GI problems, and even osteoporosis, can be related to chronic deficiencies in omega-3 fatty acids.

Omega-3 Fatty Acids and Mental Illness

The omega-3 fatty acids—ALA, EPA, and DHA—are highly concentrated in the brain and appear to be particularly important for memory, behavior, brain performance, and mental well-being. Evidence suggests that deficiencies of omega-3 fatty acids may be a factor in many psychiatric disorders, including depression, bipolar disorder, ADHD, and autism, as well as psychological traits such as hostility.

Research has shown that omega-3 supplementation is beneficial to a disorder referred to as borderline personality disorder and the personality trait of hostility. In a study published in the *American Journal of Psychiatry*, 30 female patients with moderately severe borderline personality disorder received either 1,000 mg of E-EPA daily or a placebo. After two months, those taking the E-EPA had significantly less aggression and diminished depression as compared to the patients taking the placebo.

Many studies of patients with major depressive disorder have shown deficiencies in omega-3 fatty acids. A study published in the *American Journal of Psychiatry* demonstrated that EFA abnormalities may predict risk of suicide. According to the study, low levels of DHA and elevated ratios of omega-6 to omega-3 fatty acids accurately predicted suicidal behavior in patients with major depressive disorder. The good news is that the overwhelming majority of studies in patients with major depressive disorder has shown a clinically significant improvement in depression symptoms for patients once they were supplemented with omega-3 fatty acids.

Research involving children with depression also supports a positive response to omega-3 supplementation. One study published in the *American Journal of Psychiatry* showed the benefits of EPA and DHA supplementation in childhood depression. The study involved 20 children between the ages of 6 and 12 who were suffering with, on average, a three-month period of depression. Over a 16-week period, the children either received daily doses of 400 mg of EPA and 200 mg of DHA or a placebo. Those placed on omega-3 supplementation showed a 50 percent reduction in depressive symptoms as measured by the Childhood Depression Rating Scale. The authors concluded that treatment with EPA/DHA in a 2:1 ratio was helpful in treating childhood depression.

Additional studies examining fish consumption and rates of depression confirms the beneficial effects of omega-3 fatty acids. As you recall, cold-water fish are rich in omega-3 fatty acids. Many studies have revealed that nations with high fish consumption (e.g., Iceland, Korea, and Taiwan) have much lower rates of depression than countries where fish is not eaten as often (e.g., Germany, Switzerland, and Hungary). An examination of fish and seafood consumption throughout different nations has also shown that high consumption is correlated with protection against postpartum depression, bipolar disorder, and seasonal affective disorder.

The scientific literature about EFAs and mental health is extensive and increasing. The majority of the research supports a connection between low serum and red blood cell levels of omega-3 and increased likelihood of depression. Supplementation with omega-3 fatty acids often results in clear improvement in patients.

Omega-3 fatty acid supplements may actually aid in the prevention of mental illness. A recently published study in the *Archives of General Psychiatry* found that omega-3 supplementation in patients with a history of psychiatric symptoms prevented the onset of a full-blown psychotic disorder. The study, discussed in more detail in Chapter Twenty-Seven, provides a clear, safe strategy for preventing psychiatric illnesses with essential fatty acid supplementation.

Omega-3 Fatty Acids and Physical Health

Besides its benefits on mental health, there are numerous research studies indicating the beneficial effects of omega-3 fatty acids on cardiovascular health and the reduction of inflammation and pain.

Omega-3 fatty acids are linked with the improvement of the following:

- blood pressure
- heart rhythms
- triglycerides
- cholesterol

Research scientists, physicians, the American Heart Association, and now a pharmaceutical company realize the importance of omega-3 fatty acid supplementation. Heart disease is the leading cause of death in the United States. Patients with anorexia nervosa are also at risk for cardiovascular problems. It is estimated that those suffering with anorexia nervosa have a two-fold increased risk for death from cardiovascular causes.

Essential Fatty Acids and Cholesterol

Although it may seem obvious that patients with anorexia must have low cholesterol due to strict avoidance of dietary fats, surprisingly, most patients with anorexia have high cholesterol. It's currently not understood why this is the case, but it likely may be due to poor liver function in patients with anorexia. The liver is where cholesterol is made and broken down. Due to the effects of malnutrition, the liver may not be efficiently breaking down cholesterol. Abnormalities in synthesizing estrogen, thyroid, and other hormones which are made from cholesterol may also lead to high cholesterol levels.

I have consistently found elevated cholesterol is related to decreased levels of EFAs. This inverse relationship between total cholesterol and polyunsaturated fatty acids such as omega-3 fatty acids was confirmed in a study published in the journal *Lipids*. The study examined more than 500 blood samples taken from the offspring of the participants involved in the Framingham Heart Study. In this research study, high total cholesterol correlated with low amounts of polyunsaturated fatty acids such as omega-3 fatty acids.

Do you treat high cholesterol in a patient suffering with anorexia? It would be unwise to suggest that someone struggling with anorexia should go on a low-fat or low-calorie diet to reduce their high cholesterol. Instead, patients with anorexia and high cholesterol should be encouraged to increase their EFA intake. With supplemental omega-3 fatty acids, patients with anorexia can find that their high cholesterol levels will return to normal.

Symptoms of Essential Fatty Acid Deficiencies

Many psychiatric conditions are linked to deficiencies of essential fatty acids. In examining levels of EFAs in patients with anorexia, I have consistently seen low levels of both essential omega-3 and essential omega-6 fatty acids. The signs and symptoms of EFA deficiency are readily seen and usually reflect long-standing deficiency.

The physical symptoms of EFA deficiencies include:

- Excessive thirst
- Extreme tiredness (fatigue)
- Sleep disturbances
- Poor memory
- Dry skin on the extremities
- Oily skin on the face
- Sensitivity to sunlight
- Heart arrhythmias
- Joint pain
- Unstable moods
- An inability to fight infections
- Poor circulation

Sources of Essential Fatty Acids

Meat, eggs, fish, and vegetable, seed, and nut oils are the primary dietary sources of essential fatty acids.

ALA, the precursor of EPA and DHA, is found in flaxseeds, flaxseed oil, canola oil, soybeans, soybean oil, pumpkin seeds, walnuts, and walnut oil. Because the conversion of ALA to the other forms of omega-3 fatty

Dietary Sources of Essential Fatty Acids

Omega-3 Fatty Acids		Omega-6 Fatty Acids	
ALA	Flaxseed and flaxseed oil, walnuts and walnut oil, green leafy vegetables (spinach, kale, mustard greens, etc.), winter squash, cauliflower, broccoli	LA	Sunflower, flaxseed, corn, sesame, soybean, and peanut oils
		GLA	Evening primrose oil, black currant seed oil, borage oil
EPA	Cold-water fish (salmon, tuna, cod, trout, sardines, anchovies)	AA	Animal meat, egg yolks, squid, warm-water fish
DHA	Cold-water fish and, to a smaller degree, warm-water fish		

acids can be easily compromised, most health experts recommended direct supplementation with EPA and DHA. Cold-water fish—such as salmon, mackerel, halibut, sardines, tuna, and herring—are an excellent source of both EPA and DHA. Fish oil supplements are often tested for mercury and polychlorinated biphenyl, a common pollutant in the ocean. In making these supplements, these pollutants and other impurities are removed.

Recommended Intakes of Essential Fatty Acids

The AHA recommends at least two servings of fish per week for those without a history of heart disease. Food sources of EFAs, however, vary by quite a bit, especially fish sources which are often recommended. A single 3-ounce serving of wild salmon contains up to 1.5 grams of omega-3 fatty acids. A can of tuna packed in water, on the other hand, may contain roughly one-half or 0.75 grams of the omega-3 fatty acids found in a single serving of wild salmon.

The dietary guidelines established by the USDA remain more conservative than the AHA recommendations. According to the USDA, the recommended daily intake of omega-3 fatty acids for the general adult population should be 1 gram for women and up to 1.5 grams for men. The amount of omega-6 fatty acids recommended by the government clearly reflects the skewed ratio of omega-6 fatty acids to omega-3 fatty acids present in the SAD. For omega-6 fatty acids it recommends 12 grams per day for adult women and 17 grams per day for adult men.

There are no guidelines established for patients with anorexia nervosa. I recommend supplementation with a combination of both omega-3 from fish oil and omega-6 from evening primrose oil or borage oil. The supplements should be taken two to three times a day with meals, for a day's total of approximately 3 grams of omega-3 fatty acids and 1 gram of omega-6 fatty acids.

Krill oil, despite higher cost, is an excellent source of omega-3 fatty acids, as it also contains other natural phospholipids. Krill oil, extracted from shrimp-like crustaceans, contains high amounts of EPA and DHA. There are small amounts of omega-6 fatty acids in krill oil. The oil also naturally contains several other healthy substances such as the antioxidants canthaxanthin, astaxanthin, beta carotene, vitamin E, and vitamin A.

Cod liver oil has traditionally been a commonly used source of supplemental omega-3 fatty acids. Consuming one tablespoon once a day is an excellent source of supplementation, as it also provides vitamin A and

D. Never exceed one tablespoon per day, as vitamin A and D are fat-soluble vitamins that are stored in the body. Patients with anorexia tend to already have higher levels of fat-soluble vitamins.

As you increase your intake of omega-3 fatty acids with supplementation in the range I recommend, it is important to make sure you are also taking adequate antioxidants, with at least 500 mg of vitamin C and 100 IU of vitamin E per day.

A small percentage of patients develop side effects when taking EFA supplements. Most side effects disappear with digestive enzymes or by changing brands of fish oil supplements. A few patients may develop loose stools, belching, or flatulence. Freezing or cooling fish oil supplements can minimize any side effects when starting supplementation.

Chapter Eighteen

Optimal Nutritional Support: Vitamins

Vitamins and minerals play a crucial role in health through every phase of human development. Physical health and psychological well-being are dependent on optimal nutrition. This chapter, as well as the next, describes the vitamin and mineral deficiencies associated with anorexia. Information about the function of each nutrient, how it affects anorexia, and the recommended amounts for the average person and those with anorexia will be provided.

The recommended amounts will be notated as either RDA or AI. RDA stands for recommended dietary allowance and is defined by the U.S. National Academy of Science's Food and Nutrition Board as the amount of a given nutrient considered sufficient to meet the requirements of 97 to 98 percent of healthy individuals in each gender and age group. However, certain nutrients that have been more recently recognized as important do not yet have RDAs. In these cases, the AI or adequate intake is indicated, which is defined as the level believed to be adequate for everyone in a specific age range. Some nutrients are available as individual supplements. Others, such as a number of the B vitamins, are commonly found together in one pill as a B complex vitamin supplement.

It's important to note, however, that although adhering to these guidelines can help prevent deficiencies, many experts believe these dietary intake levels are inadequate to promote optimal health.

Vitamins can be classified as either water-soluble (dissolvable in water) or fat-soluble (dissolvable in fat). The water-soluble vitamins cannot be stored by the body and therefore must be ingested on a continual basis. If more is ingested than needed, the excess water-soluble vitamins will simply be excreted in the urine. Included in the water-soluble vitamins are the B vitamins and vitamin C.

The fat-soluble vitamins, which get their name because they are absorbed from food with the help of lipids, or fats, include vitamins A, D, E, and K. Unlike water-soluble vitamins, they can be stored in the body. This means that daily intake is not as critical, and, consequently, people with anorexia are not usually deficient in them. For this reason, they will be mentioned only very briefly.

Thiamine (Vitamin B1)

In the body, thiamine is concentrated in the liver, kidneys, brain, heart, and muscles. Required for the manufacture of a small number of very important enzymes, thiamine contributes to heart health, nervous system functioning, and proper digestion, and it also helps the body produce energy from food. It is also important in the synthesis of DNA and RNA, the building blocks of life.

How it relates to anorexia: As early as the 1930s, studies have shown that thiamine deficiency can cause symptoms similar to those seen in anorexia: irritability, depression, weakness, inability to concentrate, insomnia, and decreased activity.

In a study performed in 1942, eleven women consumed a diet that contained only half of the recommended amount of thiamine. After 8 to 12 weeks, the women began to display altered mental and emotional states. The longer the diet lasted, the worse the symptoms became. Some women experienced heart abnormalities; others had difficulty even standing up. Although they maintained their body weight, all of the participants had decreased appetite and ate less, coupled with periods of nausea and vomiting. After the study ended and the women were given thiamine supplements, all of the symptoms gradually subsided.

Prolonged thiamine deficiency causes a disease called beriberi. Cerebral beriberi, also called Wernicke-Korsakoff syndrome, affects the brain and nervous system. Sufferers can experience abnormal eye movements, problems walking and standing, and a range of cognitive and psychiatric problems such as depression, panic attacks, and suicidal thoughts. Depression and panic attacks are frequently seen in anorexia.

Recommended intake for healthy people: The RDA is 1.0 mg per day for girls 14–18, and 1.1 mg for women over the age of 19.

Recommended amount for those with anorexia: For optimal nutrition, I typically recommend that individuals with anorexia take at least 50 mg of thiamine twice a day. This can be found in a B complex or multivitamin.

Niacin (Vitamin B3)

Niacin contributes to cells' energy production by breaking down carbohydrates, fats, proteins, and alcohol in the body. Healthy functioning of the digestive system, skin, and nervous system also depends on niacin. While mild niacin deficiency can result in indigestion, headaches, and a sore tongue, severe niacin deficiency causes a disease called pellagra, with its characteristic dermatitis, diarrhea, dementia, and death—the four Ds. Neuropsychiatric difficulties can include insomnia, depression, and apathy, among others.

How it relates to anorexia: As discussed in Chapter Eight, individuals with anorexia are vulnerable to deficiencies in niacin. Severe niacin deficiencies resulting in pellagra have been reported in patients with anorexia in several scientific and medical journals. Proper diagnosis of pellagra or even subclinical niacin deficiency in those suffering from anorexia remains difficult due to the individual variation in symptoms and the numerous similarities between anorexia and pellagra. Individuals with pellagra can have any number of its symptoms. For example, some pellagrins never develop the so-called tell-tale sign of pellagra, dermatitis. Also, pellagra and anorexia share similar psychological effects: depression, delusions, anxiety, fatigue, and restlessness.

Recommended intake for healthy people: The RDA for niacin is 14 mg per day for female adolescents and adults. Niacin supplements are available as niacinamide or nicotinic acid. Niacin obtained from food sources does not cause side effects, but nicotinic acid can cause flushing (redness of the skin), nausea, vomiting, and in rare cases liver abnormalities. With niacinamide supplements, flushing of the skin does not often occur.

Recommended amount for those with anorexia: I typically recommend 50 mg of niacinamide twice a day as part of a B complex or multivitamin.

Inositol

Important to biological processes in our cells such as maintaining cell membranes, inositol (which is considered a B vitamin) affects the metabolism of many neurotransmitters, including serotonin. Decreased amounts of serotonin are linked to depression, panic disorder, and OCD.

Some people with these disorders have been found to have decreased levels of inositol.

How it relates to anorexia: Depression, feelings of panic, and obsessive thoughts surrounding body image and food are psychiatric symptoms commonly seen in anorexia. Low levels of inositol in the cerebral spinal fluid have been found in individuals with depression. Treating these patients with 6 to 12 grams of inositol a day was found to significantly improve their symptoms. When the inositol treatment was stopped, their depression returned. When inositol treatment was restarted, the symptoms of depression disappeared again.

Two studies support the potential role of inositol in reducing the frequency and severity of panic attacks. One study reported that a group of patients taking inositol had significantly fewer panic attacks compared to a group taking a placebo pill. A second study compared inositol to the psychiatric medication Luvox (fluvoxamine). Subjects with active panic disorder were treated with either up to 18 grams per day of inositol or up to 150 mg per day of Luvox. The researchers found that both inositol and fluvoxamine were equally effective in treating panic disorder, but that inositol was better at reducing the number of panic attacks experienced.

Inositol can also be helpful in reducing the obsessive thinking common in those with anorexia. One study showed that people with obsessive compulsive disorder who took 18 grams per day of inositol reported experiencing fewer obsessions and compulsions. Inositol may be helpful before meals to decrease anxiety and obsessional thinking.

Recommended intake for healthy people: There is no official RDA for inositol, but it is estimated that most people ingest about 1 gram per day. A natural substance, supplemental inositol appears to be safe, even in high doses. Common side effects include nausea, bloating, insomnia, and fatigue. Because it may stimulate contractions of the uterus, it should be administered cautiously to pregnant women.

Recommended amount for those with anorexia: Although difficult to predict who will respond to inositol supplements, many who take them find significant relief from both anxiety and obsessional thoughts. I initially recommend 1/2 teaspoon (1.4 grams) of inositol taken three times a day. The dose should slowly be titrated to 8–12 grams per day. Many patients find relief at 3 teaspoons per day (8.4 grams per day). The only side effects to inositol are related to GI discomfort if the dose is titrated too quickly.

Riboflavin (Vitamin B2)

Riboflavin helps the body break down, store, and use fats, ketone bodies, and proteins, and it is necessary for processes that provide cells in the body with energy. Contributing to red blood cell production, as well as skin and eye health, riboflavin is also essential for the proper functioning of niacin, pyridoxine, and folic acid.

Symptoms of riboflavin deficiency can include problems with the digestive tract, including cracked and red lips, cracks at the corners of the mouth, and mouth ulcers. Dry, scaly skin; iron-deficiency anemia; and bloodshot, itchy and watery eyes can also occur.

How it relates to anorexia: There is no literature to support a direct relationship between riboflavin and anorexia, but adequate riboflavin is necessary for optimal health and brain function.

Recommended intake for healthy people: The RDA is 1.0 mg for girls ages 14 to 18 and 1.1 mg for adult women.

Recommended amount for those with anorexia: Riboflavin is usually contained in a B complex vitamin. I typically recommend that individuals take one 50-mg B complex or multivitamin twice a day.

Pantothenic Acid (Vitamin B5)

The word pantothenic means "from everywhere," and pantothenic acid is found in most foods, including meats, vegetables, grains, and eggs. Similar to the other B vitamins, it is necessary for the synthesis of hormones, neurotransmitters, and fatty acids.

How it relates to anorexia: People who starve themselves can become deficient in pantothenic acid, causing numbness, tingling in the hands and feet, muscle cramps, low blood glucose levels, nausea, vomiting, and sleep disturbances. A severe deficiency can also affect the adrenal glands, which are responsible for making vital hormones, such as epinephrine and corticosteroids. Adrenal insufficiency can lead to weight loss, muscle weakness, fatigue, and low blood pressure. A number of symptoms are seen in anorexia, so it is important to replenish pantothenic acid when necessary to reduce symptoms that may be due to a vitamin B5 deficiency. Fortunately, pantothenic acid supplements can reverse many of these symptoms of deficiency.

Recommended intake for healthy people: The AI for pantothenic acid is 5 mg per day for both adolescents and adults.

Recommended amount for those with anorexia: I typically recommend that individuals with anorexia take 50 mg of pantothenic acid vitamin in the morning and one in the evening in the form of a B complex or as part of a multivitamin.

Biotin

Classified as a B vitamin, biotin helps regulate blood glucose levels and is important in a number of chemical and metabolic reactions in the body. It may also be helpful in treating type 2 diabetes. Because it is important for cell growth and is beneficial for strengthening hair and nails, it is included in many beauty products.

Biotin deficiency is rare; people with certain inherited disorders may be susceptible. Symptoms of biotin deficiency can include red, scaly skin rashes (especially on the face), nausea, vomiting, lethargy, and depression.

How it relates to anorexia: There is no literature to support a direct relationship with anorexia, but adequate biotin is necessary for optimal health and brain function.

Recommended intake for healthy people: The AI for biotin is 30 micrograms (mcg) daily.

Recommended amount for those with anorexia: Biotin is usually contained in a B complex vitamin. I typically recommend that individuals take 300 mcg of biotin in a B complex or multivitamin with one in the morning and one in the evening with meals.

Pyridoxine (Vitamin B6)

Vitamin B6 aids in the production of red blood cell hemoglobin, plays a role in estrogen and testosterone function, and helps convert glucose to a form of energy that can be used by the muscles. In addition, it decreases levels of homocysteine, a harmful substance that is associated with heart disease.

A vitamin B6 deficiency can result in neurological symptoms such as depression, confusion, and irritability, as well as inflammation of the skin, soreness of the tongue, and mouth ulcers.

How it relates to anorexia: Pyridoxine is needed to make the neurotransmitters serotonin, dopamine, norepinephrine, and gamma amino butyric acid—all of which have potent effects in the brain. Psychological and psychiatric conditions such as depression, confusion, and irritability, which can be seen in anorexia, can result from a vitamin B6 deficiency.

Recommended intake for healthy people: The RDA for vitamin B6 is 1.2 mg per day for adolescent girls ages 14 to 18, and 1.3 mg per day for adults ages 19 to 50.

Recommended amount for those with anorexia: Pyridoxine is usually contained in a B complex vitamin. I typically recommend that individuals take one 50 mg B complex vitamin in the morning and one in the evening. Note: Taking more than 200 mg of vitamin B6 per day can result in numbness and pain in the arms and legs.

Folic Acid (Vitamin B9)

Folic acid, also known as folate, is well known for its involvement in DNA and RNA synthesis and cell development. Pregnant women are urged to take folic acid supplements to prevent brain and spinal cord defects in their babies. Having sufficient folic acid in the diet may protect against developing colorectal, breast, and cervical cancers. Folic acid also contributes to heart health by breaking down homocysteine, a deleterious substance associated with heart disease.

Even though cereals and flour are routinely fortified with folic acid, deficiencies do occur. Certain drugs, including oral contraceptives, seizure medications, antacids, and antibiotics, can lower folic acid levels. Some people with severely decreased food intake may not ingest enough folic acid, some may not be able to absorb it well, and others may have a genetic condition making it difficult for their bodies to effectively use folic acid once it has been absorbed.

How it relates to anorexia: Folic acid is necessary for the production of brain neurotransmitters such as serotonin and dopamine, and studies have found very low levels of folate in a large percentage of people with depression. Furthermore, antidepressant treatments, including medications and electroconvulsive therapy, may not work as well for people with an underlying folic acid deficiency; their symptoms of depression can return more frequently.

But will symptoms of depression improve if patients are treated with both medication and folic acid? According to research studies, the answer is yes. A 10-week trial of adults with depression pitted the antidepressant Prozac against Prozac plus folic acid. At the end of the study, 73 percent of those taking medication plus folic acid had recovered from their depression, compared to only 47 percent of those taking medication only.

In another study in Boston, Massachusetts, patients who remained depressed despite taking SSRI medications—including Prozac, Zoloft, Effexor, and Paxil—were given a folic acid supplement to take with their SSRIs for eight weeks. The researchers found that the patients' depression lessened after taking folic acid with their medication.

This research has direct implications with anorexia. It is important to treat any coexisting psychiatric conditions such as depression in individuals with anorexia so that treatment of the eating disorder can be as effective as possible.

Recommended intake for healthy people: 400 mcg a day is recommended for adolescents and adults ages 14 and up.

There is some concern that folate supplementation may enhance cancer risk. Folate is required for cell division and growth because of its role in DNA synthesis. If there is underlying cancer, folate may facilitate its growth. No clear studies have shown a direct link between increased cancer risk and folate supplementation. Many experts agree that the benefits of supplementation far outweigh the potential risks. Furthermore, folate in the form of L-methylfolate has been shown to have fewer potential health risks.

Recommended amount for those with anorexia: If blood levels are normal (between 2.7 and 17.0 nanograms/mL, or ng/mL), I recommend 1 mg of L-methyl folate per day. For blood levels below 2.7 ng/mL, I recommend 1 to 5 mg of folate per day in the form of L-methylfolate. Note: Excessive intake of folic acid can be problematic as too much can mask the symptoms of a vitamin B12 deficiency.

Vitamin B12

Vitamin B12 is important for DNA production, red blood cell production, and normal functioning of the central nervous system (brain and spinal cord). Low levels of the vitamin not only impair normal neurotransmitter function in the brain, but can also result in spinal cord damage. A vitamin B12 deficiency can lead to a wide range of symptoms throughout the body. People with low levels can experience neurological symptoms, such as tingling in the hands and feet, and difficulty with coordination and walking. Low levels are also associated with infertility, osteoporosis, heart disease, and stroke.

How it relates to anorexia: Vitamin B12 deficiency is one of the more common nutrient deficiencies found in anorexia and can lead to a range of psychiatric conditions including depression, anxiety, paranoia, hallucinations, memory loss, confusion, outbursts of temper, and behavioral changes. Not surprisingly, higher levels of vitamin B12 have been associated with better long-term outcomes in depression.

One of the reasons a vitamin B12 deficiency is so common in anorexia is that it is primarily found in meat products, foods that most anorexics avoid. Identifying a vitamin B12 deficiency is critical, as some of the resultant symptoms can be irreversible.

Recommended intake for healthy people: 2.4 mcg a day is recommended for adolescents and adults ages 14 and up.

Recommended amount for those with anorexia: Vitamin B12 blood levels of 200 to 900 pg/ml are considered normal, although I consider up to 1,200 pg/ml as normal. Many experts argue that these levels are inadequate. And even if they were adequate, studies have shown a poor correlation between the amount of vitamin B12 in the blood and the amount in the brain, meaning there could be a deficiency in the brain even though blood levels seem "normal." Further testing for a vitamin B12 deficiency includes blood and urine methylmalonic acid tests.

I supplement anyone with a level under 500 pg/mL. For values between 350 and 500 pg/mL, I recommend three 1,000 mcg B12 injections followed by oral liquid methyl-cobalamin 2,000 mcg per day. For values below 350 pg/mL, I recommend seven 1,000-mcg B12 injections followed by 2,000 mcg liquid methyl-cobalamin per day.

Ascorbic Acid (Vitamin C)

One of the most popular vitamin supplements, vitamin C augments the immune system and protects the body from the effects of harmful free radicals. It also aids in the absorption of iron, and plays an important part in cell reproduction and the manufacture of bones, skin, connective tissue, and blood vessels. In the liver, it helps detoxify poisons that have found their way into the body.

Anemia, easy bruisability, and impaired wound healing can be symptoms of a mild vitamin C deficiency, as can frequent infections, including colds, viruses, and respiratory illnesses. A severe vitamin C deficiency can cause a disease called scurvy, which can cause bleeding, red or purple discolorations of the skin, lethargy, severe gingivitis and gum bleeding, pain and swelling of the muscles and joints, and the loss of hair and teeth.

A vitamin C deficiency can occur in the general population, but it is more common in people who are under stress for an extended period of time—from surgery, burns, injuries, or illnesses such as anorexia—and have an increased need for vitamin C. A deficiency can be caused by a lack of fruits and vegetables in the diet, but certain medications, including oral contraceptives, non-steroidal anti-inflammatories, and sulfa antibiotics—as well as cigarette smoking—can also decrease the body's supply of the vitamin. One study found that smokers had one-third less vitamin C in their blood than nonsmokers, which may be particularly relevant for those with anorexia, as a high percentage of them smoke cigarettes.

How it relates to anorexia: Individuals with anorexia can develop scurvy. One example involves a 46-year-old woman who ate primarily boiled chicken and white rice. Admitted to the hospital for anorexia, she was noted to have a rash on both legs extending from her knees to her ankles, as well as bruising around her knees and ankles. She also had petechiae (small red areas caused by minor hemorrhages) on the roof of her mouth. A skin biopsy of the rash was found to be consistent with early scurvy. With medical treatment that included vitamin C supplements, the woman's bruising and petechiae disappeared over the course of seven days.

A second example is a 25-year-old woman with a history of anorexia who had a relatively balanced diet until she began to avoid all fruits and green vegetables, eating only high-calorie, carbohydrate foods like bread. Six months later, she developed ankle puffiness, painful swelling of her left knee, joint stiffness, and extensive bruising. Her swollen gums bled easily, and she developed shortness of breath with activity. In addition to having iron and folate deficiencies, she was also found to have a severely low level of vitamin C. With treatment and a return to eating vegetables and fruits, her symptoms improved.

Individuals with anorexia may also have subclinical scurvy, exhibiting milder symptoms. For this reason, I believe that every person with anorexia should take vitamin C.

Recommended intake for healthy people: The RDA for ascorbic acid is 65 mg per day for adolescent girls ages 14 to 18, and 75 mg per day for women over 19.

Recommended amount for those with anorexia: I generally recommend 1,000 mg of vitamin C per day. Note: At extremely high doses, vitamin C can cause gastrointestinal upset and diarrhea. There is individual variation as to what dose is considered above tolerance. This range can be anywhere between 2 and 25 grams when ill or under stress.

Fat-Soluble Vitamins and Anorexia

It's clear that the severe starvation seen in anorexia has major effects on individuals' nutritional states. Reading about vitamin deficiency disorders ranging from pellagra to scurvy in those with anorexia may lead you to believe that individuals struggling with anorexia experience universal deficiencies in all nutrients. However, that is not the case.

In most cases, individuals with anorexia actually have normal or even high levels of the fat-soluble vitamins (vitamins A, D, E, and K). Despite their restrictive diets, many more of these adolescents and adults with anorexia are meeting the DRI for fat-soluble vitamins as compared to adolescents and adults without eating disorders. (DRI encompasses four nutrient-based reference values, including both RDA and AI measurements as well as two others.) A study published in the *American Journal of Clinical Nutrition* involving 78 adolescents (half of whom have anorexia) found that a higher percentage of adolescents with anorexia were meeting the DRI for vitamins A, D, E, and K than their healthy peers. For example, 84.6 percent of the anorexic girls met the DRI for vitamin A from diet alone, compared to 67.5 percent of the group of healthy girls. Several other research studies examining the fat-soluble vitamins in individuals with anorexia have found similar results; many anorexic individuals have normal or elevated amounts of vitamins A (including its forms retinol and carotenoids), D, and E.

Clinically, it is not precisely understood why levels of fat-soluble vitamins remain high in individuals with such restricted food intake. Whatever the reason may be, girls and women suffering from anorexia often do not require supplementation of these vitamins, as they already have adequate levels. However, there are exceptions. For example, when high-dose fish oil is taken, I recommend individuals take 200 IU of vitamin E in a multivitamin or vitamin E supplement. Vitamin E should always be taken in the form of d-alpha-tocopherol, as the less expensive synthetic dl-alpha-tocopherol is not as effective.

Vitamin Dependency

Vitamins and nutrition are essential to good health. In light of this understanding, it's only fitting that the U.S. government has created a set of dietary guidelines to help us maintain our health, the RDA. The standard recommendation for consuming nutrients set by the government is based on age and gender, what the government refers to as the recommended daily allowance.

Although the government had our best interests at heart, it failed to recognize our biochemical individuality. These nutritional standards don't take into account the variability from one individual to the next in the rates at which nutrients are absorbed, used, and excreted. Simply put, each individual has different nutritional needs. The world-renowned biochemist Roger Williams noted this in his seminal 1956 book *Biochemical Individuality*. In one example, Williams recognized that at any given time there is a high degree of variability in thiamine concentrations in the blood. Williams points out that while examining the thiamine requirements for 15 individuals, the then-Director of the Division of Nutrition, Department of National Health and Welfare of Canada, Dr. L. B. Pett arrived at figures ranging from 0.40 to 1.59 mg daily. Even in a small group of participants, the thiamine needs varied nearly four-fold.

Although the RDA is a good guide for supplementation, it may not be enough. In addition to biochemical individuality creating different nutritional needs, it has been acknowledged by several physicians that long-standing nutritional deficiencies may create increased nutrient needs—a vitamin dependency.

Abram Hoffer, MD, has been a proponent in highlighting instances of vitamin dependency. As mentioned in Chapter Eight, many of the chronic pellagrins that Hoffer treated required doses of vitamin B3 well above the recommended amount for adult men and women (60 to 70 times higher, respectively). Only high doses of supplementation over the course of several months led to improvements in their illness. These individuals had dramatically increased needs for vitamin B3 due to their long-standing deficiency.

Hoffer also encountered another instance of vitamin dependency when treating a Hong Kong war veteran. During World War II, captured Canadian soldiers were interned in Hong Kong by the Japanese. At one of these imprisonment camps, George Porteous, a Canadian soldier at the time, endured 44 months of extreme stress and starvation. After liberation, Porteous and the other soldiers were emaciated and experienced severe nutritional deficiencies. Even as Porteous and the others regained weight, they never regained their health. After the war, Porteous suffered from anxiety, tension, weakness, and arthritis. He was unable to even lift his arms above his head. After a regimen of high doses of B vitamins, all of Porteous' symptoms vanished and his health improved dramatically. Porteous required B vitamins in far excess of the RDA. When Porteous lowered the doses of his vitamins, his symptoms returned.

There are other instances in which vitamin-dependency states exist, such as in genetic disorders of childhood, and prolonged starvation. Chronic nutritional deficiency and stress create increased nutrient needs described as a state of vitamin dependency. For health improvement, individuals need more than the RDA of nutrients. Only with high doses does health return.

Chapter Nineteen

Optimal Nutritional Support:
Minerals

Patients with anorexia are typically prescribed only one mineral supplement: calcium. While calcium is certainly imperative for strong bone development, it is by no means the only mineral that a starving body requires. Severely limited and restricted food intake, coupled with the lack of nutrients found in many of today's foods, makes it extremely likely that those with anorexia are not receiving the minerals their bodies need for optimal physical and psychological functioning. This chapter will explain how essential minerals affect physical, psychological, and behavioral characteristics, and how mineral supplementation may augment not only general health, but also mental health.

Calcium

Calcium is essential for blood clotting, muscle contraction, nerve transmission, and blood vessel constriction and relaxation. It is also necessary for the development and maintenance of strong bones and teeth—and not just during childhood! In adulthood, bones are constantly being remodeled, a process that involves the breakdown of old bone and the formation of new. When the rate of bone resorption (demineralization) exceeds the rate of new bone formation, osteoporosis (thinning of the bones) can occur. Osteoporosis also develops in women who do not attain peak bone mass during adolescence and young adulthood. This is common with anorexia, where decreased calcium intake results in poor initial bone development.

How it relates to anorexia: People with anorexia usually have lower bone mineral density than normal, a condition that is often measurable soon after the onset of the eating disorder. Researchers have pointed to a variety of contributing factors, such as poor nutrition, low estrogen levels, and high levels of cortisol. Whatever the reason, it leads to an increased susceptibility to bone fractures and is very hard to reverse. In fact, the only therapy that consistently benefits bone mineral density is sustained weight recovery with resumption of menstrual periods.

Because calcium and vitamin D work together to ensure optimal calcium absorption and bone development, most calcium supplements contain vitamin D or recommend they be taken with vitamin D.

Recommended intake for healthy people: The AI for adolescents ages 14 to 18 is 1,300 mg per day; and for adults ages 19 to 50, 1,000 mg per day. Note: Research suggests that in addition to calcium and vitamin D, many other nutrients are necessary for healthy bones. Magnesium, phosphorous, boron, vitamin K, iron, fluoride, and copper all contribute to bone matrix development, bone mineralization, enzyme function, or they enhance calcium's actions.

Recommended amount for those with anorexia: The recommended AI from the diet or dietary supplements is usually sufficient. A frequent concern is that calcium supplementation is recommended without adequate magnesium or other minerals required for bone health. A further concern is that high doses of calcium supplementation can negatively affect the regulation of hormones required to absorb calcium.

Magnesium

Magnesium helps maintain normal function of the muscles, nerves, heart, bones, and immune system, and it is required for the function of more than 325 enzymes in the body. It is involved in energy production, the synthesis of protein, hormones, and neurotransmitters, and in the regulation of blood glucose levels. Magnesium deficiency is associated with heart disease, osteoporosis, migraine headaches, and pre-menstrual syndrome. It can also result in psychiatric and cognitive symptoms, including fatigue, memory difficulties, problems concentrating, irritability, anxiety, depression, and the tendency to overreact emotionally.

Sometimes called the "anti-stress" mineral, magnesium has been used successfully to treat depression, anxiety, and insomnia. Unfortunately, measuring serum blood levels doesn't give a true picture of magnesium status, as less than 1 percent of the magnesium in the body is found in the blood. Most magnesium is stored in the bones (60 percent), and the remainder is found inside the body's 60 trillion cells. In fact, during starvation, total body magnesium may decrease 20 percent with no measurable change in blood levels.

One of the reasons magnesium deficiency may be common is that it is one of the first minerals to be removed when food is processed and refined. For example, refined white flour contains only 16 percent of the amount of magnesium found in whole-wheat grains. Additionally, when there is stress on the body—be it mental stress, chronic pain, or surgery—magnesium is one of the first minerals to be depleted. Increased calcium intake, alcohol, and caffeine can also reduce the body's magnesium stores.

How it relates to anorexia: People with anorexia often have a magnesium deficiency due to decreased intake or increased excretion from stress. Anorexics frequently exhibit many of the symptoms mentioned above, including depression, anxiety, insomnia, and difficulty concentrating. Magnesium supplementation has been used to successfully treat depression, anxiety, and insomnia.

Recommended intake for healthy people: The RDA for magnesium is 360 mg per day for adolescent girls ages 14 to 18, and 310 mg per day for women ages 19 to 30. Unfortunately, most people consume only about 200 mg of magnesium per day.

One of the most common forms of magnesium, called magnesium oxide, is poorly absorbed and can act as a laxative; the magnesium is excreted in the stool. More easily absorbed oral forms include magnesium glycinate, magnesium citrate, and magnesium ascorbate. In addition, the body can absorb magnesium through the skin. Magnesium creams as well as magnesium-containing Epsom or bath salts may offer an easier way to provide supplementation.

Recommended amount for those with anorexia: I recommend 400 to 600 mg of magnesium per day, from dietary sources and nutritional supplements.

Potassium

Potassium is an essential mineral necessary for nerve-impulse transmission, skeletal and smooth muscle contraction, and heart function. It has been found to lower blood pressure, minimize the risk of kidney stones, and contribute to healthy bone development.

How it relates to anorexia: The level of potassium is tightly regulated in the body, and having too much (hyperkalemia) or too little (hypokalemia) can be fatal. Hyperkalemia, which results from overuse of certain diuretics, kidney failure, or trauma, occurs when potassium intake overwhelms the kidneys' ability to excrete it. Symptoms can range from tingling of the hands and feet and muscle weakness to temporary paralysis and cardiac arrhythmias.

Hypokalemia is more commonly seen in patients with eating disorders. This can result from low magnesium consumption, prolonged vomiting or diarrhea, laxative abuse, or certain diuretics. Severely low levels of potassium in the blood can cause paralysis and cardiac arrhythmias (abnormal heart electrical rhythms) that can be fatal. Because abnormally high or low levels of potassium can become life-threatening, people with eating disorders should have their levels regularly monitored by a healthcare provider.

Recommended intake for healthy people: The AI for potassium for females 14 and older is 4,700 mg per day. Because potassium can interact with a number of medications, including asthma medications, antibiotics, and decongestants, a healthcare provider should monitor potassium supplementation.

Recommended amount for those with anorexia: Potassium levels should be monitored regularly by a physician in patients with anorexia nervosa as changes in potassium can be life-threatening.

Iron

Iron plays an integral role in the formation of hemoglobin, a protein molecule found in red blood cells that binds oxygen and carries it to the cells. Iron is essential for the makeup of hundreds of proteins and enzymes that have roles throughout the body, including cellular energy metabolism, growth and reproduction, and the detoxification of harmful free radicals.

Iron deficiency can range from mild—when iron stores are low but hemoglobin levels are normal—to more severe—when both the levels of iron and hemoglobin are affected. When iron deficiency involves low levels of hemoglobin, symptoms of anemia can occur, including fatigue, lack of energy, irritability, and depression. Low levels of iron have also been found to lead to developmental and cognitive delays in both children and adults. Accordingly, other studies have shown that iron supplements when indicated can improve cognitive function.

How it relates to anorexia: The type of iron (called heme iron) that is best absorbed by the body happens to be most plentiful in red meat, poultry, and fish, foods that people with anorexia frequently avoid. Heavy exercise and dieting—both common in anorexia—can further deplete the amount of iron in the body.

Recommended intake for healthy people: For adolescent girls ages 14 to 18, the RDA for iron is 15 mg per day; for adult women ages 19 to 50, it is 18 mg per day. Iron can inhibit the absorption of zinc when the two are taken together on an empty stomach, and iron absorption itself can be decreased when iron and calcium are taken together.

Recommended amount for those with anorexia: Many patients stop taking their iron supplements after a few days due to bothersome gastrointestinal side effects including nausea, vomiting, or constipation. Because of this, I recommend iron in the form of ferrous bisglycinate chelate. Well absorbed, without gastrointestinal side effects, this form of iron does not block the absorption of other nutrients.

For serum iron values below below 60 mcg/dL, I recommend a daily dose of at least 50 mg of iron in the form of ferrous bisglycinate, which has excellent bioavailability and does not cause constipation or GI upset. Note: Do not take more iron than is prescribed. Acute iron poisoning can be life-threatening.

Copper

Most of the copper inside the body is in the form of ceruloplasmin, a substance critical for storing and using iron. Like too little iron, a lack of copper can cause anemia, with symptoms of depression, fatigue, lack of energy, and irritability. Copper also functions as an antioxidant. Antioxidants are beneficial substances that can promote overall health by working to detoxify harmful substances called oxygen free radicals that are thought to cause cancer, heart disease, and other chronic diseases.

How it relates to anorexia: Copper is involved in the formation of brain neurotransmitters such as norepinephrine and dopamine, which are involved in psychological functioning and mental health. A copper deficiency can lead to decreased amounts of these neurotransmitters and symptoms of depression. Depression is commonly seen in individuals with anorexia. In contrast, excess copper in the body can cause too much dopamine activity resulting in psychological symptoms, including paranoia. Too much copper in the body is also associated with anxiety, hypothyroidism, insomnia, memory loss, and low zinc levels.

Recommended intake for healthy people: The RDA for copper is 890 mcg per day for adolescents ages 14 to 18, and 900 mcg per day for adults over 19 years old. Different forms of effective copper supplements exist. Too much zinc, iron, and vitamin C will inhibit copper absorption from the intestine. And too much copper can lead to low levels of vitamins C, B6, and folate, as well as the mineral manganese.

Recommended amounts for those with anorexia: The RDA is usually sufficient unless testing reveals low or elevated copper. If there are abnormal copper levels, a health professional should guide treatment.

Manganese

Manganese contributes to healthy bone and cartilage development, wound healing, and to the metabolism of carbohydrates, amino acids, and cholesterol. A deficiency of the mineral is associated with osteoporosis and diabetes.

Manganese is also critical to optimal thyroid function. When functioning normally, the thyroid gland produces two hormones called T4 (thyroxine) and T3 (triiodothyronine). Problems emerge when people have too much or too little thyroid hormone. Too much (hyperthyroidism) can cause an increase in heart rate, palpitations, muscle loss, hair loss, insomnia, and anxiety. Too little (hypothyroidism) can cause increased sensitivity to cold, weight gain, forgetfulness, sluggishness, depression, and feelings of fatigue. Manganese helps keep thyroid levels in check.

Similar to copper, manganese also functions as an antioxidant, contributing to optimal overall health. In addition, it plays a role in neurological functioning, as it appears to affect the amount of dopamine in the brain. Too much manganese has been found to cause depression, anxiety, and excessive fatigue, and may impair concentration, and toxic amounts can cause neurological symptoms similar to those of Parkinson's disease, including tremors and extremely slow movements.

How it relates to anorexia: There is no literature to support a direct relationship with anorexia, but normal manganese levels help ensure optimal brain function.

Recommended intake for healthy people: The AI of manganese for female adolescents ages 14 to 18 is 1.6 mg per day, and 1.8 mg per day for females ages 19 and older. Various effective supplemental forms exist.

Dietary and supplemental iron, as well as supplemental magnesium and calcium, have been found to reduce manganese absorption.

Recommended amounts for those with anorexia: The AI is sufficient and is usually found in a multivitamin. If testing reveals a deficiency or excess of manganese, then a health professional who is skilled in nutritional medication should guide supplementation.

Chromium

Chromium helps the body regulate blood levels of glucose, increasing the ability of the hormone insulin to transport glucose into the liver, muscle, and fat cells where it can be used as energy. By maintaining normal glucose levels in the blood, chromium may help combat "sugar cravings."

Chromium also helps with lipid (fat) metabolism. While its exact role is still unclear, the mineral has been shown to lower low-density lipoprotein (LDL) cholesterol and triglycerides, the "bad" fats that contribute to heart disease, and raise high-density lipoprotein (HDL) cholesterol, the "good" cholesterol that protects heart health.

How it relates to anorexia: Chromium appears to have antidepressant properties and may potentially help ameliorate the symptoms of depression commonly seen in individuals with anorexia. One study at the University of North Carolina School of Medicine involved subjects who were diagnosed with depression, but were not on any psychiatric medications. Although the patients' symptoms differed slightly, the one thing they had in common was an increased appetite with carbohydrate cravings. Subjects were given 400 to 600 mcg of chromium per day. The results were striking. All of these patients, who had for years failed to respond to multiple treatments, became less depressed and had better daily functioning. In another study, the subjects were patients with atypical depression and symptoms of increased appetite, weight gain, and excessive sleepiness. After being given daily doses of 600 mcg of chromium picolinate, the patients had less depression and carbohydrate cravings; some even completely stopped overeating!

Recommended intake for healthy people: The AI is 24 mcg per day for girls ages 14 to 18, and 25 mcg per day for women aged 19 to 50. Chromium supplements can be effective in different forms. Some conditions, such as infection, increased exercise, and stress can increase the need for chromium. Supplemental vitamin C can increase chromium absorption, resulting in higher levels of the mineral in the bloodstream.

Recommended amounts for those with anorexia: The RDA is sufficient and is usually found in a multivitamin. If testing reveals a deficiency or excess, then a health professional who is skilled in the use of nutritional supplements should guide supplementation.

Selenium

Selenium has been shown to slow tumor growth and protect against numerous types of cancers, including those of the lung, breast, prostate, cervix, uterus, colon, rectum, and GI system. An antioxidant, selenium also contributes to cardiovascular health, lowering the level of harmful, plaque-inducing LDL cholesterol. And, like manganese, selenium is required for normal thyroid function. Too little of this mineral can result in depression, sluggishness, fatigue, and weight gain.

How it relates to anorexia: Selenium appears to have a direct effect on brain function and mood. In one study conducted in England, subjects were given either 100 mcg of selenium or a placebo daily for five weeks. Questionnaires assessed people's moods at different points during the study. The researchers found that people taking selenium reported feeling happier and less anxious. With emerging antidepressant and anti-anxiety effects, selenium can potentially help reduce these symptoms in anorexic patients.

Recommended intake for healthy people: The RDA for selenium for those aged 14 and up is 55 mcg per day, although GI disorders can decrease the absorption of selenium, so more may be needed. Too much selenium can cause selenosis and GI upset, hair loss, white blotchy nails, and fatigue.

Recommended amounts for those with anorexia: The RDA is sufficient and is usually found in a multivitamin. If testing reveals a deficiency or excess, then a health professional should guide supplementation.

Iodine

Iodine is primarily used by the thyroid gland to make thyroid hormones (T4 and T3), which affect the metabolism, heart, and mood. It also strengthens the immune system, acting both as an antioxidant and as an anti-tumor agent, and it may decrease the pain and symptoms associated with fibrocystic breast disease.

Without enough of the mineral *in utero*, the consequent hypothyroidism can cause babies to be born deaf or with severe physical or cognitive developmental disorders. In growing children, iodine deficiency can result in intellectual impairment. Studies have demonstrated not only that iodine-deficient students are slower visual and verbal learners compared to peers who have sufficient iodine levels, but also that iodine repletion for a deficiency can improve information processing, including visual problem solving and fine motor skills.

How it relates to anorexia: There is no literature to support a direct relationship with anorexia, but normal iodine levels help ensure optimal brain function.

Recommended intake for healthy people: The RDA for iodine is 150 mcg per day. Severe deficiencies are rare, but they can exist, especially in those whose diets are vegetarian or contain no iodized salt.

Iodine deficiencies need to be corrected carefully. Excessive amounts of iodine can cause hyperthyroidism or, in those predisposed to thyroid problems, the reverse—hypothyroidism.

Recommended amounts for those with anorexia: The RDA is sufficient and is usually found in a multivitamin. If testing reveals a deficiency or excess, then a health professional should guide supplementation.

Chapter Twenty

Optimal Nutritional Support:
Proteins and Amino Acids

Proteins and their amino acid building blocks are essential for optimal brain function. To underscore their importance, let me simply say this: In my 20 years of clinical practice, the most helpful intervention I have found in treating clinical symptoms associated with anorexia and depression has been to give amino acid supplements to those who have been found to have an amino acid deficiency.

The Building Blocks of Life

Proteins are the main building blocks for all of the processes and structures of the human body. Without proteins, life would cease.

Amino Acids

Essential*	Non-Essential**
Isoleucine	Alanine
Leucine	Arginine
Lysine	Asparagine
Methionine	Aspartic Acid
Phenylalanine	Cysteine
Threonine	Glutamic Acid
Tryptophan	Glutamine
Valine	Glycine
	Histidine
	Proline
	Serine
	Tyrosine

* Must be obtained from food.
** Can be made within body from essential amino acids and cofactors.

Structural proteins are used to build and repair injured cells, including skin, hair, bones, fingernails, and internal organs. For example, proteins are responsible for replacing the lining of our intestine every seven days or so. Functional proteins are necessary to make enzymes, hormones, and neurotransmitters. These substances affect the way we function, including how messages are carried from one organ to another, how our bodies digest food, and how the brain and nervous system work.

Using the blueprint of DNA, our bodies can create more than 50,000 different protein molecules. What is more amazing, though, is that all of these proteins are comprised of various combinations of only 20 components, called amino acids. Amino acids can be classified into two types: essential and non-essential. Essential amino acids cannot be made within our bodies and are obtained only through the foods we ingest or via supplements. In order for enzymes to be made, or for new cells to be built, we need a daily supply of essential amino acids. Although non-essential amino acids can be found in foods, they can also be made within the body from essential amino acids, vitamins, and other mineral cofactors. Thus, a daily supply is not as critical. The eight essential amino acids and 12 non-essential amino acids are listed in the table on page 197.

Both animal- and plant-based foods contain amino acids, but only animal foods contain all of the essential amino acids. Some animal-based foods include meat, fish, turkey, chicken, eggs, milk, cheese and yogurt. Plant-based foods such as beans, peas, nuts, peanut butter, and seeds are also good sources of essential amino acids, but they might not contain them all in a single food. Because of this, vegetarians and vegans need to eat a variety of legumes, nuts, seeds, grains, and vegetables every day in order to obtain all of the essential amino acids.

How much protein do people need to eat each day? The general rule for protein intake is about .4 grams per pound of body weight per day. For example, a person who weighs 120 pounds would need about 48 grams of protein per day (120 x 0.4 = 48). People who exercise heavily require increased amounts of protein.

When people eat foods such as chicken or beef, what they are actually eating is large proteins comprised of peptides, or chains made up of amino acids. Once a bite of chicken, for example, is ingested, it travels from the mouth down through the esophagus to the stomach and intestines where it is digested and broken up into smaller pieces. Digestive enzymes, as well as hydrochloric acid, are needed to fully digest the proteins into smaller peptides, which the body can then absorb and break down further into individual amino acids that can be used to form new proteins.

Whenever the body needs new proteins, various enzymes act on the required amino acids and link them together to make peptides, which are then combined to create proteins. Proteins can have thousands of amino acids bonded together in specific sequences. Imagine a huge, ever-changing three-dimensional jigsaw puzzle that is constantly being put together and taken apart, depending on the changing needs of a body.

Most relevant to psychiatry and anorexia is the role of amino acids as precursors of substances called neurotransmitters.

Neurotransmitters and Mental Health

In the brain, our thoughts, emotions, and behaviors are influenced and regulated by chemical substances called neurotransmitters. When neurotransmitters are released from the ends of nerve cells, the resulting electrical impulses influence how we think, feel, and act. In anorexia, for example, individuals commonly have profound distortions in how they view their bodies. They often believe they are able to feel the fat growing on their arms or legs within hours of eating a meal. Every aspect of their lives is consumed by obsessions about weight, food, and body image, and few hours go by during which anorexics are free of these thoughts.

These obsessive thoughts and perceptual disturbances result from the malfunctioning of a starving brain. In an effort to improve patients' moods and behaviors, psychiatrists prescribe medications. Psychiatric medications affect levels of neurotransmitters in the brain in different ways. Although hundreds of neurotransmitters have been identified, there are three that have been studied extensively and have been found to have profound influences on emotion and behavior. They are dopamine, norepinephrine, and serotonin. All three are made from essential amino acid precursors obtained from the diet. The precursor for serotonin is tryptophan, and the precursor for dopamine and norepinephrine is phenylalanine. The chemical pathway from amino acid precursor to neurotransmitter is somewhat complicated and requires vitamins such as folic acid, B6, and B12, as well as minerals such as zinc, magnesium, and copper. Zinc is essential for enzymes that turn amino acids into neurotransmitters.

Most neurotransmitters are under precursor control, which means that eating extremely small amounts of amino acids in the diet will result in deficient amounts of the related neurotransmitters in the brain. This can help explain why, in general, psychiatric medications have consistently proven to be ineffective for treating anorexia nervosa. Their ineffectiveness is likely due to inadequate amounts of available amino acid precursors.

Let's consider the example of a medication like Prozac, which falls into the class of medications called SSRIs. These medications work by blocking the reabsorption of the serotonin molecules into the neurons that produced them. As a result, the serotonin can stay in the synapse (space between neurons) longer, having a more pronounced effect. Low levels of serotonin in the brain are associated with symptoms of anxiety, panic, and depression. But what happens if a person does not eat enough tryptophan in the diet? The brain will not make sufficient serotonin.

When individuals with anorexia restrict their food intake, they frequently stop eating protein. This can lead to an amino acid deficiency. But people with anorexia can become deficient in amino acids in another way. Even if they do eat protein, their bodies may be so damaged from long-term self-starvation that they do not have adequate amounts of critical digestive enzymes. When proteins cannot be digested normally, they cannot be absorbed in the gastrointestinal tract to later be used by the body.

Amino Acids and Anorexia

As part of a comprehensive nutritional evaluation for new patients, I routinely order blood or urinary amino acid tests. In testing hundreds of patients with anorexia, I have consistently found that they have low levels of essential amino acids. This probably represents a combination of poor dietary intake as well as inadequate protein digestion.

In addition to mental health symptoms such as panic, depression, obsessive thoughts, and compulsive behaviors, physical symptoms can stem from a protein and amino acid deficiency. Muscle wasting, heart abnormalities, thinning of skin, and a susceptibility to infections are common. Cuts and bruises can take longer to heal, and hair and nails can become brittle, breaking easily.

When individuals with anorexia drastically reduce their protein intake, the very little protein they do eat is used for only the most vital bodily processes. Consequently, nonessential biological functions are shut down. For example, hormone production is slowed, causing menstruation to stop.

In general, there is a paucity of research examining the relationship between anorexia and amino acid levels. The few studies that have been done substantiate the idea that individuals with anorexia commonly have amino acid deficiencies. One study found the levels of leucine, tyrosine, and lysine to be significantly lower in anorexics than in healthy control subjects. Another measured tryptophan blood levels in patients with anorexia upon admission to the hospital as well as during their refeeding treatment. Not surprisingly, the researchers found the individuals to have significantly lower tryptophan levels on admission.

Lastly, a recent study in Germany measured levels of various amino acids in three groups: weight-recovered anorexic outpatients, acutely underweight anorexics, and healthy women. Results from a one-time blood sample showed that both the weight-recovered and acutely ill subjects with anorexia had significantly lower levels of tryptophan and phenylalanine than the healthy control subjects. Clearly, a normal weight did not reflect healthy eating habits or normal amino acid levels even though the weight-recovered individuals had a normal BMI, regained menstruation, and had not binged, purged, or engaged in restrictive behaviors for at least three months. The weight-recovered individuals may have been eating diets that were nutrient-deficient. This was demonstrated in the second part of the study in which underweight patients with anorexia were followed in a highly structured inpatient treatment program with careful monitoring of dietary intake. At the end of the program, the patients had gained some weight and there was no difference between their amino acid levels and those of healthy controls.

This study supports what I see every day. The focus on weight restoration without careful monitoring of nutritional repletion leaves patients vulnerable to chronic nutritional deficiencies.

Susan was a 32-year-old executive who was on a 10-year rollercoaster ride, working as a high-functioning executive and experiencing acute relapses of her anorexia. After meeting with Susan, I recommended a comprehensive nutritional evaluation, including amino acid testing. Not too surprisingly, she was found to be deficient in most of the essential amino acids. Based on her deficiencies, we created a custom formula of the essential amino acids and vitamin cofactors.

After starting to take her amino acid supplement, Susan noticed a difference in her mood and energy levels within only a few weeks. She commented that her disordered thoughts about her eating were the "quietest" they had been in years. But it wasn't until Susan forgot to pack her supplements with her on a trip that she truly appreciated their effect. By the third day of traveling and being without her amino acids, Susan noticed that she was more fatigued as well as increasingly anxious about food and eating. She now makes sure to always bring her amino acid supplements when she travels away from home.

Amino Acid Supplementation

The brain cannot function optimally—or even normally—without an adequate supply of amino acids. However, urging an individual with anorexia to eat meat will not solve the problem. Adding large amounts of protein to a diet without giving malnourished individuals supplements and digestive enzymes will only create increased physical discomfort (bloating, diarrhea, and constipation) of the digestive tract. For this reason, until patients are eating adequately and capable of digesting protein, amino acid supplements should be taken to support nutritional recovery.

For younger adolescents who have not been ill for long and who might still have sufficient digestive enzymes and hydrochloric acid to digest protein, commercially available protein powders can be helpful and are usually well tolerated. For individuals struggling for many years, though, free-form amino acids are pivotal for recovery. As single molecules, free-form amino acids are not attached by peptide bonds to other amino acids, so they do not need to be digested. They can be absorbed easily and directly into the body, ready to help rebuild tissues, make hormones, synthesize neurotransmitters, and help reverse the physical deterioration that has taken place.

Recommendations

I have found that amino acids can be the most important supplement that individuals with anorexia can take to improve mood, decrease distorted thinking, and decrease anxiety. I routinely recommend a blend of all of the essential amino acids; this may come either in capsule or powder form. Amino acids will simply augment the body's ability to rebuild and restore health! When individuals with anorexia feel better physically and mentally, they can have an easier time partnering with their healthcare provider and family in the recovery process.

I would caution against taking supplements of isolated single amino acids. Many amino acids are sold in 500-mg strengths with marketing claims ranging from "enhanced muscle building" to "enhanced sexual stamina." These are not the supplements I recommend. Amino acid supplementation should only be done under the supervision of a healthcare professional or physician who is knowledgeable about potential side effects and drug interactions.

Optimal Nutritional Support: Antioxidants

If you walk by any supermarket shelf displaying rows of fruit juices or teas, the word "antioxidant" is everywhere. But what are antioxidants, and why are they receiving so much recent attention in health care news?

To understand what antioxidants do, you must first understand what free radicals are. Free radicals, which are atoms with an unpaired number of electrons, are created during certain chemical reactions in the body. Improperly contained free radicals, particularly oxygen free radicals, have the potential to damage our cells and DNA. They are thought to be implicated in cancer, heart disease, and other chronic diseases. Antioxidants are molecules that prevent oxidative damage from oxygen free radicals and assist our immune system. Beneficial substances, they keep us healthy by interacting with and inactivating harmful oxygen free radicals.

Previous chapters have already mentioned a number of antioxidants. Minerals such as copper, manganese, and selenium are antioxidants. They work with enzymes in the body called superoxide dismutase and glutathione peroxidase. Vitamins A, C, and E are also antioxidants. Vitamin E actually encompasses eight different antioxidants; it keeps cells healthy by preventing cell membranes from being destroyed by free radicals.

But many more antioxidants exist; they are found in fruits, vegetables, grains, flowers, green and black tea, and red wine. Antioxidants are classified into categories called polyphenols, carotenoids, and flavonoids. One important antioxidant subcategory is oligomeric proanthocyanidins (OPC). OPCs are found in the bark, leaves and blossoms of trees; skins and peels of fruit; and skins of nuts and seeds.

In over 20 years of practice I have found that antioxidants, OPCs, and specifically green tea, grape seed, pine bark, and blueberries have the most potential for enhancing brain health for anorexia nervosa and other psychiatric disorders.

Medical Benefits of Antioxidants

OPCs can have widespread and beneficial effects on a number of medical conditions. For example, OPCs help make blood vessel walls in the circulatory system stronger and strengthen connective tissue called collagen; they have been shown to provide relief for bruising, varicose veins, and hemorrhoids. Slowing the production of histamine, OPCs can also help relieve allergy symptoms. Pine bark, available as the brand Pycnogenol, can counteract damaging effects of ultraviolet radiation, help with sugar regulation in diabetes, and help prevent cardiovascular disease. Grape seed extract can help reduce high blood pressure and relieve symptoms of premenstrual syndrome. Green tea, containing a flavonoid called epigallocatechin gallate (EGCG), can help decrease tumor growth as well as prevent cancerous tumor spread. Recent research has demonstrated mood-enhancing properties of green tea.

The Effects of Antioxidants on Mental Health

Not all medications are able to cross the blood-brain barrier; in fact, that is one of the reasons it can be challenging to treat diseases affecting the brain—the medication cannot get from the blood to the cerebrospinal fluid that circulates around the brain. The antioxidants that cross the blood-brain barrier are thought to positively affect mental health by helping protect neurons (brain cells) from being damaged by free radicals. OPCs easily cross the blood-brain barrier and are unique phytochemicals for brain health.

One example of antioxidants improving mental health is the effect green tea has on mood. Two studies done in Japan assessed a number of characteristics of adults in the general population, including how much green tea they reported consuming each day as well as how they felt emotionally. In the first study, the researchers found that people living in the community over the age of 70 who drank green tea more frequently were happier and reported fewer symptoms of depression (i.e., feeling dissatisfied with life, feeling that life is empty, and feeling helpless). Those drinking more than four cups of green tea a day were 44 percent less likely to have some of these symptoms of depression. The second study found that, for individuals ages 40 and older, those who drank green tea less often reported feeling hopeless, sad, nervous, and worthless.

Key ingredients in green tea have also been shown to improve cognition and attention. A 2008 study published in *The Journal of Nutrition* examined the active ingredients in green tea (caffeine and L-theanine) and their effect on a series of tasks requiring acute attention. L-theanine, found almost exclusively in tea plants, has been shown to have antioxidant properties and neuroprotective effects. In this study, 16 participants consumed either a placebo, 100 mg of L-theanine, 50 mg of caffeine, or a combination of both L-theanine and caffeine. After ingestion they were asked to perform a series of attention tasks. The study participants performed their tasks more accurately when both L-theanine and caffeine were taken.

Helping Improve Attention and Concentration with OPCs

In addition to often experiencing symptoms of depression, individuals with anorexia frequently struggle with difficulty concentrating and paying attention. Complaints of being unable to focus are nearly ubiquitous in the patients whom I see and treat. Over the course of their treatment, many have been prescribed powerful stimulant medications such as those used in the management of ADHD. Unfortunately, this class of medications can be far from ideal in treating individuals with anorexia. One of the main side effects of stimulants is decreased appetite—the medication can facilitate individuals with anorexia to restrict food!

In my clinical research over the years, I have examined the EEG patterns of hundreds and hundreds of individuals, both with ADHD or anorexia, and found that EEGs from patients with ADHD resemble those of patients with anorexia. An EEG looks at several classes of brainwaves. Theta waves are slow and are associated with daydreaming, inattention, and disorganization. In contrast, beta wave activity is associated with an ability to focus, organize, and pay attention. Often, people with untreated ADHD as well as individuals with anorexia demonstrate high theta waves, and high theta-to-beta wave ratios. This is not surprising, as both groups similarly complain of being unable to focus and concentrate! In the case of anorexia, I believe that the high theta waves stem from the brain being starved and malnourished.

Research has found that OPCs can provide a healthier, yet still effective, treatment for the symptoms of impaired concentration and difficulty focusing. In one study, children whose ADHD was treated with Pycnogenol (pine bark) for one month showed more improvement in clinical symptoms both at school and at home than children whose ADHD was treated with a placebo. Specifically, after a month on the supplement, the children had improved attention, improved visual-motor coordination and concentration, and reduced hyperactivity.

I began using OPCs about 15 years ago in treating both children and adults with ADHD who were unable to tolerate conventional medications.

Here is one example: A 27-year-old woman came to me with complaints of being unable to concentrate to the point that her life and work were disrupted. She had foggy thinking, was unable to focus for periods of time, and had difficulty sticking with projects at work. Her laboratory testing was normal, but her brain EEG showed that she had increased theta waves as well as an increased theta-to-beta wave ratio.

I recommended she take an OPC supplement from mixed whole-food sources. Within one month, she began to feel "clearer" and found that she was able to concentrate for longer periods of time. I repeated her EEG pattern and found it to be significantly changed. On OPC supplementation, she not only had a decrease in theta wave activity, but also demonstrated an increase in her beta wave activity. Completely different, her EEG results supported her reports of being able to focus and attend better to what she was doing.

This patient is only one example. Treating hundreds of patients, I have seen improvements in school performance, work performance, and behavior with OPC supplementation.

For patients with anorexia, I frequently recommend OPCs as a source of antioxidants that can easily cross the blood-brain barrier to address problems with concentrating and focusing. For patients who cannot tolerate conventional stimulant medication, this alternative treatment has shown great success. Similar to the ADHD patients, the clinical improvement in individuals with anorexia is remarkable.

Green tea as a beverage is also a healthy alternative that can provide many benefits, including improved attention.

Gaby, a 24-year-old college student, had been struggling with eating disorders most of her life. She struggled with anorexia nervosa throughout adolescence, later developed bulimia nervosa, and more recently started restricting her food intake and exercising compulsively. As a result, Gaby started losing significant weight.

Over the course of 10 years, Gaby had multiple trials of medications, with little relief until she was treated with rEEG guided medications. The medications that provided the most relief from her anxiety and obsessive worrying about calories and weight were a combination of Lamictal and Ritalin. The stimulant medication, however, would decrease her appetite and facilitate restrictive eating behaviors. The Ritalin was discontinued and Gaby started taking OPC supplements with Lamictal. Within one month of OPC supplementation Gaby was able to not only focus better on schoolwork, but also found relief from her obsessive worrying just as she had on the stimulant medication.

Chapter Twenty-Two

Celiac Disease: The Right Food May Be the Wrong Food

For many of us, eating the foods we were told are the most nutritious may actually be causing us serious physical and psychological harm. For example, what could be more nutritious than whole-wheat bread? Isn't it one of the most healthful foods you can eat? Not if you have celiac disease. When a person with celiac disease eats foods like bread that contain gluten, a protein found in wheat and other grains, the immune system mistakes the gluten for an invading enemy and launches a full-fledged attack on this normally harmless protein. This useless battle damages the lining of the digestive tract, just as real warfare harms innocent bystanders.

Over time, the damage caused by the autoimmune reaction to gluten makes it difficult or impossible for the body to absorb certain nutrients from foods, and the person can experience severe digestive problems, nutritional deficiencies, cancer, and a significantly increased risk of early death. In one study, the mortality risk of people with undiagnosed celiac disease over a 45-year period was four times that of people without the disease!

To make matters worse, the offending substance, gluten, is among the most ubiquitous of food ingredients. Name any grain product you can think of—breads, cereals, pizza, pasta, muffins, bagels, cakes, and cookies—and gluten is almost certain to be in it. What's more, gluten is often hidden in other food products, where it's often used to bind ingredients

Grain Products that Contain Gluten

- Baking mixes
- Beer
- Bread
- Cakes and pies
- Pretzels
- Cereal

- Cookies/crackers
- Pastries
- Doughnuts
- Muffins
- Pasta

together (as in processed meats and vegetarian meat substitutes) or as a thickener for added body (used in sauces and salad dressings). See the lists in this chapter for foods that contain gluten.

Although celiac disease was once a rare problem, the incidence is rising dramatically. It's four times more common today than it was 50 years ago, a fact that may not be too surprising considering the prevalence of gluten in our SAD. Nearly one out of every 133 Americans suffers from the ailment—although many of them don't know it or have been misdiagnosed with another problem. Celiac disease is actually more common than the statistics indicate because its symptoms mimic those of so many other disorders, and that confusion can lead to a delay in diagnosis of as long as ten years!

Celiac disease, however, is not a result of high amounts of gluten in our diets. In order to have celiac disease, a person must not only have the necessary genes, but must also have activated those genes through exposure to some environmental trigger. An estimated 30 to 40 percent of people worldwide have the gene variants responsible for celiac disease; yet only 1 percent of the population develops the disease. Although it's fairly safe to say that almost everyone is exposed to gluten, the reasons most people are immune are unknown.

Celiac disease can cause symptoms in every organ and system of the body: abdominal pain and gas, diarrhea, constipation, weakness and weight loss, as well as anemia, fatigue, reproductive issues (infertility and miscarriages), joint pain, arthritis and osteoporosis, skin lesions, and changes in behavior, memory loss, mood swings, irritability, and depression.

Sarah's Story

Now 21, Sarah first started restricting her food intake and obsessively counting calories the summer before she went to college. While main-

---

Foods that May Contain Hidden Gluten

- Ice cream
- Ketchup
- Soy sauce
- Licorice
- Sauces (thickened with flour)
- Salad dressings
- Chutneys and pickles
- Instant cocoa
- Processed meats
- Meat substitutes (e.g. vegetarian burgers, nuggets, etc.)
- Spices (with anti-caking agents)

Symptoms of Celiac Disease

- Abdominal cramps and stomach pain
- Chronic diarrhea and flatulence
- An inability to absorb fats resulting in fatty stools
- Dermatitis herpetiformis: blistered, itchy skin rash
- Failure to thrive and grow in children
- Stunted growth
- Malnutrition, anemia, and fatigue
- Osteoporosis, bone pain, and bone loss
- Seizures and other neurological issues
- Lactose intolerance

taining her daily two-hour exercise regimen, she survived solely on cereal during the week, eating one bowl each for breakfast, lunch, and dinner. Weekends were spent binging on pasta, candy, cookies, and ice cream.

After meals, she often felt nauseous or overcome with stomach cramps and bloating. Worst of all, she frequently had diarrhea.

Over time, Sarah became so nervous about eating and the way it made her body feel, that she began to chew her food and spit it out before swallowing. Not eating was better than feeling the pain of digesting her food. If Sarah did allow herself to swallow, she'd likely vomit to avoid the discomfort of digesting her food.

Sarah, a junior in college, hadn't been going to class because she felt so ill and hopeless all of the time. She felt very alone, because her family, friends, and boyfriend didn't know about her struggle with eating. At 5 feet 6 inches, Sarah was about 20 pounds below her ideal weight.

After seeing a therapist for depression over a six-month span, she announced that unless she got help for the way she ate, she didn't want to live. According to Sarah, anything was better than the way she was living; she even hoped that she would be hit by a car. Sarah felt utterly hopeless when it came to eating—she couldn't stop herself from spitting out any food that she put in her mouth because she was afraid of the stomach discomfort waiting for her when she swallowed. Disgusted and feeling powerless from her inability to control her eating, Sarah sometimes cut her ankles or arms to make herself feel better.

When Sarah was referred to me, she was desperate to get better. After reviewing her medical history, I noticed all of the digestive symptoms that plagued her while she subsisted on a diet almost completely based on grain products. Blood tests confirmed that Sarah was sensitive to gluten (in wheat), and a biopsy proved positive for celiac disease.

I immediately eliminated gluten from Sarah's diet and started her on a variety of nutritional supplements, including B vitamins and zinc. After a few weeks on the diet plan, Sarah began eating better. Meals no longer ended with her bent over in pain. And so far, she has restored weight. Beyond just eating better, she's feeling better, too. Her mood has improved dramatically, she enjoys school now, and she no longer feels so alone. She's on the road to recovery.

Celiac Disease and Nutritional Deficiencies: Vitamin and Mineral Deficiencies

Damage to the lining of the gut is the main symptom of celiac disease. Once damaged, the gut can no longer digest food properly, and the absorption of macronutrients such as protein and fats is impaired. In particular, absorption of the amino acid tryptophan and the other essential amino acids is impaired. Furthermore, vitamin and mineral absorption is also impaired, resulting in deficiencies of the fat-soluble vitamins A, D, E, and K, as well as folic acid, vitamin B6, vitamin B12, and minerals such as iron, zinc, magnesium, and calcium.

As those with celiac disease begin to eliminate grain products from their diet, they may still be vulnerable to vitamin and mineral deficiencies. For instance, it's been noted that many people on a gluten-free diet will develop vitamin B deficiencies.

Celiac Disease and Nutritional Deficiencies: Low Zinc Levels

Nutritional deficiencies are common in patients with celiac disease. Zinc deficiency has been found in children and adults with celiac disease! This may be a result of poor absorption of the nutrient due to the effects of gluten on the small intestine, but it's also been theorized that zinc deficiency may contribute to celiac disease. This represents a double jeopardy for the patient with anorexia, since celiac disease and zinc deficiency are both associated with appetite changes, weight loss, GI distress, and depression.

Typically, the body's zinc level normalizes after about a year on a gluten-free diet. As you have already learned, supplementation with zinc may correct this deficiency.

Celiac Disease and Anorexia Nervosa

What does celiac disease have to do with anorexia? The two share certain characteristics, including severe digestive problems and nutritional deficiencies, weight loss, abdominal cramps, bloating, depression, anemia, skin problems, and osteoporosis, making it difficult to distinguish between the two.

In some cases, a person can be diagnosed with anorexia when the problem is actually celiac disease. In other cases, a person who has both diseases may not know it because of the overlap in symptoms. The symptoms of celiac disease can also exacerbate those seen with anorexia. For instance, celiac disease makes it physically difficult to eat, practically ensuring that those with both diseases will do their best to avoid food. To make matters worse, many of the medical consequences of celiac disease compound the health risks seen in anorexia and complicate treatment.

In short, the presence of celiac disease can confuse, delay, and compound the proper diagnosis and treatment of anorexia nervosa. And plenty of people don't even know they have this condition.

Celiac disease has far-ranging effects. Although celiac disease is known to cause many troublesome digestive problems and nutrient deficiencies, it has also been linked to neurologic and psychiatric syndromes. The deficiencies of important nutrients such as folic acid, vitamin B6, and amino acids—especially tryptophan—that are common in celiac disease, may lead to disturbances in "feel good" brain chemicals such as serotonin. A deficiency in serotonin is associated with depression and aggressive behavior. For instance, several studies have associated the digestive disorder with depression, which affects about a third of patients with celiac disease. In one research study, adolescents with celiac disease had a 31 percent risk of developing major depression, while healthy kids had a 7 percent risk. Other research has linked gluten intolerance and the nutritional deficiencies it can produce to an assortment of neurological disorders including migraine headaches, seizures, dementia, neuropathy (nerve pain), schizophrenia, developmental delays, learning disorders, behavior disorders, and autism.

Ironically, as we've seen with zinc deficiency and anorexia nervosa, the symptoms and complaints associated with celiac disease can closely mimic or exacerbate those seen with anorexia. Celiac disease creates a "double insult" to appropriate nutrition and growth when it is present alongside anorexia. Symptoms shared by the two disorders include weight loss, abdominal cramps, bloating, depression, anemia, and skin problems. As a result of malnutrition, both disorders can also cause irreversible damage to bone development and result in osteoporosis.

Symptoms Common to Celiac Disease and Anorexia

Both celiac disease and anorexia can affect nearly every organ and organ system of the body, causing a multitude of symptoms, including:

- abdominal pain
- anemia
- arthritis
- behavioral changes
- bowel gas
- constipation
- depression
- diarrhea
- fatigue
- irritability

- joint pain
- memory loss
- mood swings
- osteoporosis
- reproductive issues (infertility and miscarriages)
- skin lesions
- weakness
- weight loss

With so many symptoms in common, is it any wonder that celiac disease is often mistaken for anorexia?

Although the relationship between anorexia nervosa and celiac disease has not been studied at length, several published papers suggest that celiac disease may be a cause for the development of eating disorders such as anorexia nervosa, especially in young children. For instance, in one study published in 2008 in the journal *Psychosomatics*, the development of an eating disorder in adolescents was associated with the symptoms of celiac disease. The authors of the study suggested that young patients who suffer from the symptoms of celiac disease are more likely to develop an eating disorder. Symptoms of celiac disorder that may precede the onset of an eating disorder include a lack of desire to eat, a tendency to think about food constantly, slowed physical growth, delayed onset of puberty, a tendency to gain weight during treatment, and signs of the psychological effects of being constantly ill.

The direct relationship between celiac disease and eating disorders such as anorexia nervosa remains unclear. The similarity of symptoms of both celiac disease and anorexia can lead to confusion in the diagnosis of both disorders. Because of this confusion in the diagnostic process, it is important that adolescents who display symptoms such as unexplained weight loss or a lack of appetite be tested for celiac disease. In addition, if a child already diagnosed with anorexia nervosa does not respond to the nutritional program prescribed, the child should also be tested for celiac disease.

No formal clinical studies linking anorexia and celiac disease have been conducted to date, but several case reports published in the scientific literature highlight the connection between the two illnesses. For instance, gastroenterologists at Beth Israel Deaconess Medical Center in Boston reported on a series of 10 patients they treated with diagnoses of both celiac disease and anorexia nervosa (representing a total of 2.5 percent of the patients they saw in their clinic for celiac disease). The physicians recognized the complex interactions between the two disorders: The diagnosis of celiac disease at times masked, prompted, or exacerbated the eating disorder, or the eating disorder interfered with the treatment of celiac disease by compromising a patient's ability to follow a gluten-free diet.

These observations were confirmed by other case reports. Pediatricians at St. Vincent's Hospital and Medical Center in New York documented a challenging case of celiac disease and malnutrition in a young patient. Initially, an 11-year-old girl was diagnosed with anorexia nervosa. Several years later during a hospitalization for the eating disorder, she continued to lose weight and it was discovered that she had celiac disease. When she was placed on a gluten-free diet, however, she began to regain weight and showed signs of improved mood; she also socialized more with other patients on the ward. The authors questioned whether she ever really had an eating disorder.

Some experts have noted that the restrictive nature of the gluten-free diet may precipitate anorexia nervosa by triggering the behaviors and malnutrition that can lead to the eating disorder. In one of the few publications linking anorexia nervosa and celiac disease in the medical literature, Italian doctors reported a case of a 23-year-old young woman who was diagnosed with celiac disease before she was found to have anorexia nervosa. The researchers speculated that the dietary restrictions associated with following a gluten-free diet may have triggered the eating disorder.

In another case report, a 23-year-old woman who had been diagnosed with anorexia nervosa at the age of 14 complained of diarrhea and abdominal pain. After being diagnosed with celiac disease, she was placed on a gluten-free diet, and experienced a "prompt resolution of her symptoms." Interestingly, the diagnosis of celiac disease followed that of anorexia. As mentioned earlier, celiac disease and anorexia nervosa share similar symptoms, making it difficult to determine the onset of celiac disease. In the case of this young woman, celiac disease may have gone undiagnosed for years, making her recovery from anorexia more difficult.

Regardless of which is diagnosed first, the association between anorexia and celiac disease shouldn't be treated as a rare occurrence that's best forgotten. In my practice, I have noted that a high percentage of patients with the onset of anorexia nervosa symptoms at the early ages of 9 to 15 also have celiac disease. I recommend testing for celiac disease in all patients who report digestive discomfort and who show early signs of an eating disorder, such as obsessional thinking about food, calories, or weight.

Diagnosing Celiac Disease

Diagnosis is challenging, and many patients report suffering for months or years before being diagnosed properly. The disease is often misdiagnosed as Crohn's disease, chronic fatigue syndrome, diverticulitis, various intestinal infections, irritable bowel syndrome, or even iron-deficiency anemia.

People with celiac disease have abnormally high levels of antibodies, specialized proteins produced by the immune system, associated with the ingestion of the gluten proteins. In people with celiac disease, the immune system reacts to gluten as if it were a poison, triggering the production of an overabundance of antibodies. These antibodies proceed to mark the gluten proteins as foreign substances, and the body prepares to eliminate them. This reaction produces the associated symptoms and intestinal distress of celiac disease. The antibodies associated with the presence of celiac disease include one or more of the following: anti-gliadin, anti-endomysium, and anti-tissue transglutaminase.

When I suspect celiac disease or a sensitivity to gluten, I recommend a blood test to check for the presence of antibodies to gluten. These are usually adequate to suggest that a patient avoid gluten. However, the only way to definitively diagnose celiac disease is to perform a biopsy of the small intestine through an endoscope. This procedure not only confirms the diagnosis, but can also assess the amount of damage the disease has inflicted on the small intestine.

Managing Celiac Disease

There are no medications, supplements, or procedures to treat celiac disease. The only way to relieve the symptoms is to eliminate gluten entirely from the diet. In some people, even small amounts of gluten can cause the body to react the same way it would to large amounts of gluten, and can trigger irreversible damage to the hair-like villi of the small intestine, which are essential for the absorption of nutrients and minerals from food.

If you test positive for celiac disease, you must stay on a gluten-free diet.

Of course, it is tremendously challenging to eliminate gluten from the diet because it is found in so many products, including things you would never suspect, such as yogurt, canned products, condiments such as ketchup and mustard, and even lipstick.

I am hesitant to place any patient on a restrictive diet, unless testing confirms an intolerance or allergy to gluten; however, restriction may be life-saving: It may not only stop the damage to the small intestine, but it may prevent the digestive symptoms that can make eating so uncomfortable for many patients with anorexia. I strongly advise that patients receive counseling and nutritional support to explore how to incorporate a gluten-free diet into a healthy treatment plan.

How to Eat Gluten-Free

Patients with celiac disease must eliminate gluten from their diets. The most common sources of gluten include:
- wheat
- barley (including malt and malt flavoring)
- oats (if they're contaminated with other grains that contain gluten)
- rye

While avoiding the obvious grains above, people with celiac disease must become avid label readers and food detectives. Beyond looking for listings of the obvious sources of gluten—wheat, barley, rye, and malt—and examining food labels for the not-so-obvious gluten sources—hydrolyzed plant protein and modified food starch—those with celiac disease must ensure that food products that are gluten-free are processed separately from gluten foods. Even grains that are safe to eat such as oats may not be recommended for those with celiac disease because they can be contaminated with gluten if they are milled or processed in a facility that processes wheat, rye, or barley grains. On the positive side, it is becoming increasingly easier to ferret out gluten in products: The Food Allergen Labeling and Consumer Protection Act of 2004 requires that food manufacturers list wheat as an ingredient in any product, just as they must list if it contains other top allergens such as nuts, soybeans, fish, eggs, and milk. In addition, gluten-free products are now much more widely available.

Chapter Twenty-Three

Referenced-EEG (rEEG): An Emerging Technology Guides Medication Use

Alison had struggled with anorexia for a long time. Through the years, any improvement in her condition was soon offset by relapse into illness. Professionals often refer to patients like Alison, who don't respond to the current treatments and fail many times to sustain recovery, as treatment refractory. Between 6th and 12th grade Alison suffered multiple relapses, including hospitalizations alternating with encouraging bursts toward health. After every apparent improvement, she would become depressed—even suicidal—again.

After one period of improvement, Alison left home for college, where she unraveled again. While away from home, she found that alcohol temporarily eased her pain, and she began drinking to excess. The combination of alcohol, anorexia, and suicidal thinking made Alison's situation a desperate one. Where could she find immediate effective relief? What medication or combination of medicines would work? Prozac, Adderall, Topamax, and Klonopin were the latest in an assortment of medications, 12 that Alison remembers, that had been prescribed for her over the years, and they weren't helping.

What next?

After so many cycles of hope and disappointment, Alison gave up.

Alison was admitted to the hospital for severe depression following a suicide attempt. At age 19 Alison weighed only 90 pounds, less than 75 percent of her Ideal Body Weight.

I saw Alison after she had been admitted to the hospital. Depression had sapped her vitality; she felt defeated and helpless. Fortunately, I had a new diagnostic tool to offer her: the Referenced-EEG (rEEG).

The rEEG is a high-tech look at the brain's electrical activity that produces a personalized profile of the brain's physiology. I arranged for Alison to have the rEEG performed after her weight was stabilized. The results showed that her particular brain chemistry was resistant to the medications she had been taking. Based on the results of Alison's rEEG, I prescribed two new medicines, Neurontin and Ritalin, which have been proven effective for people with brainwave patterns similar to Alison's. Using these particular medications might normally be considered odd; few psychiatrists would have considered them useful in anorexia and depression. But thanks to these medicines, plus nutritional supplementation and a healthful diet, Alison made remarkable progress. She is now working full-time and recently became engaged. Knowing that she missed a lot during the years she was imprisoned by anorexia and depression, she is eager to embrace life once again.

Struggling with Subjectivity

Unlike other fields of medicine, psychiatry has traditionally based its treatment strategies on the self-reported or observed symptoms of mental illness. But even if the patient provides accurate information about her thoughts and feelings, and even if the doctor picks up all the signs that suggest unusual or harmful thoughts or behaviors, the diagnosis is made on the basis of subjective information. It must be made on that basis, because there is no "anorexia germ" or "OCD enzyme" to be found in the blood, or "depression spot" on the brain that can be located with an x-ray or CAT scan. In short, there is no objective way to measure anorexia, depression, or other psychological states associated with eating disorders. Thus, much of the time we are acting on the basis of educated guesswork, which is why we so often prescribe medicines that do not help our patients. It's not that we don't want to solve their problems right away: we simply do not know what will work.

It is rare for me to see patients who have not been taking multiple medications. This is because most psychiatrists prescribe one medication after another based on vague descriptions of symptoms and behaviors compiled in the Diagnostic and Statistical Manual of Mental Disorders (DSM), the handbook of the American Psychiatric Association that describes the criteria used for diagnosing mental health disorders.

The first edition, called DSM-I, was published in 1952 and defined 107 diagnoses in 132 pages. In 1994, the fourth revision of the manual, called the DSM-IV, defined 365 diagnoses in 886 pages. In what other discipline of medicine have we seen the number of diseases increase by 340 percent in four decades? Many of these diseases have precise diagnostic criteria—essentially lists of the thoughts and/or behaviors that must be displayed in order to warrant a particular diagnosis. The DSM does not, however, offer guidance on prescribing medicines. As a result, psychiatrists prescribe medication somewhat haphazardly based on lists of symptoms, hoping that something will work. Unfortunately, this kind of treatment is often unsuccessful in the treatment of anorexia, and generally demoralizes both patients and their families. They bounce between hope and discouragement, sometimes losing the will to continue trying. And even when the medicines seem to be helpful, we have no way of measuring how effective they are, understanding why they are working, or estimating how long they will continue to be effective.

From Confusion to Clarity: Referenced-EEG

Many decades ago there was hope that the electroencephalogram (EEG) might reveal the secrets of the brain and brain disorders. The EEG measures electrical activity in the brain, just as the EKG (electrocardiogram) measures the electrical activity of the heart. EKG readings—which show up as a wiggly line on a long, thin strip of paper—provide a great deal of useful information to the doctor, but EEG readings, which also show up as many wiggly lines on a paper, are not nearly as informative. Although the EEG is a helpful tool for people with seizures and certain other diseases, we have never found a brainwave pattern or certain type of electrical activity in the brain that would help us identify the origins or basis of psychiatric illness.

It seemed as if the EEG would be a very limited tool until the late 1990s when it was combined with sophisticated software to produce the rEEG, a high-tech look at the brain's electrical activity that was so complex only a computer could keep track of it. The California-based company CNS Response can now produce a personalized profile of a patient's brain physiology. This profile is referred to as a brain signature because it is unique to each individual. In addition, we can compare each person's rEEG reading to more than 17,000 medication trials from other patients compiled in an electronic database that also notes which medicines these patients were on and their results. This means we can compare a patient's EEG results to other EEGs to see which medicines were most effective for those with similar brain signatures, and which were least helpful. The rEEG gives psychiatrists the objective data needed to select therapies most likely to be effective for specific individuals, and avoid risky, expensive, and ineffective medication trials.

Performing the rEEG

The rEEG test is simple and non-invasive. Electrical signals coming from the brain are recorded, but no electricity is put into the patient's brain or body. From the patient's point of view, it's not much more complicated than having an EKG of the heart taken, although it takes longer.

To prepare for the test, the patient must be carefully tapered off of most current medications, otherwise the brainwaves measured will reflect the medication's effects rather than the brain's fundamental signature. During the test itself, a mesh hat, which resembles a bathing cap and is embedded with about 20 small electrodes, is placed on the patient's scalp, and separate clips that resemble clip-on earrings are placed on the ears. Thin wires coming from each electrode are connected to the rEEG hardware, which records the electrical activity of the brain. During the test, which takes from 30 minutes to an hour, the patient is alert and seated in a chair with eyes closed. That's all the patient has to do. Some say the only difficult part of the test is not falling asleep!

Interpreting the Test

The rEEG signals are converted to digital form, and brain biomarkers such as the amplitude of alpha waves are analyzed to identify brainwave abnormalities. The rEEG looks at 74 different biomarkers to develop a detailed and unique brain signature for each patient. Biomarkers that deviate from the norm are identified, as well as medicines that have been helpful to other patients who had similar biomarkers, deviations, or patterns.

Remember: the rEEG does not identify an "anorexic brain pattern" or anything similar. In fact, the rEEG signatures of two people with anorexia may not resemble each other much at all. And the same abnormal brainwave patterns can show up in individuals with completely different disorders or syndromes. For example, in one person, a particular abnormal pattern can manifest as depression, while in another the same pattern can manifest as OCD. The exciting thing about the rEEG is that it tells you which brain biomarkers deviate from the norm and indicates which medicines have been helpful in treating people with similar patterns. This is an amazing advance, with sometimes surprising results.

Counter-Intuitive Treatment

Certain medicines are considered improper for certain diseases. For example, common sense would lead physicians to avoid prescribing stimulants (known appetite suppressants) for patients with anorexia. But the rEEGs of some anorexic patients have predicted the likely effectiveness of stimulant medication based upon their brain patterns. And, in fact, stimulant drugs have helped many of these patients restore weight and improve mood.

Hamlin Emory, MD, and his partner Steven Suffin, MD, have performed a great deal of the original research constructing the database for the rEEG. Dr. Emory recounts the successful rEEG-guided treatment of a patient struggling with anorexia. With a history of 10 failed hospitalizations, the woman entered treatment with Dr. Emory so malnourished that she required intravenous feedings. Her rEEG revealed an abnormal brainwave profile similar to those in the database that had been normalized by stimulant medication. According to Dr. Emory, such treatment without any neurobiological basis would have been seen as "risky treatment." A few days after she began taking the stimulant, however, she felt hunger. She went on to benefit from psychotherapy and enjoyed a spectacular recovery, which has been sustained for at least eight years.

Over the years, I have found the use of common ADHD stimulant medications, including Ritalin, Adderall, and Dexedrine, to be helpful for some patients with eating disorders. However, I have also seen the negative effects of stimulant medications with patients, including decreased appetite with dramatic weight loss.

Poor sustained attention and difficulty concentrating are key symptoms of ADHD as well as symptoms of malnutrition. Misdiagnosis of malnutrition for ADHD may lead to an unnecessary prescription for stimulants. If you are not eating or not eating enough protein and essential nutrients, you may have difficulty paying attention resulting in a diagnosis of ADHD and a trial on stimulant medication. This may have disastrous effects, particularly in those who are vulnerable to eating disorders. I have seen stimulant medication exacerbate symptoms in patients who have eating disorders and in other patients stimulant medication caused the initial pattern of weight loss which triggered anorexia.

Stimulants need to be prescribed with extreme caution for patients with anorexia nervosa. With an rEEG reflecting a benefit for stimulant medication, I find that low doses carefully monitored can provide tremendous benefits to patients.

Jennifer was only 16 years old and struggling with restrictive eating patterns when I first saw her in the hospital. She had been concerned about her weight since she was 11.

Before we met, you could have described Jennifer with one word: perfect. She was a straight-A student who participated and excelled in soccer, dance, and softball. Everything appeared to be "perfect" for Jennifer and her family until she passed out and required medical hospitalization for a dangerously low heart rate.

After a week in the hospital she was transferred to an eating-disorder treatment facility. Her doctors started Jennifer on Prozac. Jennifer and her family noticed an improvement in her condition after starting the medication. They attributed her improvement to the medication and not the refeeding that had occurred. Jennifer was discharged on Prozac after 10 days in treatment.

Only six months later, Jennifer was readmitted for eating-disorder treatment. She had suffered a relapse; her weight remained low and she started purging behaviors after her meals. This time after completing the refeeding process, an rEEG test was conducted. The rEEG showed that Jennifer would benefit from a stimulant medication. Jennifer was started on a long-acting stimulant medication with positive results, including decreased obsessional thinking, improved appetite, and improved mood.

I have known Jennifer for more than four years now. After about two years of treatment with a stimulant and outpatient therapy, she has restored herself to a normal weight and has recovered from her eating disorder. Now she is currently in college, dancing and enjoying her life. She no longer requires any medication.

The rEEG identifies abnormal brainwave patterns to predict medication recommendations based on prior successes in patients with similar brainwave patterns. Essentially, this new technology allows us to personalize a prescription treatment for anorexia without having to go through trial-and-error. Without the rEEG, patients with anorexia often experience the trial and error process as an experiment in which they are a guinea pig. Frequently, patients lose hope and motivation for recovery. When medications fail to provide relief, it becomes too easy for patients to blame themselves. "If medications don't help, then it must be my fault. I should just be able to eat, but I can't!"

Referenced-EEG is a major advance in personalized medicine where physicians can tailor therapies based on the unique medication response profile of each individual patient.

Dr. Daniel Hoffman of CNS Response says, "In the post-Prozac era, we have tended to use every single drug for every single diagnosis." Because the same medications have different effects depending on an individual's brain chemistry, "We have over promised and under delivered," often prescribing "the wrong medication for the wrong brain." Now, rEEG greatly improves the odds of getting the treatment right.

One of my patients, a 24-year-old graduate student named Sage whom I treated for anorexia, anxiety, and depression, also did well with a surprising medicine regimen.

Since the age of 14, Sage had been on and off a variety of SSRI antidepressants for her depression and eating disorder. On Prozac, she was at first euphoric, then became more depressed than ever. With Celexa she experienced improvement in her depressed mood, but gained weight. Zoloft depressed her libido and caused other sexual side effects that prompted her to take herself off the medication for one year; then her depression and anorexia spiraled out of control. Sage was put back on Zoloft, but continued to feel depressed and to lack sexual desire.

"I am tired of being a guinea pig," Sage told me during her first visit to my office. Her rEEG showed that she needed an antidepressant medication, and that she would also benefit from a mood stabilizer. The rEEG helped identify a combination of medications that would benefit Sage, and indicated that just an antidepressant or a mood stabilizer alone would not be sufficient. I prescribed Lamictal, an anticonvulsant sometimes used as a mood stabilizer, and Wellbutrin, a non-SSRI antidepressant.

Sage noticed an improvement in her mood within a month, and within three months she felt better than she had in years. Her eating disorder became less a part of her life. Sage remarked, "Some days I forget I ever had anorexia."

This year she graduated from law school. "Before my rEEG, treatment was just a flip of a coin, and unfortunately it was always wrong." Then she added with a wry smile, "I can't believe how many years I wasted trying the latest medication."

Another patient who was dramatically helped by counter-intuitive rEEG results was May, a 33-year-old woman who had struggled through 13 years of an eating disorder, episodes of cutting, and suicidal thinking that came and went over the years. She also exercised excessively, abused alcohol, and was often irritable, depressed, and anxious. May was quick to jump from one therapist to another when things were not going well—which was often.

During the two years before she came to me, she had been hospitalized for inpatient psychiatric treatment four times, for a total of 70 days. At least 14 different psychiatric medications were prescribed to her at one time or another: Prozac, Zoloft, Paxil, Lexapro, Trazodone, Ativan, Ritalin, Adderall, Klonopin, Provigil, Abilify, Seroquel, Haldol, and Remeron. "There are probably others that I can't remember," she remarked.

Her rEEG report indicated that she would most likely benefit from an anticonvulsant and a tricyclic antidepressant combination, so I prescribed the anticonvulsant/mood stabilizer Trileptal and the antidepressant Nortriptyline.

Neither Nortriptyline nor Trileptal have ever been proven effective for the treatment of anorexia. Nortriptyline, a tricyclic antidepressant, and related medications (Amitriptyline) have actually been shown *not* to be helpful in anorexia, and Trileptal has never been studied for the treatment of anorexia. By itself, I do not believe it would be helpful for a majority of patients with anorexia. Yet for May this combination was perfect for her unique brain physiology.

Since her rEEG was performed and her medications adjusted (nearly two years ago), she has stayed out of the hospital and has been free of eating-disorder behavior for the first time in 13 years. She engages voluntarily in outpatient treatment and has stayed with her therapists. Her mood has stabilized and her substance craving ceased. She is able to focus at work and maintain her concentration. As May describes, "The rEEG made me feel like I can function again."

The rEEG guided the selection of two medications that might have never been combined.

The Science Behind rEEG

Although rEEG is relatively new, I am encouraged by the study results indicating that it is an effective tool for treating eating disorders. One of these studies explored the clinical effectiveness of rEEG in 81 patients with eating disorders at the Monte Nido Eating Disorder Treatment Center. The study involved patients suffering from anorexia, bulimia, or EDNOS. Among this group, more than 80 percent suffered from severe eating disorders that had not improved despite many medication trials. Patients were taken off their old medications and, based on the results of their rEEGs, new medications were prescribed for eight weeks. Ten months later, when their well-being was reassessed, more than 70 percent of the patients with anorexia were happier and had gained weight. These results show a dramatic improvement over the usual discouraging results seen in medication trials for anorexia.

Another trial involved 15 patients who had been diagnosed with refractory eating disorders and co-occurring depression. All of the participants had previously undergone outpatient treatment and had taken prescribed medications. Of the 15 patients, eight were monitored for up to two years following the rEEG. During the two years before the study, these patients had been seriously ill with depression and had spent a combined total of 588 days in the hospital. Each patient in the study had a rEEG and was given medication based on the results. All of the patients had different combinations of medications based on the rEEG. For some, the rEEG recommended a stimulant and anticonvulsant, while for others it recommended a completely different medication regimen, such as antidepressants. Following treatment guided by rEEG, there was a dramatic drop in inpatient treatment in the two years after the rEEG—just six hospitalizations for a total of 21 days!

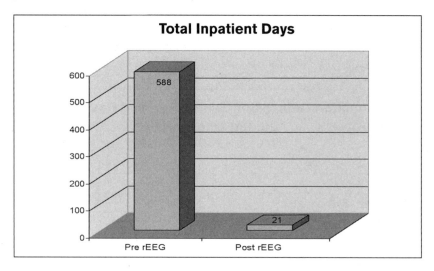

The condition of all patients improved after they began taking the new medications. Many patients went from requiring multiple hospitalizations to maintenance outpatient therapy. A striking 60 percent of those whose illness was once rated severe improved to the point that their illness could be rated as mild. Twenty-three percent of patients improved to such an extent that they no longer showed any clinical symptoms of an eating disorder. This improvement was captured on the Clinical Global Severity (CGS) scale, a tool often used by physicians to rate the severity of a patient's illness and changes in the illness over time.

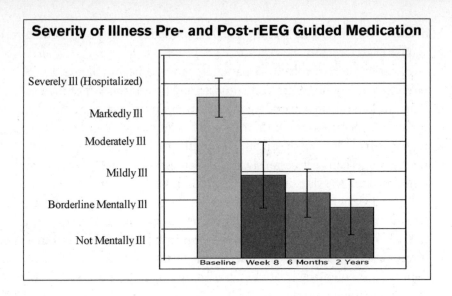

Severity of Illness Pre- and Post-rEEG Guided Medication

Another scale frequently used to measure depression is the Hamilton Rating Scale for Depression. The patients' pre- and post-rEEG guided medication Hamilton Depression Scores reinforced these findings. The severity of the patients' depression went from incapacitating to slight, and in some cases even returned to normal mood.

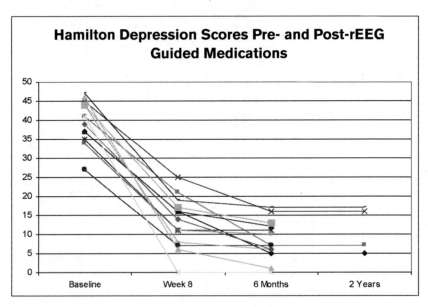

Hamilton Depression Scores Pre- and Post-rEEG Guided Medications

At the end of the trial, the patients were enthusiastic about their welcome return to health. All of them had struggled with anorexia for a long time and were now markedly improved.

Depression and Eating Disorders: Common Partners

Depression is commonly diagnosed with anorexia nervosa, with some studies estimating rates of depression at nearly 89 percent in hospitalized patients. The overall lifetime prevalence of depression has been estimated to be up to 65 percent for those with anorexia. As you learned earlier, finding effective pharmacological interventions for treatment-resistant depression is a difficult and often disappointing ordeal. But coupled with anorexia, finding effective treatment for both conditions is a Herculean task. Indeed, there are no research trials supporting the efficacy of antidepressants in treating acute depression and anorexia symptoms.

Multiple research studies have demonstrated the need for a tool such as the rEEG to guide the selection of antidepressant medication. In one study of 4,000 subjects, it was concluded that after two medications had failed them, most patients (55 percent) with depression either dropped out of treatment or relapsed, and only 13 percent achieved remission with either the third or fourth medication attempt. After the first two medications, the study could offer no predictions beyond "trial and error" as to which medications might work on any given patient.

These findings, in one of the largest studies ever conducted on evaluating medications for depression, underscore the need for a technology like rEEG.

A recent multi-center, single-blind trial proved the effectiveness of rEEG in the treatment of depression. The study, examining treatment refractory depression in 89 subjects, was conducted at 12 medical centers across the country, including Harvard, Stanford, Cornell, Rush, and the University of California-Irvine. All study participants had failed to respond to at least one antidepressant treatment, and most had failed to respond to two or more treatments. At the end of the 12-week trial, it was clear that rEEG outperformed the traditional STAR-D algorithm, a standard medication protocol used in depression research. Typically, in antidepressant studies, new effective treatments have a success rate that is about 10 percent higher than control groups. In the latest rEEG study the success rate of rEEG over the control group was 50 percent. The odds of obtaining such a dramatic response through luck or chance are less than one in 1,000 Almost all secondary measurements of depression, general health, and quality of life showed a superior response to rEEG-guided medications.

These results indicated that rEEG-guided pharmacotherapy can be highly effective in the treatment of depression. Dr. Charles DeBattista, physician at Stanford University Medical Center, and one of the lead investigators of the study summarized the findings:

"Psychiatry has lacked useful laboratory tests to select medications for depressed patients. While needing further study, this is one of the larger trials to demonstrate that there may be a role for technology that assists physicians in selecting better treatment options for their patients."

The dramatic, positive experience of patients is echoed by medical pioneers of the technology and treatment professionals experienced with its use. Dr. Hamlin Emory compares the enlightenment that comes from the ability to measure brain function with the insight that came from decoding the Rosetta Stone. Dr. Daniel Hoffman says, "After a long wait in the field of psychiatry, we finally have an objective measure to help patients achieve and sustain a durable recovery." He views rEEG as a way to "shine a flashlight in the dark, leading, we hope, to daylight." Patients with rEEG guided medication feel as though they have come back to life.

The rEEG Lowers the Cost of Care

In addition to psychological benefits, rEEG also has practical benefits. When patients improve in mood and well-being, the cost of their care is greatly reduced. As shown in the table below, the costs of hospitalization for eight patients with refractory eating disorders and depression who received rEEG-guided medication decreased an estimated $1.5 million.

The Potential of rEEG

The rEEG is the most exciting treatment breakthrough I have witnessed in 20 years of psychiatric practice, and I believe it would be difficult to overestimate its potential in the effective treatment of eating disorders.

However, the rEEG is not a magic bullet, and I do not recommend it for everyone. Those with extremely low weight or those who are rapidly losing weight will not benefit from rEEG. Patients need to be off all medication for the test, limiting its use in patients unable to taper their medications. And the rEEG does not predict the side effects that may limit a medication's use in treatment. A patient may be sensitive to a particular medication that the rEEG predicts, yet, when prescribed that medication, they may experience an unpleasant side effect. This is not uncommon for patients with eating disorders. For some it is simply the obsessive worrying about medication that limits any successful attempt at treatment with medication. For others, side effects related to chronic nutritional deficiencies limit the use of medication.

Cost of Hospitalizations Before and After rEEG-guided Medication

Hospitalization Type (In Days)	Pre-rEEG	Estimated Cost	Post-rEEG	Estimated Cost
Inpatient & Residential	789	$1,578,000	114	$228,000
Partial	210	$168,000	15	$12,000
Total Cost of Care		$1,746,000		$240,000

Note: Total Hospitalizations Pre-rEEG = 53
Total Hospitalizations Post-rEEG = 7

I have frequently found that following nutritional supplementation, patients may tolerate a medication that previously resulted in negative side effects.

Carolyn Costin, a nationally recognized expert in the eating-disorders field, believes that the opportunity to see their own brainwave patterns empowers patients. Costin observes that rEEG gives patients "a full deck of cards to play with." She has been advocating for rEEG since 1996. Costin is Director of Monte Nido, a residential treatment center in California. She is also the author of *Your Dieting Daughter...Is She Dying For Attention?* and *The Eating Disorders Sourcebook: A Comprehensive Guide to the Causes, Treatments, and Prevention of Eating Disorders.* Costin combines her personal experience of recovery from anorexia with more than 30 years of professional expertise in treating patients. Patients who come to her treatment centers often have been through several ineffective hospitalizations.

Costin observes: "People are more motivated to take their medications regularly if they understand the rationale for them. Often patients who observe the changes in other patients' lives once they've been on medications compatible with their brainwave activity come to me and ask for the test."

As one patient told her, "It helped me to see that my alpha waves needed to be normalized."

As a psychiatrist and member of a patient's treatment team, I now have something to offer besides support. I can now individualize a patient's medical treatment. Instead of the vagueness and uncertainty of choosing among unproven medications, I can use objective evidence to predict which medications are likely to help a patient get well.

The rEEG is an important tool that finally enables physicians to prescribe the proper medications with confidence. This, coupled with zinc, essential fatty acids, and balanced nutrition, offers real help and hope to those with anorexia and their families.

Referenced-EEG is a promising tool, and not just for treating patients with eating disorders and depression, but also for treating those with many other psychiatric disorders. Referenced-EEG has been helpful for patients struggling with bulimia, binge eating disorder, ADHD, substance abuse, depression, bipolar disorder, and OCD. By providing a measurable physiological basis for mental illnesses, rEEG offers the necessary guidance to personalize medication in difficult illnesses. Referenced-EEG is particularly effective in treatment-resistant depression that is non-responsive to antidepressants.

Chapter Twenty-Four

Laboratory Tests Your Doctor May Order

Underlying nutritional deficiencies in individuals with anorexia can have a dramatic effect on physical and psychological function and often contribute to the symptoms of the illness. Physicians and nutritionists may make broad assumptions about nutritional deficiencies in those with anorexia. However, it is critical that each individual's nutritional state be determined through a comprehensive metabolic evaluation, so an effective, personalized program of nutritional supplementation can be created to optimize both current functioning and long-term health.

One idea that I have tried to convey throughout this book is that of biochemical individuality: each individual's body functions differently due to his or her genetics and epigenetics. Biochemical individuality can stem from very small DNA changes called single nucleotide polymorphisms (SNPs), which involve a change at a single site in a long, long sequence of DNA. Although seemingly very minor, these minute changes cause corresponding proteins to become more or less active. Since proteins are the building blocks of all of the structures and functions of the body, including enzymes, neurotransmitters, and hormones, this means that no two individuals' bodies work exactly the same way—not even identical twins!

For example, the methylenetetrahydrofolate reductase (MTHFR) gene encodes an enzyme involved in chemical reactions with folate (also called folic acid and vitamin B9). Each person may have a slightly different DNA sequence in her MTHFR gene. About 10 percent of the population actually has differences in both copies of the MTHFR gene. In this case, the enzyme produced from the MTHFR gene is compromised and not fully functional, leading these individuals to need more dietary folate. As discussed in Chapter Eighteen, low folate levels are linked to depression. Correspondingly, changes in the MTHFR gene that reduce folate production are also associated with an increased risk of depression.

Not only do different people have varying needs for the same nutrients, but two people with the same nutrient deficiency may have different symptoms or a different progression of symptoms. For example, a vitamin B12 deficiency may be identified in three individuals after lab testing. One person might have been feeling sad, hopeless, and despondent for a few months. Another might have recently noticed bothersome numbness and tingling in her legs. The third person may not have noticed that anything was wrong! Same vitamin deficiency, different clinical manifestations.

Complicating matters further is that a person's health is not solely based on nutritional status, but also on influencing factors such as how the nutrients are digested and absorbed, other medical conditions, age, stressful influences, and toxic exposures, including alcohol and cigarettes.

This is why it is so important to have comprehensive laboratory testing done and to interpret the results within a personalized framework. In practice, optimal health is best maintained in different ways for different individuals. For instance, your body may require higher daily amounts of vitamin C to ward off a virus than your neighbor's. Only by examining a person's overall biological picture can physicians know what specific interventions a person needs.

In the nutritional assessment of a patient with anorexia, a number of tests are critical, including routine chemistry and complete blood count (CBC) and other blood and urinary tests. Unfortunately, in many cases, these simple laboratory tests are never done, or the results are ignored. Many patients with anorexia, for instance, have been told that they have iron deficiency anemia, but the doctors never prescribed iron supplements.

Many of the tests listed below are conventional and commonly performed in physicians' offices. Others are not as well known and may not be covered by a health insurance plan. However, all are important. Not only does each impart helpful information, but the results as a whole provide an overall picture of the patient's health status.

I have witnessed first hand that addressing nutrient deficiencies with specific supplements based on testing can help a patient feel better mentally and physically, enabling her to more effectively participate in treatment and achieve recovery.

Should your physician fail to order these tests, make sure to ask for them.

Getting Started

While some psychiatrists do not routinely order comprehensive metabolic laboratory testing, I believe that competent treatment of anorexia nervosa begins with an understanding of the patient's biochemical profile, focusing on any abnormalities that may be contributing to the symptoms. That's why I recommend the following tests, which can be ordered by any physician:

- Amino acids
- Complete Blood Count (CBC) with differential
- Celiac disease screening (anti-tissue transglutaminase antibody and anti-gliadin antibody tests)
- Cholesterol (total)
- Comprehensive metabolic panel
- Copper levels
- Essential fatty acids
- Folate and vitamin B12
- Homocysteine
- Iron and ferritin
- Magnesium
- Methylmalonic acid
- Red blood cell trace minerals
- Thyroid
- Urinary organic acids
- Urinary peptides
- Vitamin D (25-Hydroxy vitamin D)
- Zinc

A Brief Summary of Laboratory Tests

The following are some of the most common screening labs recommended to determine nutritional deficiencies and help target recommendations for supplementation. Not every patient requires all tests, and your healthcare provider can determine the most important ones for you.

Amino Acids

Amino acids are the building blocks of proteins found in every tissue and organ of the body. They are involved in many different processes, including regulation of neurotransmitters, formation of antibodies, and production of energy inside the cells.

Deficiencies of any of the 20 amino acids that the body uses—and in particular the eight essential amino acids that can't be manufactured by the body and must be obtained through the diet—can lead to serious health problems. For example, a deficiency of tryptophan can lead to depression, while a lack of tyrosine or phenylalanine can trigger fatigue and difficulty concentrating.

Amino acid levels can be detected in the urine or in the blood. Blood tests are conducted in one of two ways, either through a blood draw or a bloodspot test. With the blood draw, blood is drawn from a vein via a needle and analyzed for levels of amino acids. A bloodspot test requires much less blood, only the amount taken from a finger prick. Abnormally high or low levels of amino acids can be treated with supplementation or through diet modification.

Complete Blood Count (CBC) with Differential

The CBC is a blood test. This test measures red blood cell count and characteristics (called indices), white blood cell count and types (called differential), hemoglobin, hematocrit, and platelets. Low red blood cell count, hemoglobin, and hematocrit results can indicate that a person is anemic. Red blood cell indices (MCH, MCV, and MCHC) can point to the underlying nutrient deficiency causing the anemia, whether iron, copper, folate, or vitamin B12.

White blood cell levels can be abnormally high due to an infection, an allergic reaction, or leukemia, or they can be abnormally low due to medication reactions or possibly due to low zinc levels. Zinc is needed for white blood cell production, and the decreased white blood cell counts commonly seen in anorexia respond to zinc supplementation. Platelets play a role in blood clotting, and both high and low levels are abnormal. Low levels correspond with excessive bleeding and bruising.

Celiac Screening

Screening for celiac disease—a sensitivity to the gluten found in wheat and other grains—involves two blood tests for different antibodies that the body manufactures when it mistakenly sees gluten as a foreign invader. These tests search for the anti-tissue transglutaminase antibody and the anti-gliadin antibody. They are only accurate if the patient continues to eat gluten products daily until the test is performed.

The results should be negative, which means that neither of the antibodies is detected in the blood.

To confirm a positive result, or as an alternative test for those who do not eat any gluten products, a biopsy of the small intestine can be performed. An endoscope is inserted into the mouth and through the stomach to the small intestine, where tiny tissue samples are taken from its lining. These tissue samples are then examined under a microscope for characteristic changes known to be consistent with celiac disease, including flattened villi in the intestines.

Cholesterol (Total)

We normally worry about elevated cholesterol, but recent studies have found that low total cholesterol levels are associated with depression, suicidal thoughts, and/or suicidal behavior. For example, a recent study published in 2009 in the *Journal of Psychiatric Research* found that men with low serum total cholesterol (below 165 mg/dL) were seven times more likely to die prematurely from unnatural causes such as suicide and accidents than their peers with normal cholesterol levels. The authors of the study and several others in the field have suggested that low cholesterol levels decrease the amount of serotonin receptors and serotonin. Low serotonin levels are associated with depression.

Elevated cholesterol is common in anorexia nervosa, although this finding is confusing because anorexics limit or eliminate the fat in their diet. In patients with anorexia, elevated cholesterol levels reflect nutritional deficiencies and can be corrected with essential fatty acids, B vitamins, and zinc.

Comprehensive Metabolic Panel

This panel of blood tests, also called a chemistry panel, provides information about a person's electrolyte status, acid-base balance, kidney function, liver function, blood sugar, and total protein levels. All results should be within the normal range; any abnormally high or abnormally low levels should be discussed with your physician.

This panel is used as a broad screening tool to evaluate organ function and as a preliminary check for diabetes, liver disease, and kidney problems. Sometimes, people are asked to fast before their blood is drawn.

The comprehensive metabolic panel can also be useful in assessing a person's zinc status. One enzyme measured under the category of liver function tests, called alkaline phosphatase, depends on the presence of zinc for its production. Low levels of alkaline phosphatase (or alk phos) nearly always indicate a zinc deficiency.

Electrolytes are also measured in a routine chemistry panel. Abnormalities in any of the major electrolytes, such as sodium, potassium, chloride, or phosphorus, can be life-threatening and require prompt attention by a physician.

Copper

Copper is required for the synthesis of the neurotransmitters norepinephrine and dopamine, both of which modulate mental health. Low levels of copper in the blood can lead to symptoms of depression. A

---

deficiency of ceruloplasmin, a form of copper, can cause anemia. Abnormally high levels of copper can be associated with psychological symptoms such as aggression, paranoia, and anxiety.

Essential Fatty Acids

Essential fatty acids (EFAs) are critical for cell membrane structure and function, and they also regulate the inflammatory process. The EFAs the body requires can be obtained from plant and animal foods in the diet; the body can also make them by using excess dietary carbohydrates and proteins. For example, omega-6 fatty acids are derived from vegetable oils and grains; omega-3 fatty acids are found in some fish and flax oil.

People who have fatty acid deficiencies may experience symptoms of dry skin, irritability, decreased immune functioning, learning problems, hair loss, impaired wound healing, and depression.

Fatty acid levels in blood serum and in the red blood cells can be determined by a laboratory test. Results are broken down by subcategories of fatty acids, including saturated fats, monounsaturated fats, polyunsaturated fats, omega-6 fats, and omega-3 fats. Ratios of levels between some of these groups are calculated as well. Abnormally high or low levels of different fatty acids can be treated with supplementation or through dietary modification.

Folate and Vitamin B12

Examining the levels of folate and vitamin B12, which are often tested for together, can be helpful in evaluating a type of anemia called macrocytic anemia (in which the red blood cells are abnormally large), assessing general nutritional status in a malnourished patient, and searching for underlying causes of psychological or mental status changes.

Folate and vitamin B12 are B vitamins that are essential for normal psychological functioning and are often found to be deficient in patients with anorexia. Folate, or folic acid, is necessary for the proper production of brain neurotransmitters. Low levels of folate may contribute to the depression often seen in anorexia. A vitamin B12 deficiency can cause a range of psychiatric and neurological symptoms, including depression, anxiety, paranoia, hallucinations, memory loss, confusion, and numbness or tingling in the hands and feet. Identifying a vitamin B12 deficiency in the early or mild stages can help treat or even prevent these symptoms.

Homocysteine

Homocysteine is an amino acid produced by the body and found in the blood. Normally, homocysteine is quickly converted to another necessary amino acid called cysteine. However, if the conversion process falters, the body's level of homocysteine will rise. This is a harmful situation associated with increased free radical activity, irritation of the blood vessels, and the formation of blood clots. Accordingly, people with elevated homocysteine levels are at increased risk of heart attacks, strokes, and bone fractures. Folate, vitamins B12 and B6, and zinc are responsible for converting homocysteine to cysteine; therefore, those deficient in these nutrients can develop these problems. In fact, elevated homocysteine levels can indicate an early-stage deficiency of folate or vitamins B6 or B12 before blood levels even reflect these problems.

Iron and Ferritin

These two tests, often ordered together, can help evaluate if a person is anemic. The serum iron test measures the amount of iron that is traveling throughout the body in the bloodstream. The ferritin test reflects the amount of iron stored in the cells. Iron is necessary for the production of hemoglobin, which allows the red blood cells to hold onto oxygen and ferry it to all of the body's organs and tissues. Without adequate iron intake, iron-deficiency anemia will develop. Iron-deficiency anemia, which is common in those with anorexia, can be exacerbated by menstruation, pregnancy, or breast-feeding. Low iron levels may also indicate the presence of a chronic illness. Even an early iron deficiency, which can be present before an overt anemia develops, necessitates iron supplementation to prevent future symptoms of fatigue and weakness.

Elevated iron levels—which may also require treatment—can indicate an accumulation of iron in the body, possibly from multiple blood transfusions, liver disease, kidney disease, or a genetic disease called hemochromatosis.

In the early stages of iron-deficiency anemia, total iron levels may appear normal because the body has started using ferritin for hemoglobin production. In this instance, the only indication that an anemia may be developing is a low ferritin level. If ferritin levels are below normal, or even in the low-normal range, under 100 ng/mL, I recommend additional iron supplements. The ferritin level should then be rechecked after three months to make sure the anemia has been corrected and that there is not an underlying iron absorption problem.

Similar to high iron levels, increased ferritin levels can indicate inflammation, chronic infection, autoimmune disorders, or excess iron storage disorders such as hemochromatosis.

Magnesium

A magnesium blood test measures the amount of magnesium in the blood. Magnesium is an essential mineral found in every cell in the body, necessary for heart function, nerve function, and strong bones. Magnesium is also required for the function of hundreds of enzymes in the body that help with energy production and neurotransmitter synthesis. People with anorexia are often deficient in magnesium due to decreased intake and increased excretion from stress. This may contribute to their symptoms of weakness, cardiac complications, depression, anxiety, insomnia, and difficulty concentrating.

The normal range is 1.7 to 2.2 mg/dL. However, only about 1 percent of the body's total magnesium is present in the blood, which means that a blood level may not be the most accurate indicator of the total magnesium stored in all of the cells in the body. A person can have a normal blood level, but still not have enough magnesium in the body to keep all of the biological functions running smoothly.

Methylmalonic Acid (MMA)

MMA is a compound that is produced in the body, the presence of which points to an early vitamin B12 deficiency. Normally, vitamin B12 is involved in certain chemical reactions that keep the body's MMA level low. If there is not enough vitamin B12 in the body, levels of MMA are often elevated. As mentioned earlier, patients with anorexia often develop a vitamin B12 deficiency, which can cause a wide range of symptoms. Addressing a vitamin B12 deficiency as early as possible can help prevent these symptoms.

The MMA test can either be done as a blood or urine test. The results are used in conjunction with homocysteine and vitamin B12 levels to detect a mild or early vitamin B12 deficiency. Elevated levels of both MMA and homocysteine can indicate an early vitamin B12 deficiency, even if vitamin B12 blood levels are normal.

Red Blood Cell Trace Minerals

This test evaluates a number of nutrients and toxic elements that have critical functions in cells or effects on blood cell membranes. Some of the nutrient elements tested for include calcium, phosphorous, zinc, selenium, boron, and vanadium. Some of the potentially toxic elements assessed include arsenic, cadmium, lead, and mercury. A red blood cell analysis is recommended for assessing disorders specifically associated with a zinc deficiency, such as anorexia. All of the elements measured can affect biological processes such as heart function, anemia, and immune function. Results of this test can be very helpful in determining the exact nutritional supplementation a person requires for optimal health.

Normal ranges for each element vary, although the toxic elements, which are harmful to the body, should only be present in extremely low amounts.

Thyroid

The thyroid is an endocrine gland located on the front of the base of the neck. It responds to thyroid stimulating hormone (TSH), a hormone that is made by the pituitary gland at the base of the brain that senses the body's levels of thyroid hormones. Under the influence of TSH, the thyroid gland produces thyroid hormones called thyroxine (T4) and tri-iodothyronine (T3). These enter the bloodstream and travel around the body. Some T4 is also converted into T3 in the liver and other tissues. Thyroid hormones are responsible for helping the body use energy at the correct rate; problems emerge when people have too much or too little.

Hyperthyroidism (abnormally high levels of circulating thyroid hormone) can cause an increase in heart rate, palpitations, muscle loss, hair loss, insomnia, and anxiety. In contrast, hypothyroidism can cause increased sensitivity to cold, weight gain, forgetfulness, sluggishness, depression, and feelings of fatigue.

Urinary Organic Acids

Checking organic acids is important for assessing the metabolic pathways of the body. Organic acids are used by the body for a range of reactions, but they can also point to problems with biological processes, including neurotransmitter function, detoxification of biological toxins, digestive imbalances including bacterial and/or yeast overgrowth, nutrient deficiencies, and energy production. Abnormally elevated levels of organic acids accumulate when there is a blockage somewhere in one of the body's metabolic pathways. These increased levels are then excreted in the urine and measured in a urine sample.

For example, a high level of an organic acid called kynurenate is a functional sign of B6 deficiency. B6 is required for the synthesis of all major neurotransmitters, and we have no other tests to easily measure B6 levels. Kynurenate levels increase in the urine if there are inadequate amounts of B6.

This test requires a first morning urine sample; it measures a large number of different compounds indicative of overall health. Based on the results, diet modification, nutrient supplementation, or antifungal/antibiotic medications may be warranted.

Urinary peptides

A urine test can identify the presence of the urinary opiate peptides casomorphin and gliadorphin, which I discussed in Chapter Fifteen. These peptides result from the incomplete breakdown of casein and gluten, respectively, due to low levels or inactivity of the protease enzyme DPP IV in the small intestine. Abnormally high levels of these peptides cause psychological symptoms including obsessive and intrusive thoughts, which can complicate recovery from anorexia. If levels of casomorphin or gliadorphin are abnormally high in the urine, treatment involves eliminating the offending casein or gluten from the diet.

Vitamin D

Although not typically deficient in patients with anorexia, vitamin D levels should be tested as the vitamin not only works with calcium and phosphorous to maintain bone health, but has also been found to be increasingly important throughout the body. A vitamin D deficiency may be associated with high blood pressure, high blood sugar levels, and depression. A vitamin D deficiency can also cause an increased stress response in the body.

After vitamin D enters the body via sunlight or through fortified foods, it is converted in the liver to 25-hydroxy vitamin D. This is the form found in the bloodstream, and what is commonly measured to evaluate and follow an individual's vitamin D status. Low levels indicate that a person is not getting enough exposure to sunlight, is not getting enough dietary vitamin D, or has a problem with vitamin D intestinal absorption. If supplementation is necessary due to decreased levels, then an individual's 25-hydroxy vitamin D status should be monitored every three months until it is within the target range.

Zinc

As discussed in detail in Chapter Twelve, a zinc deficiency is often associated with anorexia, and correcting an underlying zinc deficiency is critical in the treatment of anorexia. However, as was also discussed in Chapter Fourteen, measuring the blood levels of zinc is not always a reliable way to detect a zinc deficiency. When blood levels are evaluated, though, a normal serum zinc level is given as any value between 60 and 120 g/ml.

A better assessment of zinc status is the Zinc Taste Test, described in Chapter Fourteen, which can identify even a subtle deficiency. For the Zinc Taste Test, a Category 1 or 2 response indicates the person likely has a significant zinc deficiency.

Chapter Twenty-Five

An Integrative Approach
to Anorexia Nervosa

Integrative medicine is a therapeutic approach to healing based on biochemical individuality, and the understanding that the body, mind, and spirit are all interconnected. Rather than simply attempting to eliminate signs and symptoms of a disorder, the aim of integrative medicine is to restore balance in the body by adjusting the factors, both internal and external, that nurture or repair the whole being. Both traditional and complementary therapies can be incorporated into an integrative approach.

After almost 20 years of treating patients, I am convinced that there is a prominent place for nutritional supplements in the treatment of mental illness, in particular anorexia nervosa, a disorder of self-starvation. In this chapter, I also present other aspects of an integrative approach to anorexia, including complementary therapies that decrease the effects of stress. Two of these—Kundalini yoga and Emotional Freedom Technique (EFT)—can decrease anxiety and relieve symptoms of OCD.

Nutritional Supplementation:
Lab Tests and Repletion Recommendations

While I do not suggest that nutritional supplements are magic bullets that can simply arrest anorexia nervosa, supplements are safe and cost-effective strategies that can dramatically affect outcomes. A nutritionally optimal environment makes recovery easier and plays a major role in the prevention of relapse. When the brain is receiving proper nourishment, symptoms may be relieved, and patients will feel more motivated to participate in psychotherapy.

Creating a nutritionally optimal environment begins with discovering what nutrients are missing, in excess, or out of proportion. Some of that can be done through a careful physical examination; for example, certain problems with the skin suggest deficiencies of essential fatty acids. Much of the process, however, depends on laboratory testing. I recommend that laboratory testing and the ZTT be completed before

Starting Protocol

**If the ZTT results in a 1 or 2
Getting Started: For 2 Weeks**

Supplement	Dose	Time of Day	Total Dose
Liquid Zinc (Aqueous Monohydrate)	4 mg per 1 Tsp	3 Tsp before each meal	36 mg per day
Plant-Based Comprehensive Digestive	2 pills	With each meal	6 per day
Probiotics	5 to 10 billion CFU per pill	Before 2 meals	2 per day

Vitamin B$_{12}$, Iron, Vitamin D, and amino acid supplements can be added at any time if individual lab testing shows deficiency.

nutritional supplements are started. Ask your physician to order the blood tests described in Chapter Twenty-Four. The results of the lab tests should then be discussed with your physician in detail.

After completing the ZTT and working with your physician to understand your unique metabolic profile, you can safely start following a core supplement program.

The starting protocol should be continued for at least two weeks or until you develop a strong metallic taste (Category 3 or 4) on the Zinc Taste Test. Once you have a strong taste on the ZTT (a 3 or a 4), then follow Starting Protocol B with a multivitamin mineral supplement that includes zinc chelate.

After two weeks of zinc, digestive enzymes, and probiotics, the Basic Supplement Schedule can be started. Minimal fat-soluble vitamins are recommended in the supplement schedule as patients with anorexia have consistently been shown to have high or normal levels of vitamin A, D, and E. It is always advisable to start slowly and add a new supplement every three days. I would recommend working with a health professional who is knowledgeable in nutrition, and I would not advise nutritional supplementation without professional consultation. The supplement

Starting Protocol B

Getting Started: For 2 Weeks

Supplement	Dose	Time of Day	Total Dose
Multivitamin/Mineral	1 pill	With each meal (3 times per day)	3 per day
Zinc Chelate	15 mg	With two meals (2 times per day)	30 mg per day
Plant-Based Comprehensive Digestive Enzymes with DPP IV	2 pills	With each meal (3 times per day)	6 per day
Probiotics	5 to 10 billion CFU per pill	Before each meal (2 times per day)	2 per day

Vitamin B12, Iron, Vitamin D, and amino acid supplements can be added at any time if individual lab testing shows deficiency.

schedule is a guide only, and any vitamin and mineral supplementation should be taken with professional guidance.

Complementary Therapy Approaches for Anorexia Nervosa

Individual, family, and group therapy play a vital role in the treatment of anorexia. As described in Chapter Five, good evidence supports the use of family therapy in treatment for adolescents. The Maudsley approach is one example. Offering parents a concrete plan when dealing with their child's illness, it is being increasingly implemented with successful results. Individual and group therapy are also critical parts of a comprehensive treatment plan.

While this book does not focus on behavioral health strategies, the therapies described in this section deserve consideration. Aimed at decreasing anxiety, panic, and OCD, these therapies can often help patients with anxiety around food. However, these therapies are rarely

Guidelines for a Basic Supplement Schedule

Time of Day	Supplement	Dose
Upon Waking	Calcium Citrate with Vitamin D	250 to 500 mg calcium citrate
	Probiotic	5-10 billion CFU per pill
Breakfast	Zinc chelate	15 mg
	Plant-Based Digestive Enzymes with DPP IV	2
	Multivitamin with Minerals	1
	Vitamin C	500 to 1,000 mg
	Vitamin B complex	50 to 75 mg (of each B vitamin)
	Essential Fatty Acids	1 to 2 g (EPA/DHA/GLA)
	Magnesium Glycinate	100 to 200 mg
Lunch	Digestive Enzymes with HCl and DPP IV	2
	Essential Fatty Acids	1 to 2 g (EPA/DHA/GLA)
Dinner	Zinc chelate	15 mg
	Plant-Based Digestive Enzymes with DPP IV	2
	Multivitamin with Minerals	1
	Vitamin C	500 to 1,000 mg
	Vitamin B complex	50 to 75 mg (of each B vitamin)
	Magnesium glycinate	100 to 200 mg
	Essential Fatty Acids	1 to 2 g (EPA/DHA/GLA)
Before Bed	Calcium Citrate with Vitamin D	250 to 500 mg calcium and 100 to 200 IU vitamin D
	Probiotic	5 to 10 billion CFU per pill

effective in the malnourished minds of patients who are actively struggling with anorexia nervosa. Nutritional repletion with individualized recommendations provides the foundation for the effective use of all therapies, including complementary therapies.

A Four-Step Behavioral Technique

The following is one behavioral technique designed to counteract and change the intrusive, distorted thoughts and behaviors common in anorexia.

Created by Dr. Jeffrey Schwartz, author of *Brain Lock*, this protocol was devised to assist patients with OCD. However, it can also be used by individuals with anorexia to decrease obsessional thoughts and compulsive behaviors, supporting sustained recovery. According to Dr. Schwartz, this biobehavioral approach will teach an individual to "prevent habitual compulsive responses and replace them with new, more constructive behaviors" as the person comes to understand that thoughts and urges have a biological basis. People do not need a therapist for this technique; they can learn the four steps themselves. Very briefly, here they are:

1. **Relabel.** In the first step, individuals need to recognize and be aware that obsessive and/or intrusive thoughts and urges are not real, but only symptoms of their psychiatric condition. They are false messages coming from the brain.
2. **Reattribute.** Individuals need to remind themselves that the intensity and intrusive nature of the thoughts and urges are due to a biochemical imbalance in their brain.
3. **Refocus.** This step involves shifting attention away from an intrusive urge or thought to a more pleasant action (i.e., taking a walk or listening to music). Upon experiencing a compelling urge, an individual should relabel and reattribute the feeling, and then shift her attention to another behavior for as long as she can before attending to the thought or urge. It may be necessary to build up this amount of elapsed time; the goal is 15 minutes.
4. **Revalue.** Mastering the first three steps can then lead to an individual's realization that the obsessive thoughts and compulsions are caused by a medical condition and are not significant; in other words, they are not as important as once believed. For example, an individual might remind oneself, "These thoughts are my anorexia talking. I do not need to pay attention to them."

The description of Dr. Schwartz's plan is abbreviated here; more information can be found in the Resources Section.

Dr. Schwartz's plan, a form of intensive CBT, can produce changes in brain function in patients with OCD. A 2009 study published in the journal *Molecular Psychiatry* examined brain scans of 10 patients with OCD before and after four weeks of intensive individual CBT consisting of a 90-minute individual CBT session five days a week. The study found significant changes in brain activity after just four weeks of treatment. Compared to SSRI treatment or standard weekly CBT sessions, changes occurred much faster with the intensive CBT treatment. The brain patterns of the patients who received intensive CBT were similar to neuroimaging results seen in studies of OCD treatment with pharmacotherapy or neurosurgery. The intensive CBT elicits a similar response to treatment as pharmacotherapy.

Relaxation Response/Prayer/Meditation

Eastern meditative techniques can offer powerful benefits for people practicing them.

Jon Kabat-Zinn, Professor of Medicine Emeritus and founding director of the Stress Reduction Clinic and the Center for Mindfulness in Medicine, Health Care, and Society at the University of Massachusetts Medical School, has focused his career on bringing the practice of mindfulness into mainstream medicine. Through his techniques and established centers, Kabat-Zinn promotes the mind-body interaction for healing and coping with stress, pain, and illness.

Over the past several decades, Dr. Herbert Benson, an associate professor of medicine at Harvard Medical School, has introduced an extension of this mindfulness concept to Western society in the form of the relaxation response. Once a person can elicit the relaxation response, heart and breathing rates become slower, blood pressure decreases, and muscle tension dissipates.

The relaxation response can be induced by a simple meditation involving the following two general actions:

- Repeating a word continuously for a few minutes.
- Ignoring any thoughts that occur during the meditation and focusing solely on one's breathing.

Kundalini Yoga

While the relaxation response emphasizes clearing the mind, Kundalini yoga is distinctly different. Kundalini yoga is a centuries-old system of highly structured and controlled meditation and breathing techniques. This type of yoga embraces the philosophy that energy and consciousness resides at the base of the spine. Through specific postures, breathing, and visualization exercises, this energy is harnessed and consciousness is elevated—both of which result in improved physical well-being. Most relevant to anorexia is the fact that certain Kundalini yoga breathing and postural techniques target different psychiatric disorders, including major depressive disorder, anxiety disorders, and OCD.

Two studies by David Shannahoff-Khalsa, Director of The Research Group for Mind-Body Dynamics, Institute for Nonlinear Science at the University of California, San Diego, demonstrate the effect that Kundalini yoga can have on reducing symptoms of OCD. In the first study, five patients with severe OCD learned and practiced Kundalini yoga for a year. After this time, the patients all showed significant clinical improvement, as measured by a standard OCD research scale. Further, three patients were able to discontinue their medications, and the other two were able to reduce their anxiety medications by half.

The second study, described in *The Journal of Alternative and Complementary Medicine*, involved two groups of patients with severe OCD; half were placed on a Kundalini yoga protocol, and the other half learned and practiced the relaxation response plus meditation for three months. Only the group practicing Kundalini yoga demonstrated significant clinical improvement. After three months, participants in both groups were then asked to follow the Kundalini yoga protocol. After a year of practicing Kundalini yoga, all of the participants experienced a decrease in their OCD symptoms, and their improvements were more dramatic than what is typically seen as a result of OCD medication!

Although these studies were not conducted with patients with anorexia, the high occurrence of OCD in eating disorder patients is striking. Research has estimated that OCD can occur in as many as 69 percent of patients with anorexia.

I have always found this statistic somewhat humorous as the core symptoms of anorexia nervosa are obsessive thinking about food and body image and compulsive ritualistic behaviors around food! Yet, if the criteria in the DSM checklist for OCD are not complete, patients are not diagnosed with OCD. I try to utilize all tools available to help patients relieve the obsessive thoughts so prominent in anorexia.

Shannahoff-Khalsa asserts that Kundalini yoga can produce both quick, temporary relief as well as long-term improvement and remission. More information can be found in the Resources Section.

Emotional Freedom Technique (EFT)

A tool in the new field of Energy Psychology, EFT is a needle-free version of acupuncture that people can learn to perform on themselves to address anxiety and psychological stress. Similar to acupuncture and acupressure, EFT makes use of the meridian system in the body, and is based on an understanding that there is a connection between people's health, their emotions, and electromagnetic energy in the body.

Whereas acupuncture uses needles, EFT does not. Instead, an individual lightly taps on set points on her head and upper body with her fingertips while consciously thinking about a troubling problem and speaking a positive affirmation. Individuals assess their subjective distress initially (using a scale of 1–10), and then again after performing EFT for a few minutes, with a goal of decreasing the intensity of the problematic thoughts. While EFT may sound complicated, in reality, it is very simple to learn. Performing this powerful technique, even for a few minutes at a time, can dramatically reduce the intensity of a person's emotions and thoughts.

It is important to understand what is meant by a positive affirmation. With EFT, positive affirmations are based in reality and address where a person is at the present moment. EFT affirmations are not statements that the individual knows to be false and will not believe. An affirmation such as "I am wonderful!" is not likely to be believed by many patients with low self-esteem, and research has actually demonstrated that this may cause a person with low self-esteem to feel worse about herself.

An example of an EFT affirmation is the following: "Even though I am feeling worried and frightened about lunch, I deeply and completely accept myself." Phrased in this way, this statement reflects reality—what the person knows and feels—and has a greater chance of being well-received and helpful to the individual.

EFT can be done in any place and at any time (although people are likely to feel self-conscious while tapping on themselves in public). To perform it, a person repeats the affirmation while going through a number of tapping cycles. Over the course of a few minutes, the intensity of the emotion the person is experiencing should lessen.

I have found that EFT can help alleviate the anxiety associated with meals and help patients become more attuned to feelings associated with anxiety. As strange as it may sound, for example, tapping before meals can result in less anxiety.

Karen, a 26 year-old patient, had made significant progress with the help of nutritional supplementation in her recovery after 10 years with anorexia. Although married and working, Karen continued to struggle with anxiety around meals, and if she was not "reminded," she would frequently miss meals.

In preparation for a vacation to the Caribbean, I talked to Karen about EFT with suggestions about phrases to use during her tapping. Karen had the time, energy, and motivation during this vacation to explore this and returned to the office a "believer."

During a walk on the beach, sitting by the pool, and before meals in her room, Karen developed a pattern of tapping that decreased her anxiety around eating. It was a pattern that she could easily integrate into her life as she returned home. Over the next year, Karen found tapping a significant stress reducer as meals became easier and her treatment progressed more quickly.

I encourage exploration of EFT in conjunction with psychotherapy as the process of tapping elicits many thoughts and emotions that can be powerful tools for personal growth and self-awareness. The combination of tapping specific points on the meridians and voicing realistic affirmations has helped patients decrease anxiety and enhance health and well-being.

Research has shown that EFT can improve many psychological problems in addition to anxiety, such as depression and post-traumatic stress disorder.

In a study published in *The International Journal of Healing and Caring*, seven veterans with post-traumatic stress disorder (PTSD) symptoms such as depression and anxiety were treated with EFT. After completing six sessions of EFT, their overall anxiety decreased by 46 percent, depression decreased by 49 percent, and the symptom intensity of their PTSD decreased by 50 percent. This significant improvement was retained up to three months after their last EFT session.

More information about EFT can be found in the Resources Section of this book.

Chapter Twenty-Six

Avoiding Relapse

Research has clearly demonstrated that genetically determined personality and temperament traits contribute to a person's vulnerability to developing anorexia nervosa. Many patients may recover, although the outcome for some is an endless struggle with pathological eating, depression, anxiety, and chronic delusional thoughts related to body image. The physiological changes and nutritional deficiencies that resulted from the initial pathological eating sustain the illness and likely accelerate the downward spiral, impairing successful treatment and often leading to a relapsing course of anorexia.

Relapses are a hallmark of the long-term course of anorexia nervosa. While in a hospital or treatment program, individuals often experience a lessening of their symptoms and gain enough weight to be released home. However, about one-third of them will relapse, lose the weight again, and sink back into the behaviors of disordered eating. The highest risk of relapse was found by some researchers to be between 6 and 17 months following discharge. Further complicating matters, about 30 percent of patients who are initially treated for anorexia will "cross over" and later develop symptoms of binge eating and bulimia.

Frustratingly, a sustained, full recovery from anorexia can take years. At the University of California at Los Angeles, individuals who had initially been treated in a treatment program were followed for more than a decade. It took some patients as long as 10 to 15 years after leaving the program to recover fully from their eating disorders. And even after all that time, recovery was still not universally achieved: only 76 percent of participants in the study met the criteria for full recovery.

I frequently encounter the tragedy of this "revolving-door treatment." A family spends an exorbitant amount of money for a highly recommended 90-day treatment center. Their loved one attends the program, cooperates, gains weight, and is discharged. However, some time between 30 days and 12 months later, the illness returns with a vengeance.

Why? I believe one reason is that the underlying nutrient deficiencies that contributed to the development of the illness were never addressed or corrected. Standard treatment programs involve refeeding, medication, and education. Participants learn better coping skills, how their emotions affect their eating behaviors, and basic nutrition education. But since anorexia is a physiological disorder that arises as a result of nutritional deficiencies, educational activities cannot put back what's missing. Nor can coping skills restore the brain's neurochemical balance. Although body weight may be temporarily restored following an intensive period of refeeding and education, the odds are against a sustained recovery.

Ironically, the refeeding process itself can inadvertently compound nutritional deficiencies. Research has shown that deficiencies in certain nutrients, including omega-3 fatty acids and zinc, can actually become worse as patients are being refed. As patients recover from starvation during refeeding, the body's physiology changes dramatically. After the initial adjustment to increased food intake, metabolic processes in the body increase, and the body develops higher nutrient and caloric requirements. For example, one study found that patients who took the daily recommended amount of zinc and gained weight while in the hospital paradoxically developed a relative zinc deficiency prior to discharge. Their increasing metabolism required more zinc than their body was taking in!

The importance of breaking the cycle of illness cannot be overstated: The longer an individual struggles with relapses, the more likely she is to die from medical complications associated with anorexia. And the more protracted the recovery process, the greater the despair and loss of hope in individuals and their families. Thus, parents and family members need to recognize impending signs of a possible relapse and address them early and aggressively.

Researchers have found that patients with the following characteristics return to disordered eating more often:

- Substance abuse
- Severe obsessive and compulsive symptoms
- History of suicide attempts
- Excessive exercise
- Greater body image disturbance
- Residual concerns about weight, shape, and eating

The Plan

To help families whose loved ones are working toward full recovery but are thwarted by repeated relapses, I have developed a relapse prevention plan. Following these recommendations will give your child or other loved one an advantage in the recovery process—physically, mentally, and emotionally. The five steps for avoiding relapse include:

1. Optimal nutritional support.
2. Assessing and treating co-occurring mental health disorders and substance abuse.
3. Monitoring, re-evaluating, and supporting during times of increased stress.
4. Developing trust and honest communication through unconditional listening.
5. Finding meaning in life beyond anorexia.

Optimal Nutritional Support

My clinical experience has convinced me that when supplementation with zinc and certain other nutrients is introduced early in the treatment process, the deadly downward spiral of anorexia can be stopped. Continuing with a sound program of nutritional supplementation for 6 to 12 months after recovery is critical to preventing relapse. To review, the nutritional support should include:

- **Zinc:** Low levels of zinc are associated with decreased appetite, weight loss, altered taste perception, depression, and amenorrhea (missed menstrual periods).
- **B vitamins:** Deficiencies can lead to a number of psychological and neurological problems often associated with anorexia.
- **Omega-3 fatty acids:** These fatty acids are crucial for normal metabolism, insulin regulation, and prevention of rapid weight gain.
- **Digestive enzymes:** By aiding the digestive process, digestive enzymes can help alleviate the gastrointestinal distress common in anorexia.
- **Probiotics:** Probiotics help restore normal functioning and decrease inflammation within the gastrointestinal system. They may also help with anxiety and depression.
- **Amino acids:** Amino acids are the precursors to neurotransmitters such as serotonin, which regulate mood and appetite.

A comprehensive metabolic workup can also determine whether an individual has underlying celiac disease or abnormal levels of amino acids, fatty acids, organic acids, or urinary peptides. A common finding is a vitamin B12 deficiency, which can only be assessed by a blood test.

Even if an individual has had an initial medical workup, some repeat laboratory testing may be necessary. Some of the fat-soluble vitamins, like vitamin D, can accumulate to dangerous levels in the body, so testing should be repeated after three months of nutrient supplementation. It is also important to repeat lab work to make sure that the nutrients in the supplements an individual is taking are actually being properly absorbed and used by the body. I have seen patients take handfuls of supplements only to learn later that they remained nutrient deficient because they lacked the hydrochloric acid or digestive enzymes necessary for vitamin or mineral absorption.

If your child or other loved one has not yet undergone comprehensive metabolic testing, arrange to have it performed immediately! Once the testing is done, be sure to follow up with your healthcare provider.

Assessing and Treating Co-occurring Mental Health Disorders and Substance Abuse

People with anorexia frequently have other mental health conditions that may not be immediately recognized, including ADHD, substance abuse disorders, depression, panic disorder, or OCD. If not treated, persistent symptoms of other psychiatric conditions can derail recovery and increase the likelihood of relapse.

As has been mentioned, the obsessive thoughts, compulsive behaviors, and feelings of panic that are so prevalent in anorexia can make it almost impossible for a healthy approach to food and eating to occur. Did you know that some researchers found that almost 70 percent of women with anorexia also have an anxiety disorder? The link between anxiety disorders and anorexia is very strong; higher rates of OCD have been found in family members of individuals with anorexia than in the general population.

Depression is another frequently co-occurring condition that needs to be addressed in order for an individual to fully recover. Feelings of despair, worthlessness, and hopelessness certainly won't make it easier for an individual to engage fully in therapy or a treatment plan.

Individuals with anorexia also often turn to alcohol and/or illicit drugs to combat the pervasive feelings of anxiety and panic tormenting their brains. In fact, about half of individuals with an eating disorder report being dependent upon drugs or alcohol. Substance abuse is not only a confounding treatment factor, but also a deadly one; the deaths of patients with anorexia frequently involve substance abuse. In addition, anorexics who are discharged from a hospital or treatment program and then restart or begin abusing alcohol or drugs fare extremely poorly. Not only does their overall recovery take longer, but they also have a significantly greater risk of dying than do anorexics who do not abuse drugs or alcohol after discharge.

If you think that your loved one with anorexia is struggling with substance abuse, get help immediately. A physician or mental healthcare provider can guide you through the types of treatment available.

To determine if an individual has any other psychiatric disorders that should be addressed, a comprehensive psychiatric assessment should be performed by a competent mental health professional or psychiatrist. After a diagnosis is made, appropriate treatment can be started. This may include medications, individual therapy, and/or family therapy. Family therapy, in which all of the members of the family work to correct unhealthy interactions, has been shown to be particularly helpful for adolescents.

If psychiatric medications are indicated, obtaining an rEEG can be invaluable. This non-invasive brainwave test can determine with a high degree of accuracy which medications—given an individual's unique brain chemistry—will work best for a patient. For patients already taking medications, it can often be important to obtain a follow-up rEEG to make sure that the current medications are still the most beneficial. Over time, the neurochemistry of an individual's brain can change, especially with hormonal changes (including growth spurts and the onset of menstrual periods) and improvement of nutritional status. Other medications might turn out to be more effective at different points along the recovery process.

Monitoring and Reevaluating During Times of Increased Stress

Our lives can be disrupted from stress at any time, and an adolescent's life is no exception! Teenagers graduate from high school, leave for college, end relationships, and lose friends. They may have someone close to them die, or their parents may get divorced. Mental angst takes its toll on the body. Chronic stress can suppress the immune system, raise blood pressure, increase the risk of developing diabetes, and cause depression. The body loses essential nutrients, either through excessive excretion or from newly increased needs. The nutrients that are often depleted are the ones known for fighting stress: the B vitamins, vitamin C, and magnesium.

Stress can also have dire psychological effects. Recent research published in the journal *Science* has shown that stress can essentially rewire the brain to promote a vicious cycle of continual stress. Researchers studied laboratory animals that were under chronic stress and found that the animals had smaller than normal areas in their brain that were associated with decision-making and goal-directed behaviors. In contrast, they had larger-than-normal brain areas that were linked to habit formation. When presented with new tasks, the chronically stressed animals were not able to try new actions or make new decisions; instead, they fell back on safe, familiar routines, even when those familiar actions were not called for. Generalizing to human behavior, the results mean that persistent stress causes individuals to return to familiar habits—even if those habits are detrimental or not productive. For example, when under stress, individuals who are recovering from anorexia may return to their prior disordered habits.

Developing a safety net with a treatment team that would involve physicians, therapists, and nutritionists can help prevent relapses in recovering patients during times of acute stress. While restoring the body's supply of the B vitamins, vitamin C, and magnesium can help begin to mitigate stress, other interventions may also be warranted. Your treatment team can determine which ones—outpatient therapy, inpatient treatment, medication, or other nutritional supplements—might be most beneficial.

Institute an Unconditional Listening Process

Relapse is always associated with shame and guilt; because of this, individuals struggling with an eating disorder may not be honest with family members about a reemergence of their thoughts or behaviors. In my experience, when individuals relapse, it is because they are increasingly anxious and obsessively worrying about their body or food. However, as patients may recognize that these thoughts are irrational, they avoid sharing and discussing them.

Research supports that anorexia nervosa is stigmatized. In contrast to other mental health disorders, including severe depression, panic attacks, schizophrenia, and dementia, eating-disorder patients were more likely to be blamed for their illness. Believing that the condition is self-inflicted, it can be hard for frustrated and angry family members and friends to be empathic.

That is why I recommend a process called unconditional listening. A powerful tool that brings family members together, unconditional listening offers individuals the chance to openly share their thoughts. The way the method works is as follows: the individual and her family members (parents, guardians, spouse, or partner) all decide the logistics of when and where they will convene. During this scheduled time and in this "safe" place, the individuals are encouraged to share thoughts and feelings. Family members must sit and listen in a genuine and nonjudgmental manner. They may not respond at all—not even two hours after the fact!

I suggest that families work toward 15-minute "sessions." Five minutes may be an appropriate first try. During this time, patients are encouraged not to focus on weight, meal plans, or food. Instead, family members are asked to listen to their loved one talk about thoughts and feelings unrelated to core obsessions of their illness. This may be difficult at first, and the rule of silent, nonjudgmental listening may need repeating, but eventually you will hear what it's like to be imprisoned with an eating disorder. The goal of this exercise is to help families understand the importance of listening and for patients to feel heard.

Remarkably, this technique allows everyone to feel better. Family members are afforded the opportunity to glimpse their loved one's thought processes, and the individual is able to share thoughts without repercussions. By talking about what she is thinking and feeling, the individual may begin to understand that her irrational thoughts are not part of her, but part of the illness, and she may begin to emotionally connect with others.

Unconditional listening is most effective for adults and adolescents over the age of 17. For younger adolescents it is important to work with a family therapist about learning how to listen better, and communicate directly, and if eating is still irregular, the Maudsley approach should be considered (more about the Maudsley approach on page 50).

Finding Meaning in Life beyond Anorexia

When a person has anorexia, the calories, self-loathing thoughts, and restricting behaviors overshadow all aspects of daily life. To escape the clutches of the illness and journey towards health, it is critical that an individual's attention and energy be focused elsewhere. Whether they focus on school, work, hobbies, or spending time helping others, patients need to find and pursue other positive aspects of their lives.

One only needs to look to the Internet to see the strangling hold anorexia can have on individuals. Hundreds of pro-anorexia (called "pro-ana") websites can be easily accessed by a simple web search. Created by and for people with anorexia, these sites extol the virtues of restricted eating, promote anorexia as a lifestyle choice, and provide a supportive community for those severely restricting their calorie intake. In short, their goal is to help individuals with anorexia maintain and conceal their illness. Commonly, the sites contain sections including "tips and advice" about dieting and calorie restriction; "thinspirational" messages with religious metaphors; photo galleries; "medical" information; online support; and personal stories and poems.

Recent clinical research has demonstrated just how potentially harmful pro-ana websites can be. Studying a wide array of sites, researchers found that the tips and tricks sections, which promote fasting and laxative abuse, poses the most serious medical risk for individuals. In addition, these sections offer advice about how to be deceptive, describing ways individuals can lie to their families and healthcare professionals about the extent of their disordered eating behaviors!

The danger of these online communities cannot be stressed enough. If your child or loved one has found her way to a pro-ana website, not only do you need to have a discussion about why she shouldn't visit the site, but you also need to figure out a way to prevent your child's return to these types of sites.

Giving up the identity of anorexia is extremely difficult at any age. Anorexia may often be comforting to patients; it provides their lives with structure, purpose, and a means to be successful. While many claim that they hate having anorexia, they often fear "giving up" the illness.

To be able to seek meaning in life, a person first needs the biological relief from this illness. Medications and proper nutrition will typically arrest the underlying physiological dynamics and health consequences of anorexia.

Seeking meaning in life as a goal in therapy was a principle first explored by Victor Frankl. A Holocaust survivor, he developed the philosophy of logotherapy based on his experiences in a concentration camp. Logotherapy is a psychological perspective that is based first and foremost on the principle that life under all circumstances has meaning, and that every human being seeks meaning in life. The meaning is there, and we want it—it will enrich our lives and make us feel whole. But most of the time, we are struggling to find that meaning.

People who have low self-esteem or psychological disorders, whether anxiety, depression, or another underlying condition that renders them vulnerable to an eating disorder, are fundamentally thwarted in their search for meaning. They believe they can never be successful at finding meaning in life.

To help your loved one begin to find something meaningful in his or her life other than the anorexia, encourage participation in daily activities, hobbies, or social action. But take it slowly! While having a full life is the goal, reentering a world of daily activities immediately after treatment should be done in moderation and with the support of therapy. It may not be a good idea, for instance, to send a child who is only a few months into recovery across the country to begin college without solid family and professional supports.

Similarly, expectations upon returning to school may need to be modified. Participating in three sports and taking a course load of advanced classes immediately after treatment may not be the wisest choice.

Chapter Twenty-Seven

Prevention Is Possible

Anorexia nervosa steals lives. It robs its victims of their health and vitality and has the potential to affect every organ system in the body. Some of the medical complications of the illness such as osteoporosis and heart and kidney damage may even be irreversible.

The lengthy and difficult recovery process, as well as the lack of proven conventional medical treatment, begs the question: Why are we waiting for anorexia to develop instead of preventing it? There are a growing number of eating-disorder prevention programs available, but the incidence of anorexia continues to increase. Clearly these programs are not nearly as effective as we would like them to be.

In this book, I have put forth a new model of anorexia as a disorder likely resulting from nutrient deficiencies in genetically vulnerable individuals. A disorder of malnutrition demands a nutrition-related solution. Prevention measures must also focus on optimizing an individual's nutritional status.

Awareness of Risk Factors

Prevention begins with awareness that a problem is likely to occur due to a growing number of the risk factors. As discussed in Chapter Two, the greater the number of the following characteristics, the greater the risk of developing anorexia nervosa:

- Female
- Age 13 to 25
- Family history of anorexia and/or other eating disorders
- Complications at birth, such as low birth weight, preterm delivery, and/or a difficult delivery
- Obsessive-compulsive personality traits such as perfectionism, inflexibility, and the need for order and symmetry
- Low self-esteem, depression, and/or anxiety
- History of childhood eating issues including feeding problems as an infant and undereating in late childhood
- Current dieting behaviors

If your child exhibits three or more of the above characteristics, you will need to monitor him or her closely. Keep an eye out for worrisome behaviors or comments that may point to disordered thoughts about food, meals, weight, and/or body image. For example, is she preoccupied with her weight? Does she talk about wanting to have a completely empty stomach? Does she obsess over calories? You also need to be aware of how and what your child is eating. Does she eat in secret? Has she stopped eating meat?

Be especially vigilant if she suffers from depression, anxiety, or OCD. Any suspicious eating behaviors or mental health problems should be investigated and treated by a mental health professional with medications, behavioral plans, and/or therapy, as deemed appropriate.

Nutritional Prevention

Especially in individuals with an inherently higher risk for developing anorexia, making sure the body receives an ongoing supply of essential nutrients now can likely prevent symptoms later. The idea of preventive measures is nothing new; after all, people brush their teeth every day to prevent future cavities and gum disease. Prophylactic medications are also widely prescribed. For example, people with chronic asthma may take a daily anti-inflammatory inhaler in order to prevent airway inflammation that can contribute to an acute asthma exacerbation. Along the same lines, good nutrition can be thought of as a prevention measure. And just as people can take preventative medications to avoid developing medical conditions, they can incorporate nutrient supplements into their daily routine to help ward off potential future psychiatric illnesses.

A relevant study was published in 2010 in the *Archives of General Psychiatry* on just this topic. Researchers wanted to see if omega-3 fatty acids (described in Chapter Seventeen) given prophylactically would prevent at-risk adolescents and young adults from later developing a psychotic disorder, or a mental illness characterized by highly distorted thinking and/or a loss of contact with reality. Just as risk factors for anorexia exist, so do risk factors for psychotic disorders. Participating subjects had a history of mild or short-lived psychotic symptoms or episodes, a schizophrenia-like personality disorder, or a first-degree relative with a diagnosed psychotic disorder such as schizophrenia. Subjects were divided into two groups. For 12 weeks, one group received a capsule containing fish oil with omega-3 fatty acids; the other group received an inactive placebo capsule. After 12 weeks, the subjects discontinued taking all capsules. For the next 40 weeks, the researchers carefully monitored the participants' psychiatric behaviors and overall functioning.

The results were dramatic! At the end of the study, only 5 percent of the subjects who received the omega-3 supplements had transitioned to a full-blown psychotic disorder, compared to 27.5 percent of the placebo group. In addition, the group receiving omega-3 supplements were found to have higher overall functioning and fewer psychotic episodes, such as delusions and hallucinations. Reassuringly, there were no significant side effects seen with the omega-3 supplements.

This idea that nutrition can be neuroprotective has significant implications, not only for psychotic disorders, but also for anorexia nervosa. I hope you have learned how maintaining optimal nutritional health by taking nutrient supplements can help decrease symptoms associated with anorexia. Reducing abdominal discomfort, depression, anxiety, or intrusive thoughts can allow individuals with anorexia to feel better, so they can more effectively participate in their recovery. Likewise, the vital role of optimal nutritional health in preventing the relapse of anorexia should be common sense.

I want to expand even further on this idea, and discuss how optimal nutrition can help prevent the development of anorexia. If your child or loved one has a higher than normal risk of developing anorexia based on the criteria above, think "nutritional insurance." Eating a variety of nutrient-dense foods and taking the nutritional supplements I recommend will begin to create a state of optimal health in your child. And a body and brain in which adequate levels of nutrients are maintained, even through times of stress and the advent of puberty, will not be as prone to developing anorexia.

Following are the categories of supplements that I feel are most critical:

- A comprehensive multivitamin and mineral
- Essential fatty acids
- Probiotics

Because every individual has differing biochemical needs, a professional with experience in the field of nutrition can help you decide the specific types of these supplements that can best support your child or loved one's nutritional needs.

You may have heard from other health professionals about the importance of taking a daily multivitamin. I wholeheartedly concur. Taking a multivitamin is one of the best things your child or other loved one can do for her health. Especially in today's society of overly processed, nutrient-depleted foods, rarely do individuals' diets contain all of the necessary vitamins and minerals. Take the B vitamins, for instance, which are important for preventing not only psychological problems such as depression, fatigue and irritability, but also medical symptoms, including muscle weakness, digestive problems, and heart disease. Taking a multivitamin will ensure that an individual gets enough of the B vitamins each day.

The importance of EFAs is becoming increasingly popular in the scientific literature. While EFAs play a vital role in the body, including preventing osteoporosis, dry skin, and cardiac abnormalities, the role of EFAs in brain development and function is even more critical. EFA deficiencies can lead to a host of psychological problems, such as depression, fatigue, sleep disturbances, and unstable moods. These symptoms can make an individual vulnerable, and psychologically vulnerable adolescents may be more likely to develop an eating disorder. To avoid an EFA deficiency, and to help the brain function at full capacity, supplements are invaluable. In addition, omega-3 fatty acids can help stabilize a person's metabolism and weight, which may lessen any desire to diet. The less dieting behavior, the less potential for anorexia.

When antibiotics are taken for a bacterial illness such as strep throat, the medication not only targets the bacteria causing the infection, but it also wipes out bacteria indiscriminately, including the good bacteria that live in a person's intestine. As mentioned earlier in the book, the role of these friendly bacteria is crucial in maintaining an individual's health. They protect the body from infection by providing a barrier against germs; decrease inflammation in the gastrointestinal system; and aid in food digestion. Without enough friendly bacteria, problems ensue, including abdominal discomfort, fatigue, increased allergies, and— recently discovered—depression and anxiety. Taking probiotics whenever antibiotics are taken is necessary to replenish these friendly bacteria, and to avoid symptoms that just may push a person teetering on the edge of an eating disorder over the cliff.

Laboratory Testing May Become Necessary

Let's assume that you are addressing your child or loved one's nutritional needs. Your child is eating healthily and taking the recommended supplements. And, yet, red flags begin to appear. Maybe your child declares she is becoming a vegetarian, or she dips below a healthy weight.

Or maybe her weight is normal, but she has developed obsessive thoughts about feeling fat, or compulsive rituals around cleanliness or eating. When concerns or behaviors such as these become evident, I recommend a more detailed work-up as listed below. Obtaining a complete picture of your child's nutritional status is crucial. She may have a deficiency of other essential nutrients, including zinc. Or she may have an underlying medical condition, such as inactivity of the digestive enzyme DPP IV, which can ultimately result in obsessive thoughts and compulsive behaviors. Again, a professional with nutrition experience can help you interpret the test results and determine the specific nutritional interventions or diet modifications that are warranted.

- **Comprehensive laboratory testing.** Evaluating an individual's over-all metabolic profile, including checking iron and vitamin B12 levels, via blood and urinary testing can identify a nutrient deficiency or an underlying medical condition such as celiac disease. Chapter Twenty-Four provides a list and description of all of these tests.
- **Zinc Taste Test.** You should be able to perform a zinc taste test at home to determine if zinc deficiency might be one of the reasons, for example, that your child has stopped eating meat. As discussed earlier, a zinc deficiency can be aggravated by the growth spurt and the increased biological and psychological demands of puberty. See Chapter Fourteen for details about this test.
- **Testing for urinary opiate peptides.** Many of my patients, especially between the ages of 8 and 12, with symptoms of OCD are found to have elevated casomorphin and/or gliadorphin levels in their urine. Treating these individuals with a DPP IV digestive enzyme supplement and diet modification can make a world of difference—the intrusive, obsessive thoughts and compulsive rituals and behaviors disappear within months! In individuals who already have anorexia, this helps them on the road to recovery. But it would be even more beneficial to identify and treat these OCD symptoms early, before an individual even begins to restrict her food intake. Chapter Fifteen has more information about casomorphin and gliadorphin.

Promoting a Healthful Lifestyle at Home

In addition to addressing nutritional needs, parents can do a great deal to promote the physical and psychological health of their children by incorporating the following practices in their home and daily life.

- **Build your child's self-esteem.** Help your child learn to accept herself for who she is by emphasizing her strengths other than physical appearance. Start early! Healthy self-esteem at age 10 is predictive of good mental health in adolescence, which includes a lower risk of developing anorexia.
- **Adopt a healthy attitude toward your own body.** When a parent discusses his or her own weight in a negative or self-deprecating manner, a child not only notices, but tends to become more critical of her own body shape and weight. Interestingly, one risk factor for anorexia is having a father who is dissatisfied with his body weight. Communicate a healthy and accepting attitude toward your body, especially when your child is in the pre-pubescent years and when her mind is most malleable, to help dispel the kinds of thinking that lead to disordered eating. If necessary, seek help to change your own negative self-perceptions.
- **Avoid battles over food with your child.** Studies have shown that when parents try to control their child's eating, the child is more likely to become preoccupied with becoming thin.
- **Don't pressure your child to attain a certain weight or size.** According to a study of children in middle school, 26 percent of girls and 22 percent of boys believe they are significantly overweight, and an even higher percentage of children are trying to lose weight. Dissatisfaction with one's size and shape, in combination with the stresses of puberty, can trigger disordered eating. In addition, activities encouraging children to maintain a certain weight or body type, such as ballet, can serve as springboards to anorexia.
- **Eat as a family.** Try to schedule some sit-down meals for the entire family each week. A recent study conducted by the Center on Addiction and Substance Abuse at Columbia University found sharing a family dinner to be the single most important factor protecting against many adolescent high-risk behaviors, including eating disorders.
- **Involve your child's primary care physician.** A healthcare provider who routinely examines and weighs your child is in a unique position to detect a developing eating disorder. Let your healthcare provider know about any concerns you might have regarding your child's eating behaviors. You should also ask your healthcare provider to monitor your child's zinc levels.
- **Know the websites your child is viewing.** Girls without eating disorders—especially those with a higher drive for thinness and

perfection—have been found to visit pro-anorexia or pro-ana web-sites, sites created by anorexics to promote and encourage food restriction. Please be aware that these sites exist and are dangerous! One study found that after a site like this was viewed even only one time, immediate and negative effects resulted. The women looking at it felt worse, had lower self-esteem, and perceived themselves as heavier afterward compared with women looking at fashion and home décor websites. In addition, after seeing the site, the women reported that they were more likely to exercise and think about their weight in the near future.

- **Get help at the first signs of trouble.** Keep in mind that the shorter the duration of anorexia, the greater the possibility of a full recovery. As soon as trouble arises, ask your healthcare provider to refer your child to an eating disorders specialist.

If Your Child Decides to Become a Vegetarian

Chapter Nine on diet and nutrition broached the scenario of a 10-year-old girl voicing her sudden decision to become a vegetarian. As described in Chapter Thirteen, a zinc nutritional deficiency can lead to abnormalities of taste, especially with meat. In addition, some children become vegetarian as a socially acceptable way of restricting food intake. If your child unexpectedly decides to become a vegetarian, it is important to try to determine where the decision stems from—if it is an ideological choice, an excuse to restrict food, or due to a zinc-deficient state. Here are some questions you can ask your child that may help tease these causes apart:

- Can you tell me why you have made this decision?
- Does meat taste strange or different to you?
- Does your stomach hurt when you eat meat?
- Does eating meat make you feel nauseated?
- Have you been reading or learning about cruelty to animals? If so, is that important to you?
- Are you comfortable with the way your body looks?
- Have you thought about losing weight?

In addition, if your child does indeed stop eating meat, you will likely have concerns about your child's nutrition. If your child allows you to prepare her meals, and eats what you have prepared, you can better ensure that she eats a well-balanced diet of protein, fruits, vegetables, and whole grains. If, however, your child is like many other teenage vegetarians and subsists primarily on white-flour-based products, sugar, and fruit, you will want to begin discussing the following areas with your child:

- The importance of getting enough vitamins, minerals, essential fatty acids, and antioxidants in the diet, and what diseases or symptoms can develop when the diet is deficient in these nutrients (see Chapters Seventeen to Twenty-One).
- How a zinc deficiency can cause decreased appetite, weight loss, depression, and altered taste perception—all of which may lead to the development of anorexia (see Chapter Thirteen).
- How eating adequate amounts of protein is important for normal physical and psychological development (Chapter Twenty).
- The need to take certain nutrient supplements to avoid nutritional deficiencies and stay healthy.

Where to Begin

First of all, just reading and understanding this book is an enormous first step. Knowledge is power!

Second, bear in mind that any intervention is better than doing nothing at all. It is certainly not necessary for you to implement all aspects of a prevention plan at once; you can address each one individually.

Finally, while you are deciding how to proceed, begin by giving your child zinc, EFAs, and a multivitamin supplement. The importance of these nutrients cannot be emphasized enough, and they can go a long way in helping your child feel better and get better.

Preventing nutritional deficiencies in high-risk individuals requires a commitment to your loved one's health, and restoring nutritional balance to patients with anorexia requires time and patience.

In the book *Superimmunity for Kids: What to Feed Your Children to Keep Them Healthy Now, and Prevent Disease in Their Future*, Dr. Leo Galland wrote, "The gift of optimal nutrition is a gift that lasts a lifetime." Take that message to heart! Health is based on the food that we eat and our ability to digest and absorb nutrients. Optimal individualized nutrition can, indeed, help prevent anorexia.

Pieces of the Puzzle: Finding the Edges and Separating the Colors

The human body is a complex symphony of biology, chemistry, physics, and perhaps some magic. Molecular magic is the only way I can conceive of the intricate changes that occur in the trillions of cells that provide energy, life, and human potential.

Anorexia nervosa is a profound disturbance of the body's ability to sustain this molecular magic. Malorexia is perhaps a better term for this illness, for it points more clearly to the profound state of malnutrition and malabsorption underlying the psychological and physiological symptoms that cause the spiral downward to disease.

Psychiatrists, who have come to rely increasingly on pharmaceutical interventions, have tried over and over to relieve their patients' bad feelings with medication. Since most anorexic patients find that their symptoms are not relieved by one medication, the psychiatrist writes another prescription. It is common for physicians to prescribe two, five, even seven medications in an effort to relieve the anorexic patient's suffering. Each new drug trial initiates a new cycle of guarded anticipation that this time the medication will work, followed by a return of the bad feelings when it doesn't.

Anorexia is one of the most serious health problems facing adolescents and young men and women today. Life with anorexia is an unrelenting struggle with obessional thoughts around eating and weight. A new treatment model must enhance treatment success, decrease risk for relapse, and support a model of prevention.

A Message of Hope

I believe the approach I have outlined in this book offers lasting hope for those who suffer from anorexia. My approach is a form of integrative medicine drawing on new scientific research about the way the brain works, as well as on wisdom from the field of nutrition. An integrative approach allows us to use all the tools of medicine and healing to treat this complex disorder. Indeed, standard treatment for anorexia has not been consistently effective.

There is no doubt that the quality of nutrients we consume affects the functioning of our bodies and contributes to differences in our health risks. That's why a sound nutritional approach provides hope for restoring the biological foundation of optimal functioning. The goal is to provide the body with foods from which essential nutrients can be extracted and used to prevent the malnourishment that sets the stage for anorexia. This inclusive approach differs from conventional medicine, which views each body system as an isolated entity and disconnects psychiatry and physiology. As a consequence, psychiatrists base their professional diagnoses on a lists of symptoms—lists that grow each year.

By emphasizing nutrition and its effect on brain health, I do not intend to minimize the complicated psychological factors that may contribute to the development of disordered eating. Food, dieting, and body image have powerful cultural connotations that take on multiple meanings for all of us within our families and throughout life. It is important for professionals to help patients with anorexia interpret the meaning of their symptoms and behaviors in the context of their personal history and their current life. Increasing their insight into their illness can help the transition towards recovery.

Remember the critical insight revealed more than half a century ago by Dr. Ancel Keys in his study of healthy male volunteers who severely restricted their eating for three months. At the end of the study, the men had lost the expected amount of weight. But they also exhibited signs of depression, anxiety, and OCD, despite the fact that at the beginning of the study all these men had been considered psychologically healthy. It only took three months of restricted eating and nutrient deficits to trigger some of the same symptoms that plague our anorexic patients. Keys' study makes clear, to anyone who looks with an open mind, that semi-starvation causes nutritional deficiencies which then bring on psychological problems that can set the stage for anorexia.

That malnutrition underlies the anorexic's psychological problems is also clear from the mixed results of standard therapy. A majority of patients try variations of psychotherapy over the course of many years. Individual, family, DBT, and group therapy can indeed help patients get better: The therapeutic relationship can itself become a powerful lever for growth, and DBT offers critical skills for emotional self-regulation and tolerance of distress. Yet I frequently hear the same refrain: even on a quiet evening, the eating disorder remains a powerful monster lurking in the closet; at more turbulent times it wreaks havoc. Despite psychological intervention, the eating disorder retains the power to disrupt homes and lives.

I do not suggest that nutritional supplements are magic bullets that can erase psychological stresses or negative emotions. Instead, I propose that a nutritionally optimal environment facilitates a sustained recovery. The healthier the brain, the less the anxiety. Patients can more freely use psychotherapy to understand the psychological factors that may contribute to disordered eating.

Anorexia nervosa is a complex disorder that requires an equally complex approach for treatment. An integrative approach, such as the one I have outlined in this book, joins nutritional supplementation to treat malnutrition with personalized medicine to relieve the psychiatric symptoms that challenge the recovery process.

The treatment of anorexia nervosa has to improve. The lives of our children and family members are at stake. Anorexia nervosa has the highest mortality rate of any psychiatric illness. Something has to change. I sincerely hope that we take a step back from our current treatment paradigm and turn the telescope around the right way to see the malnourished mind of anorexia nervosa.

A more detailed list can be found at www.AnswerstoAnorexia.com

Introduction

Kaye, W. (2009). Eating disorders: Hope despite mortal risk. *American Journal of Psychiatry, 166*(12), 1309-1311.

Chapter 1: A New Approach

Bergh, C., Ejderhamn, J., & Sodersten, P. (2003). What is the evidence basis for existing treatments of eating disorders?. *Current Opinion in Pediatrics, 15*(3), 344-345.

Bulik, C.M., Sullivan, P.F., Tozzi, F., Furberg, H., Lichtenstein, P., & Pederson, N.L. (2006). Prevalence, heritability, and prospective risk factors for anorexia nervosa. *Archives of General Psychiatry, 63*(3), 305-312.

Papadopoulos, F.C., Ekbom, A., Brandt, L., & Ekselius, L. (2009). Excess mortality, causes of death and prognostic factors in anorexia nervosa. *British Journal of Psychiatry, 194*(1), 10-17.

Chapter 2: Anorexia 101

American Psychiatric Association. (2006). *Practice guideline for the treatment of eating disorders* (3rd ed.). Washington, D.C.: American Psychiatric Publishing.

Crow, S.J., Peterson, C.B., Swanson, S.A., Raymond, N.C., Specker, S., Eckert, E.D., & Mitchell, J.E. (2009). Increased mortality in bulimia nervosa and other eating disorders. *American Journal of Psychiatry, 166*(12), 1342-1346.

Fairburn, C.G., Cooper, Z., Bohn, K., O'Connor, M.E., Doll, H.A., & Palmer, R.L. (2007). The severity and status of eating disorder NOS: Implications for DSM-V. *Behaviour Research and Therapy, 45*(8), 1705-1715.

Gura, T. (2007). *Lying in weight: The hidden epidemic of eating disorders in adult women.* New York: HarperCollins Publishers.

Kaye, W. (2008). Neurobiology of anorexia and bulimia nervosa. *Physiology & Behavior, 94*(1), 121-135.

Monteleone, P., Fabrazzo, M., Martiadis, V., Serritella, C., Pannuto, M., & Maj, M. (2005). Circulating brain-derived neurotrophic factor is decreased in women with anorexia and bulimia nervosa but not in women with binge-eating disorder: Relationships to co-morbid depression, psychopathology and hormonal variables. *Psychological Medicine, 35*(6), 897-905.

Tozzi, F., Thornton, L.M., Klump, K.L., Fichter, M.M., Halmi, K.A., Kaplan, A.S., . . . Kaye, W.H. (2005). Symptom fluctuation in eating disorders: Correlates of diagnostic crossover. *American Journal of Psychiatry, 162*(4), 732-740.

Chapter 3: Misplaced Blame

Derenne, J.L., & Beresin, E.V. (2006). Body image, media, and eating disorders. *Academic Psychiatry, 30*(3), 257-261.

Guisinger, S. (2003). Adapted to flee famine: Adding an evolutionary perspective on anorexia nervosa. *Psychology Review, 110*(4), 745-761.

Kalm, L.M., & Semba, R.D. (2005). They starved so that others be better fed: Remembering Ancel Keys and the Minnesota experiment. *Journal of Nutrition, 135*(6), 1347-1352.

Monteleone, P., & Maj, M. (2008). Genetic susceptibility to eating disorders: Associated polymorphisms and pharmacogenetic suggestions. *Pharmacogenetics, 9*(10), 1487-1520.

Zandian, M., Ioakimidis, I., Bergh, C., & Södersten, P. (2007). Cause and treatment of anorexia nervosa. *Physiology & Behavior, 92*(1-2), 283-290.

Chapter 4: Confusing Cause and Effect

Bemporad, J.R. (1996). Self-starvation through the ages: Reflections on the pre-history of anorexia nervosa. *International Journal of Eating Disorders, 19*(3), 217-237.

Gull, W.W. (1874). Anorexia nervosa (apepsia hysterica, anorexia hysterica). *Transactions of the Clinical Society of London, 7*, 22-28.

Jackson, A.A. (2001). Human nutrition in medical practice: The training of doctors. *Proceedings of the Nutrition Society 60*(2), 257-263.

Chapter 5: Therapy Not the Answer

Bergh, C., Osgood, M., Alters, D., Maletz, L., Leon, M., & Sodersten, P. (2006). How effective is family therapy for the treatment of anorexia nervosa?. *European Eating Disorders Review, 14*(6), 371-373.

Bulik, C.M., Berkman, N.D., Brownley, K.A., Sedway, J.A., & Lohr, K.N. (2007). Anorexia nervosa treatment: A systematic review of randomized controlled trials. *International Journal of Eating Disorders, 40*(4), 310-320.

Lock, J., & le Grange, D. (2005). Family-based treatment of eating disorders. *International Journal of Eating Disorders, 37 Suppl*, S64-S67.

McCabe, E.B., & Marcus, M.D. (2002). Question: Is dialectical behavior therapy useful in the management of anorexia nervosa?. *Eating Disorders, 10*(4), 335-337.

Robins, C.J., & Chapman, A.L. (2004). Dialectical behavior therapy: Current status, recent developments, and future directions. *Journal of Personality Disorders, 18*(1), 73-89.

Chapter 6: Trial and Error Polypharmacy

Bergh, C., Ejderhamn, J., & Sodersten, P. (2003). What is the evidence basis for existing treatments of eating disorders?. *Current Opinion in Pediatrics, 15*(3), 344-345.

Bulik, C.M., Berkman, N.D., Brownley, K.A., Sedway, J.A., & Lohr, K.N. (2007). Anorexia nervosa treatment: A systematic review of randomized controlled trials. *International Journal of Eating Disorders, 40*(4), 310-320.

Crow, S.J. (2006). Fluoxetine treatment of anorexia nervosa: Important but disappointing results. *The Journal of the American Medical Association, 295*(22), 2659-2660.

Crow, S.J., Mitchell, J.E., Roerig, J.D., & Steffen, K. (2009). What potential role is there for medication treatment in anorexia nervosa?. *International Journal of Eating Disorders, 42*(1), 1-8.

Halmi, K.A., Eckert, E., LaDu, T.J., & Cohen, J. (1986). Anorexia nervosa. Treatment efficacy of cyproheptadine and amitriptyline. *Archives of General Psychiatry, 43*(2), 177-181.

Kaye, W.H., Nagata, T., Weltzin, T.E., Hsu, L.K., Sokol, M.S., McConaha, C., . . . Deep, D. (2001). Double-blind placebo-controlled administration of fluoxetine in restricting and restricting-purging-type anorexia nervosa. *Biological Psychiatry, 49*(7), 644-652.

Walsh, B.T., Kaplan, A.S., Attia, E., Olmsted, M., Parides, M., Carter, J.C., . . . Rockert, W. (2006). Fluoxetine after weight restoration in anorexia nervosa: A randomized controlled trial. *The Journal of the American Medical Association, 295*(22), 2605-2612.

Chapter 7: Beyond Calorie Counts and Meal Plans

Gomez-Pinilla, F. (2008). Brain foods: The effects of nutrients on brain function.

Nature Reviews Neuroscience, 9(7), 568-578.

Hoffer, A. (1970). Pellagra and schizophrenia. *Psychosomatics, 11*(5), 522-525.

Kyle, U.G., & Pichard, C. (2006). The Dutch Famine of 1944-1945: A pathophysiological model of long-term consequences of wasting disease. *Current Opinions in Clinical Nutrition and Metabolism Care, 9*(4), 388-394.

Prousky, J.E. (2003). Pellagra may be a rare secondary complication of anorexia nervosa: A systematic review of the literature. *Alternative Medicine Review, 8*(2), 180-185.

Williams, R. (1956). *Biochemical individuality: The basis for the genetotrophic concept.* New York: McGraw-Hill.

Chapter 8: How Diet and Nutrition Can Start, Worsen, or Stop Anorexia

Attia, E., Wolk, S., Cooper, T., Glasofer, D., & Walsh, B.T. (2005). Plasma tryptophan during weight restoration in patients with anorexia nervosa. *Biological Psychiatry, 57*(6), 674-678.

Briefel, R.R., Wilson, A., & Gleason, P.M. (2009). Consumption of low-nutrient, energy-dense foods and beverages at school, home, and other locations among school lunch participants and nonparticipants. *Journal of the American Dietitic Association, 109*(2 Supplement), S79-S90.

Donovan, U.M., & Gibson, R.S. (1996). Dietary intakes of adolescent females consuming vegetarian, semi-vegetarian, and omnivorous diets. *Journal of Adolescent Health, 18*(4), 292-300.

Haddad, E.H., & Tanzman, J.S. (2003). What do vegetarians in the United States eat?. *American Journal of Clinical Nutrition, 78*(3 Suppl), 626S-632S.

Kessler, D.A. (2009). *The end of overeating: Taking control of the insatiable American appetite.* New York: Macmillan.

Robinson-O'Brien, R., Perry, C.L., Wall, M.M., Story, M., & Neumark-Sztainer, D. (2009). Adolescent and young adult vegetarianism: Better dietary intake and weight outcomes but increased risk of disordered eating behaviors. *Journal of the American Dietetic Association, 109*(4), 648-655.

Chapter 9: Anorexia, Genes, and Nutrients

Church, D. (2009). *The genie in your genes: Epigenetic medicine and the new biology of consciousness.* Santa Rosa, CA: Energy Psychology Press.

Cloud, J. (2010, Jan. 6). Epigenetics: Why your DNA isn't your destiny. *Time.* Retrieved from http://www.time.com/time/health/article/0,8599,1951968,00.html

Craig, G. (2009). The timeless EFT principles (and why EFT is always on the cutting edge). Retrieved January 5, 2010, from http://www.emofree.com/timeless-eft-principles.htm

Stuffrein-Roberts, S., Joyce, P.R., & Kennedy, M.A. (2008). Role of epigenetics in mental disorders. *Australian and New Zealand Journal of Psychiatry, 42*(2), 97-107.

Tsankova, N., Renthal, W., Kumar, A., & Nestler, E.J. (2007). Epigenetic regulation in psychiatric disorders. *Nature Reviews Neuroscience, 8*(5), 355-367.

Chapter 10: Malorexia

Bulik, C.M., Klump, K.L., Thornton, L., Kaplan, A.S., Devlin, B., Fichter, M.M., . . . Kaye, W.H. (2004). Alcohol use disorder comorbidity in eating disorders: A multicenter study. *Journal of Clinical Psychiatry, 65*(7), 1000-1006.

Bulik, C.M., Sullivan, P.F., Fear, J.L., & Joyce, P.R. (1997). Eating disorders and antecedent anxiety disorders: A controlled study. *Acta Psychiatrica Scandica, 96*(2), 101-107.

Dellava, J.E., Thornton, L.M., Hamer, R.M., Strober, M., Plotnicov, K., Klump, K.L., . . . Bulik, C.M. (2010). Childhood anxiety associated with low BMI in women with anorexia nervosa. *Behaviour Research and Therapy, 48*(1), 60-67.

Ellison, Z., Foong, J., Howard, R., Bullmore, E., Williams, S., & Treasure, J. (1998). Functional anatomy of calorie fear in anorexia nervosa. *The Lancet*, *352*(9135), 1192.

Keel, P.K., Dorer, D.J., Eddy, K.T., Franko, D., Charatan, D.L., & Herzog, D.B. (2003). Predictors of mortality in eating disorders. *Archives of General Psychiatry*, *60*(2), 179-183.

Klein, D.A., Bennett, A.S., Schebendach, J., Foltin, R.W., Devlin, M.J., & Walsh, B.T. (2004). Exercise "addiction" in anorexia nervosa: Model development and pilot data. *CNS Spectrums*, *9*(7), 531-537.

Kodirov, S.A., Takizawa, S., Joseph, J., Kandel, E.R., Shumyatsky, G.P., & Bolshakov, V.Y. (2006). Synaptically released zinc gates long-term potentiation in fear conditioning pathways. *Proceedings of the National Academy of Sciences*, *103*(41), 15218-15223.

Redgrave, G.W., Coughlin, J.W., Heinberg, L.J., & Guarda, A.S. (2007). First-degree relative history of alcoholism in eating disorder inpatients: Relationship to eating and substance use psychopathology. *Eating Behaviors*, *8*(1), 15-22.

Root, T.L., Pisetsky, E.M., Thornton, L., Lichtenstein, P., Pedersen, N.L., & Bulik, C.M. (2009). Patterns of co-morbidity of eating disorders and substance use in Swedish females. *Psycholoigcal Medicine*, *40*(1), 105-115.

Strober, M. (2004). Pathologic fear conditioning and anorexia nervosa: On the search for novel paradigms. *International Journal of Eating Disorders*, *35*(4), 504-508.

The National Center on Addiction and Substance Abuse at Columbia University. (2003). *Food for thought: Substance abuse and eating disorders*. New York: The National Center on Addiction and Substance Abuse at Columbia University.

Thompson-Brenner, H., Eddy, K.T., Franko, D.L., Dorer, D., Vashchenko, M., & Herzog, D.B. (2008). Personality pathology and substance abuse in eating disorders: A longitudinal study. *International Journal of Eating Disorders*, *41*(3), 203-208.

Chapter 11: The Plan: A New Approach to Anorexia

Bakan, R. (1979). The role of zinc in anorexia nervosa: Etiology and treatment. *Medical Hypotheses*, *5*(7), 731-736.

Birmingham, C.L., & Gritzner, S. (2006). How does zinc supplementation benefit anorexia nervosa?. *Eating and Weight Disorders*, *11*(4), e109-111.

Gomez-Pinilla, F. (2008). Brain foods: The effects of nutrients on brain function. *Nature Reviews Neuroscience*, *9*(7), 568-578.

Hellzén, M., Larsson, J.O., Reichelt, K.L., & Rydelius, P.A. (2003). Urinary peptide levels in women with eating disorders. A pilot study. *Eating and Weight Disorders*, *8*(1), 55-61.

Hoffman, D.A. (n.d.). *Referenced-EEG® (rEEG®): A biomarker assessment system to guide pharmacotherapy*. Retrieved Mar. 9, 2009, from http://cnsresponse.com/doc/CNSR%20rEEG%20Research%20Summary.pdf

Karwautz, A., Wagner, G., Berger, G., Sinnreich, U., Grylli, V., & Huber, W.D. (2008). Eating pathology in adolescents with celiac disease. *Psychosomatics*, *49*(5), 399-406.

Kidd, P.M. (2007). Omega-3 DHA and EPA for cognition, behavior, and mood: Clinical findings and structural-functional synergies with cell membrane phospholipids. *Alternative Medicine Review*, *12*(3), 207-227.

Pacholok, S.M., & Stuart, J.J. (2005). *Could it be B12?: An epidemic of misdiagnoses*. Fresno, CA: Quill Driver Books.

Rubio-Tapia, A., Kyle, R.A., Kaplan, E.L., Johnson, D.R., Page, W., Erdtmann, F., . . . Murray, J.A. (2009) Increased prevalence and mortality in undiagnosed celiac disease. *Gastroenterology*, *137*(1), 88-93.

Schauss, A., & Costin, C. (1989). *Zinc and eating disorders: Discover the fascinating role of a mineral nutrient in anorexia nervosa bulimia obesity and pica*. New Canaan, Connecticut: Keats Publishing, Inc.

Van West, D., Monteleone, P., Di Lieto, A., De Meester, I., Durinx, C., Scharpe, S., . . . Maes, M. (2000). Lowered serum dipeptidyl peptidase IV activity in patients with anorexia and bulimia nervosa. *European Archives of Psychiatry and Clinical Neuroscience, 250*(2), 86-92.

Chapter 12: The Link to Zinc

Bakan, R. (1979). The role of zinc in anorexia nervosa: Etiology and treatment. *Medical Hypotheses, 5*(7), 731-736.

Beumont, P., Hay, P., Beumont, D., Birmingham, L., Derham, H., Jordan, A., . . . Royal Australian and New Zealand College of Psychiatrists Clinical Practice Guidelines Team for Anorexia Nervosa. (2004). Australian and New Zealand clinical practice guidelines for the treatment of anorexia nervosa. *The Australian and New Zealand Journal of Psychiatry, 38*(9), 659-670.

Bhatnagar, S., & Taneja, S. (2001). Zinc and cognitive development. *British Journal of Nutrition, 85* (Suppl 2), S139-S145.

Birmingham, C.L., Goldner, E.M., & Bakan, R. (1994). Controlled trial of zinc supplementation in anorexia nervosa. *International Journal of Eating Disorders, 15*(3), 251-255.

Black, M.M. (2003). The evidence linking zinc deficiency with children's cognitive and motor functioning. *Journal of Nutrition, 133*, 1473S-1476S.

Brandao-Neto, J., Stefan, V., Mendonca, B.B., Bloise, W., & Castro, A.V.B. (1995). The essential role of zinc in growth. *Nutrition Research, 15*(3), 335-358.

Bryce-Smith, D., & Simpson, R.I. (1984). Case of anorexia nervosa responding to zinc sulphate. *The Lancet, 2*(8398), 350.

Katz, R.L., Keen, C.L., Litt, I.F., Hurley, L.S., Kellams-Harrison, K.M., & Glader, L.J. (1987). Zinc deficiency in anorexia nervosa. *Journal of Adolescent Health Care, 8*(5), 400-406.

Lask, B., Fosson, A., Rolfe, U., & Thomas, S. (1993). Zinc deficiency and childhood-onset anorexia nervosa. *Journal of Clinical Psychiatry, 54*(2), 63-66.

McClain, C.J., Stuart, M.A., Vivian, B., McClain, M., Talwalker, R., Snelling, L., & Humphries, L. (1992). Zinc status before and after zinc supplementation of eating disorder patients. *Journal of the American College of Nutrition, 11*(6), 694-700.

Safai-Kutti, S. (1990). Oral zinc supplementation in anorexia nervosa. *Acta Psychiatrica Scandinavia. Supplementum, 361*(82), 14-17.

Schauss, A., & Costin, C. (1989). *Zinc and eating disorders: Discover the fascinating role of a mineral nutrient in anorexia nervosa bulimia obesity and pica.* New Canaan, Connecticut: Keats Publishing, Inc.

Schauss, A.G., & Bryce-Smith, D. (1987). Evidence of zinc deficiency in anorexia nervosa and bulimia nervosa. In W.B. Essman (Ed.), *Nutrients and brain function* (pp. 151-162). Basel, Switzerland: Karger.

Spear, L. (2007). The developing brain and adolescent-typical behavior patterns: An evolutionary approach. In D. Romer & E.F. Walker (Eds.), *Adolescent psychopathology and the developing brain: Integrating brain and prevention science* (pp. 9-30). New York: Oxford University Press.

Van Voorhees, A.S., & Riba, M. (1992). Acquired zinc deficiency in association with anorexia nervosa: Case report and review of the literature. *Pediatric Dermatology, 9*(3), 268-271.

Ward, N.I. (1990). Assessment of zinc status and oral supplementation in anorexia nervosa. *Journal of Nutritional & Environmental Medicine, 1*(3), 171-177.

Yamaguchi, H., Arita, Y., Hara, Y., Kimura, T., & Nawata, H. (1992). Anorexia nervosa responding to zinc supplementation: A case report. *Gastroenterologia Japonica, 27*(4), 554-558.

Chapter 13: The Functions of Zinc

Akhondzadeh, S., Mohammadi, M.R., & Khademi, M. (2004). Zinc sulfate as an adjunct to methylphenidate for the treatment of attention deficit hyperactivity disorder in children: A double blind and randomized trial. *BMC Psychiatry, 4*, 9.

Amani, R., Saeidi, S., Nazari, Z., & Nematpour, S. (2009). Correlation between dietary zinc intakes and its serum levels with depression scales in young female students. *Biological Trace Element Research*, [Epub ahead of print].

Arnold, L.E., & DiSilvestro, R.A. (2005). Zinc in attention-deficit/hyperactivity disorder. *Journal of Child and Adolescent Psychopharmacology, 15*(4), 619-627.

Bediz, C.S., Baltaci, A.K., & Mogulkoc, R. (2003). Both zinc deficiency and supplementation affect plasma melatonin levels in rats. *Acta Physiologica Hungarica, 90*(4), 335-339.

Bilici, M., Yildirim, F., Kandil, S., Bekaro lu, M., Yildirmi , S., De er, O., ... Aksu, H. (2004). Double-blind, placebo-controlled study of zinc sulfate in the treatment of attention deficit hyperactivity disorder. *Progress in Neuro-Psychopharmacology & Biological Psychiatry, 28*(1), 181-190.

Chou, H.C., Chien, C.L., Huang, H.L., & Lu, K.S. (2001). Effects of zinc deficiency on the vallate papillae and taste buds in rats. *Journal of the Formosan Medical Association, 100*(5), 326-335.

Essatara, M.B., Morley, J.E., Levine, A.S., Elson, M.K., Shafer, R.B., & McClain, C.J. (1984). The role of the endogenous opiates in zinc deficiency anorexia. *Physiology & Behavior, 32*(3), 475-478.

Levenson, C.W. (2003). Zinc regulation of food intake: New insights on the role of neuropeptide Y. *Nutrition Reviews, 61*(7), 247-258.

Maes, M., D'Haese, P.C., Scharpé, S., D'Hondt, P., Cosyns, P., & De Broe, M.E. (1994). Hypozincemia in depression. *Journal of Affective Disorders, 31*(2), 135-140.

Nowak, G., Szewczyk, B., & Pilc, A. (2005). Zinc and depression. An update. *Pharmacological Reports, 57*(6), 713-718.

Sawada, T., & Yokoi, K. (2010). Effect of zinc supplementation on mood states in young women: A pilot study. *European Journal of Clinical Nutrition*. [Epub ahead of print]

Siwek, M., Dudek, D., Paul, I.A., Sowa-Ku ma, M., Zieba, A., Popik, P., ... Nowak, G. (2009). Zinc supplementation augments efficacy of imipramine in treatment resistant patients: A double blind, placebo-controlled study. *Journal of Affective Disorders, 118*(1-3), 187-195.

Tamai, H., Takemura, J., Kobayashi, N., Matsubayashi, S., Matsukura, S., & Nakagawa, T. (1993). Changes in plasma cholecystokinin concentrations after oral glucose tolerance test in anorexia nervosa before and after therapy. *Metabolism, 42*(5), 581-584.

Chapter 14: Zinc Deficiency and How to Avoid It

Dinsmore, W.W., Alderdice, J.T., McMaster, D., Adams, C.E., & Love, A.H. (1985). Zinc absorption in anorexia nervosa. *The Lancet, 1*(8436), 1041–1042.

Freeland-Graves, J.H., Bodzy, P.W., & Eppright, M.A. (1980). Zinc status of vegetarians. *Journal of the American Dietetic Association, 77*(6), 655-661.

Gibson, R.S., Heath, A.L., Limbaga, M.L., Prosser, N., & Skeaff, C.M. (2001). Are changes in food consumption patterns associated with lower biochemical zinc status among women from Dunedin, New Zealand?. *British Journal of Nutrition, 86*(1), 71-80.

Klump, K.L., Burt, S.A., McGue, M., & Iacono, W.G. (2007). Changes in genetic and environmental influences on disordered eating across adolescence: A longitudinal twin study. *Archives of General Psychiatry, 64*(12), 1409-1415.

Tannhauser, P.P. (2002). Anorexia nervosa: A multifactorial disease of nutritional origin?. *International Journal of Adolescent Medicine and Health, 14*(3), 185-191.

Tannhauser, P.P., Latzer, Y., Rozen, G.S., Tamir, A., & Naveh, Y. (2001). Zinc status and meat avoidance in anorexia nervosa. *International Journal of Adolescent Medicine and Health, 13*(4), 317-326.

Chapter 15: Casomorphin and Gliadorphin: Little Known Link to Anorexia

Hellzén, M., Larsson, J.O., Reichelt, K.L., & Rydelius, P.A. (2003). Urinary peptide levels in women with eating disorders: A pilot study. *Eating and Weight Disorders, 8*(1), 55-61.

Hildebrandt, M., Rose, M., Mönnikes, H., Reutter, W., Keller, W., & Klapp, B.F. (2001). Eating disorders: A role for dipeptidyl peptidase IV in nutritional control. *Nutrition, 17*(6), 451-454.

Chapter 16: Digestive Health: The Foundation of Recovery

Benton, D., Williams, C., & Brown, A. (2007). Impact of consuming a milk drink containing a probiotic on mood and cognition. *European Journal of Clinical Nutrition, 61*(3), 355-361.

Molin, G. (2001). Probiotics in foods not containing milk or milk constituents, with special reference to Lactobacillus plantarum 299v. *American Journal of Clinical Nutrition, 73*(2 Suppl), 380S-385S.

Nova, E., Toro, O., Varela, P., Lopez-Vidriero, I., Morande, G., & Marcos, A. (2006). Effects of a nutritional intervention with yogurt on lymphocyte subsets and cytokine production capacity in anorexia nervosa patients. *European Journal of Nutrition, 45*(4), 225-233.

Rao, A.V., Bested, A.C., Beaulne, T.M., Katzman, M.A., Iorio, C., Berardi, J.M., & Logan, A.C. (2009). A randomized, double-blind, placebo-controlled pilot study of a probiotic in emotional symptoms of chronic fatigue syndrome. *Gut Pathogens, 1*(1), 6.

Chapter 17: Optimal Nutritional Support: Essential Fatty Acids

Amminger, G.P., Schäfer, M.R., Papageorgiou, K., Klier, C.M., Cotton, S.M., Harrigan, S.M., . . . Berger, G.E. (2010). Long-chain omega-3 fatty acids for indicated prevention of psychotic disorders: A randomized, placebo-controlled trial. *Archives of General Psychiatry, 67*(2), 146-154.

Ayton, A.K. (2004). Dietary polyunsaturated fatty acids and anorexia nervosa: Is there a link?. *Nutritional Neuroscience, 7*(1), 1-12.

Ayton, A.K., Azaz, A., & Horrobin, D.F. (2004). Rapid improvement of severe anorexia nervosa during treatment with ethyl-eicosapentaenoate and micronutrients. *European Psychiatry, 19*(5), 317-319.

Holman, R.T., Adams, C.E., Nelson, R.A., Grater, S.J.E, Jaskiewicz, J.A., Johnson, S.B., & Erdman, J.W. Jr. (1995). Patients with anorexia nervosa demonstrate deficiencies of selected essential fatty acids, compensatory changes in non-essential fatty acids and decreased fluidity of plasma membranes. *Journal of Nutrition, 125*(4), 901-907.

Kris-Etherton, P.M., Harris, W.S., & Appel, L.J. (2002). Fish consumption, fish oil, omega-3 fatty acids, and cardiovascular disease. *Circulation, 106*(21), 2747-2757.

Matzkin, V., Slobodianik, N., Pallaro, A., Bello, M., & Geissler, C. (2007). Risk factors for cardiovascular disease in patients with anorexia nervosa. *International Journal of Psychiatric Nursing Research, 13*(1), 1531-1545.

Nemets, H., Nemets, B., Apter, A., Bracha, Z., & Belmaker, R.H. (2006). Omega-3 treatment of childhood depression: A controlled, double-blind pilot study. *American Journal of Psychiatry, 163*(6), 1098-1100.

Zanarini, M.C., & Frankenburg, F.R. (2003). Omega-3 fatty acid treatment of women with borderline personality disorder: A double-blind, placebo-controlled pilot study. *American Journal of Psychiatry, 160*(1), 167-169.

Chapter 18: Optimal Nutritional Support: Vitamins

Benjamin, J., Levine, J., Fux, M., Aviv, A., Levy, D., & Belmaker, R.H. (1995). Double-blind, placebo-controlled, crossover trial of inositol treatment for panic disorder. *American Journal of Psychiatry, 152*(7), 1084-1086.

Christopher, K., Tammaro, D., & Wing, E.J. (2002). Early scurvy complicating anorexia nervosa. *Southern Medical Journal, 95*(9), 1065-1066.

Fava, M., & Mischoulon, D. (2009). Folate in depression: Efficacy, safety differences in formulations, and clinical issues. *Journal of Clinical Psychiatry, 70* (Suppl 5), 12-17.

George, G.C., Zabow, T., & Beumont, P.J. (1975). Letter: Scurvy in anorexia. *South African Medical Journal, 49*(35), 1420.

Haagensen, A.L., Feldman, H.A., Ringelheim, J., & Gordon, C.M. (2008). Low prevalence of vitamin D deficiency among adolescents with anorexia nervosa. *Osteoporosis International, 19*(3), 289-294.

Pacholok, S.M., & Stuart, J.J. (2005). *Could it be B12?: An epidemic of misdiagnoses.* Fresno, CA: Quill Driver Books.

Palatnik, A., Frolov, K., Fux, M., & Benjamin, J. (2001). Double-blind, controlled, crossover trial of inositol versus fluvoxamine for the treatment of panic disorder. *Journal of Clinical Psychopharmacology, 21*(3), 335-339.

Williams, R.D., Mason, H.L., Smith, B.F., & Wilder, R.M. (1942). Induced thiamine (vitamin B1) deficiency and the thiamine requirement of man. *Archives of Internal Medicine, 69*(5), 721-738.

Chapter 19: Optimal Nutritional Support: Minerals

Davidson, J.R., Abraham, K., Connor, K.M., & McLeod, M.N. (2003). Effectiveness of chromium in atypical depression: A placebo-controlled trial. *Biological Psychiatry, 53*(3), 261-264.

Eby, G.A., & Eby, K.L. (2006). Rapid recovery from major depression using magnesium treatment. *Medical Hypotheses, 67*(2), 362-370.

McLeod, M.N., & Golden, R.N. (2000). Chromium treatment of depression. *The International Journal of Neuropsychopharmacology, 3*(4), 311-314.

Murray-Kolb, L.E., & Beard, J.L. (2007). Iron treatment normalizes cognitive functioning in young women. *American Journal of Clinical Nutrition, 85*(3), 778-787.

Chapter 20: Optimal Nutritional Support: Protein and Amino Acids

Attia, E., Wolk, S., Cooper, T., Glasofer, D., & Walsh, B.T. (2005). Plasma tryptophan during weight restoration in patients with anorexia nervosa. *Biological Psychiatry, 57*(6), 674-678.

Ehrlich, S., Franke, L., Schneider, N., Salbach-Andrae, H., Schott, R., Craciun, E.M., . . . Lehmkuhl, U. (2009). Aromatic amino acids in weight-recovered females with anorexia nervosa. *International Journal of Eating Disorders, 42*(2), 166-172.

Palova, S., Charvat, J., Masopust, J., Klapkova, E., & Kvapil, M. (2007). Changes in the plasma amino acid profile in anorexia nervosa. *Journal of International Medical Research, 35*(3), 389-394.

Chapter 21: Optimal Nutritional Support: Antioxidants

Barnham, K.J., Masters, C.L., & Bush, A.I. (2004). Neurodegenerative diseases and oxidative stress. *Nature Reviews Drug Discovery, 3*(3), 205-214.

Carper, J. (1998). *Miracle cures: Dramatic new scientific discoveries revealing the healing powers of herbs, vitamins, and other natural remedies.* New York: Harper Paperbacks.

Hozawa, A., Kuriyama, S., Nakaya, N., Ohmori-Matsuda, K., Kakizaki, M., Sone, T., . . . Tsuji, I. (2009). Green tea consumption is associated with lower psychological distress in a general population: The Ohsaki Cohort 2006 Study. *American Journal of Clinical Nutrition, 90*(5), 1390-1396.

Trebatická, J., Kopasová, S., Hradecná, Z., Cinovský, K., Skodácek, I., Suba, J., . . . Duracková, Z. (2006). Treatment of ADHD with French maritime pine bark extract, Pycnogenol. *European Child & Adolescent Psychiatry, 15*(6), 329-335.

Chapter 22: Celiac Disease – The Right Food May be the Wrong Food

Ferrara, A., & Fontana, V.J. (1966). Celiac disease and anorexia nervosa. *New York State Journal of Medicine, 66*(8), 1000-1005.

Hallert, C., Grant, C., Grehn, S., Grännö, C., Hultén, S., Midhagen, G., . . . Valdimarsson, T. (2002). Evidence of poor vitamin status in coeliac patients on a gluten-free diet for 10 years. *Alimentary Pharmacology & Therapeutics, 16*(7), 1333-1339.

Hallert, C., Svensson, M., Tholstrup, J., & Hultberg, B. (2009) Clinical trial: B vitamins improve health in patients with coeliac disease living on a gluten-free diet. *Alimentary Pharmacology & Therapeutics, 29*(8), 811-816.

Högberg, L., Danielsson, L., Jarleman, S., Sundqvist, T., & Stenhammar, L. (2009). Serum zinc in small children with coeliac disease. *Acta Paediatrica, 98*(2), 343-345.

Karwautz, A., Wagner, G., Berger, G., Sinnreich, U., Grylli, V., & Huber, W.D. (2008). Eating pathology in adolescents with celiac disease. *Psychosomatics, 49*(5), 399-406.

Leffler, D.A., Dennis, M., Edwards George, J.B., & Kelly, C.P. (2007). The interaction between eating disorders and celiac disease: An exploration of 10 cases. *European Journal of Gastroenterology and Hepatology, 19*(3), 251-255.

Ludvigsson, J.F., Reutfors, J., Osby, U., Ekbom, A., & Montgomery, S.M. (2007). Coeliac disease and risk of mood disorders— A general population-based cohort study. *Journal of Affective Disorders, 99*(1-3), 117-126.

Pynnönen, P.A., Isometsä, E.T., Aronen, E.T., Verkasalo, M.A., Savilahti, E., & Aalberg, V.A. (2004). Mental disorders in adolescents with celiac disease. *Psychosomatics, 45*, 325-335.

Pynnönen, P.A., Isometsä, E.T., Verkasalo, M.A., Savilahti, E., & Aalberg, V.A. (2002). Untreated celiac disease and development of mental disorders in children and adolescents. *Psychosomatics, 43*(4), 331-334.

Ricca, V., Mannucci, E., Calabrò, A., Bernardo, M.D., Cabras, P.L., & Rotella, C.M. (2000). Anorexia nervosa and celiac disease: Two case reports. *International Journal of Eating Disorders, 27*(1), 119-122.

Singhal, N., Alam, S., Sherwani, R., & Musarrat, J. (2008). Serum zinc levels in celiac disease. *Indian Pediatrics, 45*(4), 319-321.

Yucel, B., Ozbey, N., Demir, K., Polat, A., & Yager, J. (2006). Eating disorders and celiac disease: A case report. *International Journal of Eating Disorders, 39*(6), 530-532.

Chapter 23: Referenced-EEG (rEEG): An Emerging Technology Guides Medication Use

Costin, C. (2006). *The eating disorders sourcebook: A comprehensive guide to the causes, treatments, and prevention of eating disorders* (3rd ed.). New York: McGraw-Hill.

Greenblatt, J., Sussman, C., & Jameson, M. (2008). *EEG guided medication predictions in treatment refractory eating disorder patients with comorbid depression.* Poster Presented at US Mental Health and Psychiatric Congress.

Worcester, S. (2005). rEEG system helps guide prescribing. *Clinical Psychiatry News, 33*(2), 1 & 6.

Chapter 24: Laboratory Tests Your Doctor May Order

Boscarino, J.A., Erlich, P.M., & Hoffman, S.N. (2009). Low serum cholesterol and external-cause mortality: Potential implications for research and surveillance. *Journal of Psychiatric Research, 43*(9), 848-854.

Holick, M.F. (2007). Vitamin D deficiency. *New England Journal of Medicine, 357*(3), 266-281.

Hyman, M., Baker, S.M., & Jones, D.S. (2005). Biochemical individuality and genetic uniqueness. In D.S. Jones (Ed.), *Textbook of functional medicine* (pp. 71-73). Gig Harbor, WA: Institute for Functional Medicine.

Chapter 25: An Integrative Approach to Anorexia

Benson, H., & Klipper, M.Z. (1976). *The Relaxation Response.* New York: HarperTorch.

Schwartz, J.M., & Beyette, B. (1997). *Brain lock: Free yourself from obsessive-compulsive behavior* (1st ed.). New York: Harper Perennial.

Shannahoff-Khalsa, D.S. (2004). An introduction to Kundalini yoga meditation techniques that are specific for the treatment of psychiatric disorders. *Journal of Alternative and Complementary Medicine, 10*(1), 91-101.

Shannahoff-Khalsa, D.S., Ray, L.E., Levine, S., Gallen, C.C., Schwartz, B.J., & Sidorowich, J.J. (1999). Randomized control trial of yogic meditation techniques for patients with obsessive compulsive disorders. *CNS Spectrums, 4*(12), 34-47.

Swingle, P.G. (2001). *Emotional freedom technique (EFT) and theta suppressing harmonic markedly accelerates SMR treatment of seizure disorder.* Raleigh, N.C.: Association for Applied Psychophysiology and Biofeedback.

Chapter 26: Avoiding Relapse

Carter, J.C., Blackmore, E., Sutandar-Pinnock, K., & Woodside, D.B. (2004). Relapse in anorexia nervosa: A survival analysis. *Psychological Medicine, 34*(4), 671-679.

Johnson, J.G., Cohen, P., Kotler, L., Kasen, S., & Brook, J.S. (2002). Psychiatric disorders associated with risk for the development of eating disorders during adolescence and early adulthood. *Journal of Consulting and Clinical Psychology, 70*(5), 1119-1128.

Keel, P.K., Dorer, D.J., Franko, D.L., Jackson, S.C., & Herzog, D.B. (2005). Postremission predictors of relapse in women with eating disorders. *American Journal of Psychiatry, 162*(12), 2263-2268.

Norris, M.L., Boydell, K.M., Pinhas, L., & Katzman, D.K. (2006). Ana and the internet: A review of pro-anorexia websites. *International Journal of Eating Disorders, 39*(6), 443-447.

Strober, M., Freeman, R., & Morrell, W. (1997). The long-term course of severe anorexia nervosa in adolescents: Survival analysis of recovery, relapse, and outcome predictors over 10-15 years in a prospective study. *International Journal of Eating Disorders, 22*(4), 339-360.

Tierney, S. (2006). The dangers and draw of online communication: Pro-anorexia websites and their implications for users, practitioners, and researchers. *Eating Disorders, 14*(3), 181-190.

Chapter 27: Prevention is Possible

Amminger, G.P., Schäfer, M.R., Papageorgiou, K., Klier, C.M., Cotton, S.M., Harrigan, S.M., . . . Berger, G.E. (2010). Long-chain omega-3 fatty acids for indicated prevention of psychotic disorders: A randomized, placebo-controlled trial. *Archives of General Psychiatry, 67*(2), 146-154.

Fairburn, C.G., Cooper, Z., Doll, H.A., & Welch, S.L. (1999). Risk factors for anorexia nervosa: Three integrated case-control comparisons. *Archives of General Psychiatry, 56*(5), 468-476.

Favaro, A., Tenconi, E., & Santonastaso, P. (2006). Perinatal factors and the risk of developing anorexia nervosa and bulimia nervosa. *Archives of General Psychiatry, 63*(1), 82-88.

Conclusion

Burford-Mason, A. (2009).Vitamins on trial: Bad science- misleading conclusions. *Journal of Orthomolecular Medicine, 24*(1), 47-48.

Kalm, L.M., & Semba, R.D. (2005). They starved so that others be better fed: Remembering Ancel Keys and the Minnesota experiment. *Journal of Nutrition, 135*(6), 1347-1352.

Williams, R. (1956). *Biochemical individuality: The basis for the genetotrophic concept.* New York: McGraw-Hill.

www.AnswerstoAnorexia.com

This site serves as a companion and supplement to *Answers to Anorexia*. A helpful resource, the website contains easy-to-understand information about eating disorders that you can read, print out, and share with your friends and family. If your loved one has recently been diagnosed with anorexia nervosa, this website will help you get started with planning the most appropriate treatment. The website includes:

- Comprehensive reference list (more than 300) by chapter for *Answers to Anorexia*.
- Up-to-date research in the field of eating disorders, anorexia nervosa, and Integrative Medicine.
- Regularly updated columns and blogs.
- Dr. Greenblatt's conference and speaking schedule.

Outpatient Care

Comprehensive Psychiatric Resources, Inc. (CPR)

20 Hope Ave, Suite 107
Waltham, Massachusetts 02453
Phone: 781-647-0066
Fax: 781-899-4905
www.comprehensivepsychiatricresources.com

Located in Waltham, Massachusetts, Comprehensive Psychiatric Resources (CPR) provides patient-centered, science-based care to individuals suffering from all mental health disorders. Founder and Medical Director Dr. Greenblatt has developed an Integrative Mental Health practice at CPR that specializes in the comprehensive treatment of eating disorders. The staff at CPR understands that because each individual is unique, a person's treatment must be individualized in order to be successful. With that tenet in mind, each patient's genetic, environmental, biochemical, and nutritional status is evaluated. Based on this information, a person's treatment is then tailored specifically for him or her. This integrative approach views the body as a complex network of interacting systems, in which each system can influence the individual as a whole.

To create personalized treatment plans, CPR incorporates the following:

- Referenced-EEG to determine which medication or medications have the best chance of working for an individual, based on the person's distinct brain wave patterns.
- Comprehensive nutritional testing to determine if underlying metabolic disturbances are contributing to an individual's illness and what an individual's nutritional needs are, so that appropriate nutritional recommendations can be made.
- Dedicated staff and clinicians with specialized experience in integrative psychiatry and nutritional biochemistry.
- A focus on restoring optimal physical and mental health and vitality instead of simply reducing symptoms.
- High-quality nutritional supplements for optimal health for patients.

In addition to specializing in the treatment of eating disorders, CPR uses an Integrative Medicine approach for the treatment of all mental illnesses, including anxiety, depression, attention-deficit hyperactive disorder (ADHD), chronic pain, obsessive-compulsive disorder (OCD), schizophrenia, bipolar disorder, substance abuse, and addictions.

Inpatient Eating Disorder Treatment

Walden Behavioral Care
9 Hope Avenue, Suite 500
Waltham, Massachusetts 02453
Phone: 781-647-6700
www.waldenbehavioralcare.com
Located in Massachusetts, Walden Behavioral Care provides a complete "continuum of care" for treating patients with eating disorders and psychiatric disorders by integrating medical, behavioral, and nutritional care.

Referenced-EEG

CNS Response (Corporate Headquarters)
26895 Aliso Creek Rd | # B-450
Aliso Viejo, CA 92656 | USA
Phone: 949-420-4400
Fax: 866-294-2611
www.cnsresponse.com
CNS Response offers information and referral information regarding Referenced-EEG, including information about the nearest treatment providers.

Web Resources for Eating Disorders

Multiservice Eating Disorders Association, Inc. (MEDA)
92 Pearl Street
Newton, MA 02158
Phone: 617-558-1881
www.medainc.org
The Multi-service Eating Disorders Association (MEDA) is a national nonprofit organization based in Newton, Massachusetts, that treats people who suffer from eating disorders and works to prevent the proliferation of eating disorders within our society. MEDA takes a three-pronged approach to diminishing the pervasiveness of eating disorders, uniquely offering a combination of education, prevention and treatment. It provides education through professional training and scholastic teaching, recovery and treatment through assessments, referrals, and support group sessions, and prevention through academic and public education.

Rosalia Cerrone Foundation for Adult Anorexia
420 Lexington Avenue, Suite 1701
New York, NY 10170
Phone: 212-922-0092, 877-500-5577
www.rcfaa.org
The Rosalia Cerrone Foundation is dedicated to the creation of a new culture for treating adult anorexia in the medical community. Their goal is to confront the biological, psychological, and cultural issues that promote self-denial and impede treatment.

Academy for Eating Disorders (AED)
60 Revere Dr.
Northbrook, IL 60662
Phone: 847-498-4274
Fax: 847-480-9282
www.aedweb.org
The Academy for Eating Disorders is an association dedicated to eating disorders research, education, treatment, and prevention.

National Eating Disorder Association (NEDA)

603 Steward St., Suite 803
Seattle, WA 98101
Phone: 206-382-3587
Treatment Referral: 800-931-2237
www.nationaleatingdisorders.org

NEDA, a non-profit organization, offers support to those affected by eating disorders through providing education and resources to the public and members of the eating disorders field.

Integrative Medicine Resources

Comprehensive Human Resources (CHR)

www.CHRFoundation.org

CHR is a nonprofit foundation started by Dr. Greenblatt to educate professionals, families, and patients on the understanding and clinical practice of integrative medicine for mental health. CHR is dedicated to the prevention of mental illness.

American Board of Integrative Holistic Medicine (ABIHM)

5313 Colorado Street
Duluth, MN 55804-1615
Phone: 218-525-5651
FAX: 218-525-5677
www.holisticboard.org/

ABIHM is an association which establishes and promotes standards for Integrative Holistic Medicine. ABIHM is also a resource for physicians desiring certification in Integrative Holistic Medicine as well as for those who seek physicians certified in Holistic Medicine.

American Holistic Medical Association (AHMA)

23366 Commerce Park, Suite 101B
Beachwood, Ohio 44122
Phone: 216-292-6644
Fax: 216-292-6688
www.holisticmedicine.org/

AHMA is an association dedicated to the advancement of holistic and integrative medicine in healthcare. AHMA is committed to increasing the awareness and understanding of integrative, complementary, and alternative medicine techniques.

American College for Advancement in Medicine (ACAM)
Corporate Headquarters

8001 Irvine Center Drive, Ste 825
Irvine, CA 92618
Phone: 1-800-532-3688
Fax: 949-309-3535
www.acam.org

ACAM is a non-profit association dedicated to educating physicians and other health care professionals on the latest findings and emerging procedures in complementary, alternative, and integrative medicine.

International College of Integrative Medicine

Box 271, Bluffton, OH 45817
Phone: 866-464-5226
Fax: 610-680-3847
www.icimed.com

The ICIM is a community of dedicated healthcare professionals advancing emergent innovative therapies in integrative and preventive healthcare. They conduct educational sessions, support research and publications, and cooperate with other professional and scientific organizations.

Institute of Functional Medicine
4411 Pt. Fosdick Drive NW, Suite 305
P.O. Box 1697
Gig Harbor, WA 98335
Phone: 800-228-0622
Fax: 253-853-6766
www.functionalmedicine.org
A resource for training physicians and patients about the principles of functional medicine. IFM also provides referrals to functional medicine practitioners.

Whole Health Web
www.wholehealthus.com
This informative website provides general health information with an emphasis on natural health. There is also free audio downloads on select health topics and a directory of natural health practitioners around the country.

Natural Medicine Comprehensive Database
www.naturaldatabase.com
Information on natural products for the treatment of a variety of medical disorders. Includes a database of potential interactions between prescription medications and supplements.

Emotional Freedom Techniques (EFT)
http://www.emofree.com/
A resource providing the essentials to understand and practice EFT. Included in the website is research supporting the use of EFT in the treatment of various conditions.

Kundalini Yoga
http://www.kundaliniyoga.org/
Provides an introduction to the practice of Kundalini yoga with a free online course as well as information regarding additional resources about Kundalini yoga.

Books

The Relaxation Response by Herbert Benson and Miriam Klipper
The Guide to a Dairy-Free Diet by David Brownstein, MD
The Guide to a Gluten-Free Diet by David Brownstein, MD
The Guide to Healthy Eating by David Brownstein, MD
The Genie in Your Genes: Epigenetic Medicine and the New Biology of Intention by Dawson Church, PhD
The Eating Disorders Sourcebook: A Comprehensive Guide to the Causes, Treatments, and Prevention of Eating Disorders by Carolyn Costin
Your Dieting Daughter...Is She Dying For Attention? by Carolyn Costin
Nutrition Made Simple by Robert Crayhon, MS
The Four Pillars of Healing by Leo Galland, MD
Power Healing by Leo Galland, MD
Eating Disorders: The Journey to Recovery Workbook by Laura J. Goodman and Mona Villapiano
Nutrigenomics by Mark Hyman, MD
The Ultramind Solution by Mark Hyman, MD
Could it be B12? by Sally M. Pacholok, RN, Jeffrey Stuart, DO
Omega-3 Oils, a Practical Guide by Donald Rucin, MD, Clara Felix
Brain lock: Free yourself from obsessive-compulsive behavior: A four-step self-treatment method to change your brain chemistry by Jeffrey Schwartz, MD, and Beverly Beyette
The Crazy Makers: How the food Industry is Destroying our Brains and Harming our Children by Carol Simontacchi
Eating Disorders: Time For Change: Plans, Strategies, and Worksheets by Mona Villapiano and Laura J. Goodman

Biochemical Individuality by Roger J. Williams, PhD
You Are Extraordinary by Roger J. Williams
Why Stomach Acid is Good for You by Jonathan V. Wright, MD, Lane Lenard, PhD

Gluten-Free Resources

GFCF Diet
http://www.gfcfdiet.com
Large online database with answers to many questions about gluten-free and dairy-free living.

Celiac.com
www.celiac.com

Celiac Disease Foundation
www.celiac.org

Celiac Sprue Association
www.csaceliacs.org

Gluten Free Living
www.glutenfreeliving.com

Gluten Intolerance Group of North America
www.gluten.net

National Foundation for Celiac Awareness
www.celiaccentral.org

Nearly Normal Cooking
www.nearlynormalcooking.com

University of Maryland Center for Celiac Research
www.celiaccenter.org

Dairy-Free Resources

GFCF
http://www.gfcf.com
A good place to start for information on food buying and cooking.

Go Dairy Free
http://www.godairyfree.org
Online source for shopping tips, recipes, reviews of dairy free products, cookbook guides and book recommendations.

Testing Laboratories

Great Plains Laboratory
www.greatplainslaboratory.com
A broad range of nutritional and metabolic testing is offered through Great Plains including opioid peptide testing for casomorphin and gliadorphin.

Doctor's Data
www.doctorsdata.com
Specialists in testing for heavy metal toxicity as well as nutritional and metabolic testing.

Index

Also Available from Sunrise River Press

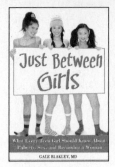

Just Between Girls
What Every Teen Girl Should Know About Puberty, Sex, and Becoming a Woman

Gale Blakley, MD The adolescent years are a time of endless questions for girls: Why have my friends all gotten their periods and I haven't? How long should I wait to have sex? Why are my emotions so out of control? *Just Between Girls* tells young women how to stay sexually healthy as they transition through adolescence, puberty, and young adulthood. It is told through the eyes of a teenage girl, Rachel. After each fictional story, the author— a gynecologist and obstetrician—answers Rachel's and her friends' questions about their physical and emotional changes. She discusses contraceptive methods, abstinence, safe sex, and how to avoid becoming a victim of dating violence. Blakley captures the reader with her vivid story telling and characters, and she encourages the reader to talk openly with a trusted adult and to make responsible choices. Softbound, 6 x 9 inches, 200 pages. **Item # SRP613**

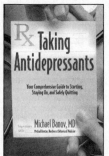

Taking Antidepressants
Your Comprehensive Guide to Starting, Staying On, and Safely Quitting

by Michael Banov, MD Antidepressants are the most commonly prescribed class of medications in this country. Yet, consumers have few available resources to educate them in a balanced fashion about starting and stopping antidepressants. Dr. Michael Banov walks the reader through a personalized process to help them make the right choice about starting antidepressants, staying on antidepressants, and stopping antidepressants. Readers will learn how antidepressant medications work, what they may experience while taking them, and will learn how to manage side effects or any residual or returning depression symptoms. Softbound, 6 x 9 inches, 304 pages. **Item # SRP606**

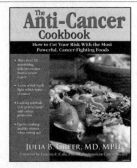

The Anti-Cancer Cookbook
How to Cut Your Risk with the Most Powerful, Cancer-Fighting Foods

by Dr. Julia Greer, MD, MPH Dr. Julia Greer explains what cancer is and how antioxidants work to prevent pre-cancerous mutations in your body's cells, and then describes which foods have been scientifically shown to help prevent which types of cancer. She then shares her collection of more than 220 scrumptious recipes for soups, sauces, main courses, vegetarian dishes, sandwiches, breads, desserts, and beverages, all loaded with nutritious ingredients chock-full of powerful antioxidants that may slash your risk of a broad range of cancer types. Softbound, 7.5 x 9 inches, 224 pages. **Item # SRP149**

Working Parents, Thriving Families
10 Strategies That Make a Difference

David J. Palmiter, Jr., PhD Finally, here is a down-to-earth parenting book for busy, working parents who simply don't have the time to try to apply the complicated recommendations found in other parenting books. Board-certified child psychologist David J. Palmiter distills the complex science of good parenting into 10 specific, effective, and time-efficient strategies for promoting wellness in children. These 10 strategies, proven effective through evidence-based research, will help your child develop a healthy self-esteem, feel safe and connected to the family, make healthy decisions, and develop independence and resilience. Your full-time job and other responsibilities don't have to keep you from giving your children the happy, well-adjusted childhood they deserve. Softbound, 6 x 9 inches, 256 pages. **Item # SRP614**